AMBEDKAR AND FIGHT AGAINST UNTOUCHABILITY

AMBEDKAR AND FIGHT AGAINST UNTOUCHABILITY

Dr. Surendra Kumar Singh

CENTRUM PRESS
NEW DELHI-110002 (INDIA)

CENTRUM PRESS
H.O.: 4360/4, Ansari Road, Daryaganj,
New Delhi-110002 (India)
Tel: 23278000, 23261597, 23255577, 23286875
B.O.: No. 1015, Ist Main Road, BSK IIIrd Stage,
IIIrd Phase, IIIrd Block, Bangalore-560085 (INDIA)
Tel: 080-41723429
Email: centrumpress@gmail.com
Visit us at: www.centrumpress.com

Ambedkar and Fight against Untouchability

First Edition, 2011

ISBN 978-93-80836-41-6

PRINTED IN INDIA

Printed at Mehra Offset Press, Delhi

Contents

Preface

The Hindu religious belief that "All human beings are not born equal" creates caste-based discrimination against the Dalits that leads to various forms of violence against them including public humiliation, torture, rape, beating and killing. Reacting to the values of Hinduism, Rabindranath Gore wrote,

We do not value Hinduism, we value human dignity... We want equal rights in the society. We will achieve them as far as possible while remaining within the Hindu fold or if necessary by kicking away this worthless Hindu identity.

Ambedkar was a great supporter of women's liberation. He blamed the verna system, which has not only subjugated Dalits but also women. He questioned *Manu Smriti* (Laws of Manu), the law book (Dharam-Shastra) of Brahminic Hinduism and attributed to Manu, the legendary first man and lawgiver. *Manu Smriti* prescribed the Dharma of each Hindu, stating the obligations attached to his or her social class and stage of life. It was hostile to the interest of lower caste people and women. It prohibited re-marriage of widows. He felt that *Manu Smriti* was solely responsible for the downfall of Hindu women. He encouraged the Dalits to embrace Buddhism to liberate their own selves from Hindu subjugation. Hence he fought for the right to choose ones' faith. After embracing Buddhism, Ambedkar said, "[U]nfortunately for me I was born a Hindu Untouchable... I solemnly assure you I will not die as a Hindu." He practiced what he advocated and became a Buddhist in 1956.

He also wrote about the French revolution ideas of fraternity, liberty and equality. He thought that the French and Russian revolutions failed to realize all three ideas. He believed that they could not all be realized except through the way of the Buddha.

He adopted various means to safeguard dalit rights. Ambedkar launched a movement against dalit discrimination by creating public opinion through his writings in several periodicals such as *Mook Nayak, Vahishkrit Bharat, and Equality Janta*, which he started for the protection of dalit rights.

The book, which provides a rare opportunity to debate and discuss the contribution of Dr. Ambedkar in nation-building, will be great interest to all sections of people.

—Dr. Surendra Kumar Singh

1

Ambedkar on Untouchability

Untouchability: Its Source

It is usual to hear all those who feel moved by the deplorable condition of the Untouchables unburden themselves by uttering the cry "We must do something for the Untouchables". One seldom hears any of the persons interested in the problem saying 'Let us do something to change the Touchable Hindu'. It is invariably assumed that the object to be reclaimed is the Untouchables. If there is to be a Mission, it must be to the Untouchables and if the Untouchables can be cured, untouchability will vanish. Nothing requires to be done to the Touchable. He is sound in mind, manners and morals. He is whole, there is nothing wrong with him. Is this assumption correct? Whether correct or not, the Hindus like to cling to it. The assumption has the supreme merit of satisfying themselves that they are not responsible for the problem of the Untouchables.

How Natural is such an Attitude is Illustrated by the Attitude of the Gentile towards the Jews: Like the Hindus the Gentiles also do not admit that the Jewish problem is in essence a Gentile problem. The observations of Louis Goulding on the subject are therefore very illuminating. In order to show how the Jewish problem is in its essence a Gentile problem, he says:

> *"I beg leave to give a very homely instance of the sense in which I consider the Jewish Problem in essence a Gentile Problem. A close acquaintance of mine is a certain Irish terrier of mixed pedigree, the dog Paddy,*

who is to my friend John Smith as the apple of both his eyes. Paddy dislikes Scotch terriers; it is enough for one to pass within twenty yards of Paddy to deafen the neighbourhood with challenges and insults. It is a practice which John Smith deplores, which, therefore, he does his best to check—all the more as the objects of Paddy's detestation are often inoffensive creatures, who seldom speak first. Despite all his affection for Paddy, he considers, as I do, that Paddy's unmannerly behaviour is due to some measure of original sin in Paddy. It has not yet been suggested to us that what is here involved is a Scotch Terrier Problem and that when Paddy attacks a neighbour who is peacefully engaged in inspecting the evening smells it is the neighbour who should be arraigned for inciting to attack by the fact of his existence."

There is here a complete analogy between the Jewish Problem and the problem of the Untouchables. What Paddy is to the Scotch Terrier, the Gentile is to the Jews, and the Hindu is to the Untouchables. But there is one aspect in which the Jewish Problem stands in contrast to the Gentile Problem. The Jews and the Gentiles are separated by an antagonism of the creeds. The Jewish creed is opposed to that of the Gentile creed. The Hindus and the Untouchables are not separated by any such antagonism. They have a common creed and observe the same cults.

The second explanation is that the Jews wish to remain separate from the Gentiles. While the first explanation is chauvinistic the second seems to be founded on historical truth. Many attempts have been made in the past by the Gentiles to assimilate the Jews. But the Jews have always resisted them. Two instances of this may be referred.

The first instance relates to the Napoleonic regime. After the National Assembly of France had agreed to the declaration of the 'Rights of man' to the Jews, the Jewish question was again reopened by the guild merchants and religious reactionaries of Alsace. Napoleon resolved to submit the question to the consideration of the Jews themselves. He convened an Assembly of Jewish Notables of France, Germany and Italy in order to ascertain whether the principles of Judaism were compatible with the requirements of citizenship as he wished to fuse the Jewish element with the dominant population. The Assembly consisting of III deputies, met in the Town Hall of Paris on the 25th of July 1806, and was required to frame replies to twelve questions relating mainly to the possibility of Jewish patriotism, the permissibility of inter-marriage between Jew and Non-Jew, and the legality of usury.

So pleased was Napoleon with the pronouncements of the Assembly that he summoned a Sanhedrin after the model of the ancient council of Jerusalem to convert them into the decree of a Legislative body. The Sanhedrin, comprising of 71 deputies from France, Germany, Holland and Italy met under the presidency of Rabbi Sinzheim, of Strassburg on 9th February 1807, and adopted a sort of Charter which exhorted the Jews to look upon France as their fatherland, to regard its citizens as their brethren, and to speak its language, and which also pressed toleration of marriages between Jews and Christians while declaring that they could not be sanctioned by the synagogue. It will be noted that the Jews refused to sanction intermarriages between Jews and non-Jews. They only agreed to tolerate them.

The second instance relates to what happened when the Batavian Republic was established in 1795. The more energetic members of the Jewish community pressed for a removal of the many disabilities under which they laboured. But the demand for the fuller rights of citizenship made by the progressive Jews was at first, strangely enough, opposed by the leaders of the Amsterdam community, who feared that civil equality would militate against the conservation of Judaism and declared that their co-religionists renounced their rights of citizenship in obedience to the dictates of their faith. This shows that the Jews preferred to live-as strangers rather than as members of the community.

Whatever the value of their explanations the Gentiles have at least realized that there rests upon them a responsibility to show cause for their unnatural attitude towards the Jews. The Hindu has never realised this responsibility of justifying his treatment of the Untouchables. The responsibility of the Hindus is much greater because there is no plausible explanation he can offer in justification of untouchability. He cannot say that the Untouchable is a leper or a mortal wretch who must be shunned. He cannot say that between him and the Untouchables, there is a gulf due to religious antagonism which is not possible to bridge. Nor can he plead that it is the Untouchable who does not wish to assimilate with the Hindus.

But that is not the case with the Untouchables. They too are in a different sense an eternal people who are separate from the rest. But this separateness, their segregation is not the result of their wish. They are punished not because they do not want to mix. They are punished because they want to be one with the Hindus. In other words, though the problem of the Jews and of the Untouchables is similar in nature—inasmuch as the problem is created by others—it is essentially different. The Jew's case is one of the voluntary isolation. The case of the Untouchables is that of compulsory segregation. Untouchability is an infliction and not a choice.

Untouchables: Their Numbers

Before one tries to know what it is to be an Untouchable one would like to know what is the total population of the Untouchables of India. For this one must go to the Census Report. The first general census of India was taken in the year 1881. Beyond listing the different castes and creeds and adding up their numbers so as to arrive at the total figure of the population of India the Census of 1881 did nothing. It made no attempt to classify the different Hindu castes either into higher and lower or touchable and untouchable. The second general census of India was taken in the year 1891. It was at this census that an attempt to classify the population on the basis of caste and race and grade was made by the Census Commissioner for the first time. But it was only an attempt.

The third general census of India was taken in 1901. At this census a new principle of classification was adopted namely "Classification by Social precedence as recognised by native public opinion". To this serious opposition was raised by high caste Hindus to the enumeration by caste in the Census Report. They insisted on the omission of the question regarding caste.

This objection did not have any effect on the Census Commissioner. In the opinion of the Census Commissioner enumeration by caste was important and necessary. It was argued by the Census Commissioner that "whatever view may be taken of the advantages or disadvantages of caste as a social institution, it is impossible to conceive of any useful discussion of the population questions in India in which caste would not be an important element.

Caste is still 'the foundation of the Indian social fabric' and the record of caste is still 'the best guide to the changes in the various social strata in the Indian Society' Every Hindu (using the term in its most elastic sense) is born into a caste and his caste determines his religious, social, economic and domestic life from the cradle to the grave. In western countries the major factors which determine the different strata of society *viz.* wealth, education and vocation are fluid and catholic and tend to modify the rigidity of birth and hereditary position.

In India spiritual and social community and traditional occupation override all other factors. Thus where in censuses of western countries an economic or occupational grouping of the population affords a basis for the combination of demographic statistics, the corresponding basis in the case of the Indian population is the distinction of religion and caste. Whatever view may be taken of caste as a national and social institution it is useless to ignore it, and so long as caste continues to be used as one of the distinguishing features of an individual's official and social identity it cannot be claimed that a decinnial enumeration helps to perpetuate an undesirable institution.

This Census of 1901 did not result in fixing the total population of the Untouchables at any exact figure. This was due to two reasons. In the first place no exact tests were applied to determine who is an Untouchable. Secondly a class of the population which was economically and educationally backward but not Untouchable was mixed up with those who were actually Untouchables.

The Census of 1911 went a step further and actually laid down ten tests to mark off the Untouchables from those who were Touchable. Under these tests the Census Superintendents made a separate enumeration of castes and tribes who (1) denied the supremacy of the Brahmins; (2) did not receive the Mantra from Brahmana or other recognised Hindu Guru; (3) denied the authority of the Vedas; (4) did not worship the great Hindu Gods; (5) were not served by good Brahmanas;

(6) have no Brahmin priests at all; (7) have no access to the interior of the ordinary Hindu temple; (8) cause pollution; (9) bury their dead and (10) eat beef and do not reverence the cow.

The separation of the Untouchables from the Hindus was insisted upon by the Muslims in a memorial to the Government dated 27th January 1910 in which they claimed that their representation in the political bodies of the country should be in proportion to the population of Touchable Hindus and not Hindus as a whole because they contended that the Untouchables were not Hindus.

Be that as it may the Census of 1911 marks the beginning of the ascertainment of the population of the Untouchables. Efforts in the same direction were continued at the Census of 1921 and 1931. As a result of these efforts the Simon Commission which came to India in 1930 was able to state with some degree of surety that total population of Untouchables in British India was 44.5 millions.

Suddenly, however, in 1932 when the Lothian Committee came to India to investigate the question of franchise for the reformed Legislatures and began its investigation, the Hindus adopted a challenging mood and refused to accept the figure given by the Simon Committee as a true figure of the Untouchables of India. In some provinces the Hindus went to the length of denying that there were any Untouchables at all. This is due to the fact that the Hindus had by now realised the danger of admitting the existence of the Untouchables. For it meant that a part of the representation enjoyed by the Hindus will have to be given up by them to the Untouchables.

The Census of 1941 must be left out of consideration. It was taken during the war and it was a sort of a rough measure. The latest Census is that of 1951. The following figures are taken from the statement issued by the Census Commissioner. The Census Commissioner gives the population of the Scheduled Castes in India as 513 lakhs. The total population of India, as shown by the 1951 census is 3,567 lakhs, excluding 1.35 lakhs, the enumeration records in whose case were destroyed by fire in the Census Tabulation Office at Jullundur. Out of the total population of 3,567 lakhs, 2,949 lakhs live in rural areas and 618 lakhs in the urban areas.

The Scheduled Castes in rural areas total 462 lakhs and in urban areas their figures are 51 lakhs. Non-agricultural classes for the whole population total 1,076 lakhs, the Scheduled Castes 132 lakhs. Cultivators of land, wholly or mainly owned, and their dependants total 1,674 lakhs for the whole population, 174 lakhs for the Scheduled Castes. Cultivators of land, wholly or mainly unowned and their dependants are 316 lakhs for the whole of India, 56 lakhs for the Scheduled Castes. Cultivating labourers and their dependants are 448 lakhs for the whole of India, 148 lakhs for the Scheduled Castes. Figures for non-agricultural classes are as follows:

Production other than Cultivation: Total 377 lakhs. Scheduled Castes 53 lakhs.

Commerce: Total 213 lakhs. Scheduled Castes 9 lakhs. Transport: Total 56 lakhs. Scheduled Castes 6 lakhs. Other services and miscellaneous sources: Total 430 lakhs, Scheduled Castes 64 lakhs.

Out of a total Scheduled Caste population of over 513 lakhs, 114 lakhs live in North India (Uttar Pradesh); 128 lakhs in East India (Bihar, Orissa, West Bengal, Assam, Manipur and Tripura); 110 lakhs in South India (Madras, Mysore, Travancore-Cochin and Coorg); 31 lakhs in West India (Bombay, Saurashtra and Kutch); 76 lakhs in Central India (Madhya Pradesh, Madhya Bharat, Hyderabad, Bhopal and Vindhya Pradesh); and 52 lakhs in North-West India (Rajasthan, Punjab, Patiala and East Punjab States Union, Ajmer, Delhi, Bilaspur and Himachal Pradesh).

Slaves and Untouchables

Far from being ashamed of untouchability, the Hindus try to defend it. The line of their defence is that the Hindus have never upheld slavery as other nations have done and that in any case, untouchability is not worse than slavery. This argument was used by no less a person than the late Lala Lajpat Rai in his book called 'Unhappy India'. It would have been unnecessary to waste one's time in refuting this countercharge had it not been that on account of its plausibility the world at large not having witnessed anything worse than slavery is likely to believe that untouchability cannot be worse than slavery.

The first reply to the countercharge is that it is quite untrue that slavery was not recognised by the Hindus. Slavery is a very ancient institution of the Hindus. It is recognised by Manu, the Hindu lawgiver and has been elaborated and systematised by the other Smriti writers who followed Manu. Slavery among the Hindus was never merely ancient institution, which functioned, only in some hoary past. It was an institution which continued throughout Indian history down to the year 1843 and if it had not been abolished by the British Government by law in that year, it might have continued even today.

As to the relative merits of slavery and untouchability, the best way to meet the countercharge is to compare and contrast untouchability with slavery as it existed in ancient Rome and in modern America. What was the *de facto* condition of the slaves in the Roman Empire? The best description I know of is to be found in Mr. Barrow's *Slavery in the Roman Empire.* Says' Mr. Barrow:

> *"Hitherto, it is the repulsive side of household slavery that has been sketched. There is also another aspect. The literature reveals the vast household as normal. It is, of course, the exception. Large slave staffs undoubtedly existed, and they are generally to be found in Rome. In Italy and the Provinces there was less need of display; many of the staff of the Villa were engaged in productive work connected with land and its produce. The old-fashioned relationship between foreman and slave remained there; the slave was often a fellow worker. The kindliness of Pliny towards his staff is well known. It is in no spirit of self-righteousness, and in no wish to appear in a favourable light in the eyes of the future generations which he hoped would read his letters that he tells of his distress at the illness and death of his slaves. The household (or Pliny) is the slaves' republic. Pliny's account of his treatment of his slaves is sometimes regarded as so much in advance of general or even occasional practice as to be valueless as evidence. There is no reason for this attitude.*
>
> *From reasons both of display and genuine literary interest, the rich families attached to their households, slaves trained in literature and art. Clavisices Sabinus*

is said by Seneda to have had eleven slaves taught to recite Homer, Hesioid, and nine lyric poets by heart. 'Book cases would be cheaper', said a rude friend. 'No, what the household knows the master knows' was the answer. But, apart from such abuses, educated slaves must have been a necessity in the absence of printing;.... The busy lawyer, the dilettante poet, the philosopher and educated gentlemen of literary tastes and need of copyists and readers and secretaries. Such men were naturally linguistic also; a librarius *who dies at the age of twenty boasts that he was 'literatus Graecis Latinis'.* Amanuenses *were common enough; librarians are to be found in public and private libraries.... Shorthand writing was in common use under the Empire, and slave* Notarii *were regularly employed. Many freemen, rhetoricians and grammarians are collected by Snetonius in a special treatise. Verrius Flaccus was tutor to Austus's grandsons, and at death was publicly honoured by a statue. Scribonius Aphrodisius was the slave and disciple of Orbilius and was afterwards freed by Scribenia. Hyginus was librarian of the Palatine Library, in which office he was followed by Julius Modestus, his own freeman. We hear of freemen historians of a slave philosopher who was encouraged to argue with his master, friends of slaves and freed architects. Freemen as doctors occur frequently in the inscriptions, some of them specialists, they had been trained in big households as slaves, as is shown by one or two examples; after Manumission they rose to eminence and became notorious for their high fees."' The tastes of some section of society demanded that dancer, singers, musicians, mountebanks, variety artists, athletic trainers and messieurs should be forthcoming. All these are to be found in slavery often trained by teachers who had acquired some reputation."*

The age of Augustus was the beginning of a period of commercial and industrial expansion.... Slaves had indeed been employed (in arts and crafts) before, but the sudden growth of trade.... their employment in numbers that would otherwise have been unnecessary. Romans engaged more freely and more openly in various forms of commercial and industrial venture. Yet, even so, the agent became more important, for commercial activities became more widespread; and such agents were almost necessarily slaves.... (this is so) because the bonds of slavery (are elastic). (They could be) so relaxed as to offer an incentive to the slave to work by the prospect of wealth and freedom, and so tightened as to provide a guarantee to the master against loss from the misconduct of his slave.

In business contracts between slave and master or third person seem to have been common, and the work thus done, and no doubt, the profits were considerable.... Renting of land to the slave has already been noticed.... and in industry much the same system was used in various forms; the master might lease a bank, or a business of the use of a ship, the terms being a fixed return or the slave being paid on a commission basis.

The earnings of the slave became in law his peculium was saved it might be used to a variety of purpose. No doubt in many cases this fund was expended in providing food or pleasure. But peculium must not be regarded merely as petty savings, casually earned and idly spent. The slave who made his master's business yield profits, to his own profit too, very often, had a keen sense of the best use to make up his own money. Often he reinvested it in his master's business or in enterprises entirely unrelated to it. He could enter into business relations with his master, from whom he came to be regarded as entirely distinct, or he could make contracts with a third person. He could even have procurators to manage his own property and interests. And so with the peculium may be found not only land, houses, shops, but rights and claims.

The activities of slaves in commerce are innumerable; numbers of them are shopkeepers selling every variety of food, bread, meat, salt, fish, wine, vegetables, beans, lupine-seed, honey, curd, ham, ducks and fresh fish; others deal in clothing—sandals, shoes, gowns and mantles. In Rome, they plied their trade in the neighbourhood of the Circus Mamimus, or the Porticus Trigemimus; or the Esquiline Market, or the Great Mart (on the Caolian Hill) or the Suburra .... The extent to which slave secretaries and agents acted for their masters is shown very clearly in the receipts found in the house of Caecillius Jucundus at Pompei.

That the State should possess slaves is not surprising; war, after all, was the affair of the State and the captive might well be State-property. What is surprising is the remarkable use made of public slaves under the Empire and the extraordinary social position occupied by them....

"'Public slave' came to mean before the Empire a slave of the State employed in its many offices, and the term implied a given occupation and often social position. The work of slaves of the State, slaves of the townships, and slaves of Caesar comprises much of what would now fall to parts of the higher and the whole of the lower branches of the civil services and of the servants of Municipal Corporations, working both with head and hands.... In the subordinate levels (of the Treasury) there worked numbers of clerks and financial officers, all freedmen and slaves. The business dealt with must have been of vast range.... The Mint.... the immediate head was a knight, in charge of the minting processes.... a freedman was placed; under him served freedmen and slaves.... From one branch of State service, at any rate, slaves were rigorously excluded, except on one or two occasions of exceptional stress. They were not allowed to fight in the Army because not thought worthy of honour. Doubtless other motives were present also; it would be dangerous experiment to train too many slaves systematically in the use of Arms. If, however, slaves served rarely in the fighting line, they are regularly to be found in great numbers behind it employed as servants, and in the commissariat and transport. In the fleet slaves were common enough."

Let us turn to the *de facto* position of the Negro in the United States during the period in which he was slave in the eye of the law. Here are some facts which shed a good deal of light on his position:

"Lafayette himself had observed that white and black seamen and soldiers had fought and messed together in the Revolution without bitter difference. Down in Granville County, North Carolina, a full blooded Negro, John Chavis, educated in Princeton University, was conducting a private school for white students and was

a licentiate under the local Presbytery, preaching to white congregations in the State. One of his pupils became Governor of North Carolina, another the State's most prominent Whig senator. Two of his pupils were sons of the Chief Justice of North Carolina. The father of the founder of the greatest military Academy of the State attended his school and boarded in his home..... Slave labour was used for all kinds of work and the more intelligent of the Negro slaves were trained as artisans to be used and leased. Slave artisans would bring twice as much as an ordinary field hand in the market. Master craftsmen owned their staff. Some masters, as the system became more involved, hired slaves to their slave artisans. Many slave artisans purchased their freedom by the savings allowed them above the normal labour expected."

"The advertisements for runaways and sales are an index to this skill. They received the same or better wages than the poor white labourer and with the influence of the master got the best jobs. The Contractors for masons' and carpenters' work in Athens, Georgia in 1838 were petitioned to stop showing preference to Negro labourers. "The white man is the only real, legal, moral, and civil proprietor of this country and state. The right of his proprietorship reached from the date of the studies of those whitemen, Copernicus and Galileo, who indicated the sphericity of the earth; which sphericity hinted to another white man, Columbus, the possibility by a westerly course of sailing, of finding land. Hence by whitemen alone was this continent discovered, the whitemen alone, aye, those to whom you decline to give money for bread or clothes for their famishing families, in the logical manner of withholding work from them defending Negroes too in the bargain." In Atlanta in 1858 a petition signed by 2 white mechanics and labourers sought protection against the black slave artisans of masters who resided in other sections. The very next year sundry white citizens were aggrieved that the City Council tolerated a Negro dentist to remain and operate in their midst. 'In justice to ourselves and the community it ought to be abated. We, the residents

of Atlanta, appeal to you for justice'. A Census of free Negroes in Richmond County, Georgia, in 1819 showed carpenters, barbers, boatcorkers, saddlers, spinners, millwrights, holsters, weavers, harness makers, sawmill attendants and steamboat pilots. A Negro shoemaker made by hand the boots in which President Munrow was inaugurated. Harriet Martineau marvelled at the slave workmanship in the delicately tiled floors of Thomas Jefferson's home at Monticello. There still stands in the big house of the old plantation, heavy marks of the hands of these Negro craftsmen, strong mansions built of timber hewn from the original oak and pinned together by wooden pins. Negro women skilled in spinning and weaving worked in the mills. Buckingham in 1839 found them in Athens, Georgia, working alongside with white girls without apparent repugnance or objection. Negro craftsmen in the South, slave and free fared better than their brothers in the North. In 1856 in Philadelphia, of 1637 Negro craftsmen recorded, less than two-thirds could use their trades; 'because of hostile prejudice'. The Irish who were pouring into America from the very beginning of the nineteenth century were being used in the North on approximately the same motives of preference, which governed Negro slavery. 'An Irish Catholic, it was argued in their favour, seldom attempts to rise to a higher condition than that in which he is placed, while the Negro often makes the attempt with success. Had not the old Puritan Oliver Cromwell, while the traffic in black slaves was on, sold all the Irish not killed in the Drogheda Massacre, into Barbados? Free and fugitive Negroes in New York and Pennsylvania were in constant conflict with this group and the bitter hostility showed itself most violently in the draft riots of the New York. These Hibernians controlled the hod carrying and the common labour jobs, opposing every approach of the Negro as a menace to their slight hold upon America and upon a means of livelihood."

Such was the *de facto* condition of the Roman slave and the American Negro slave. Is there anything in the condition of the Untouchables of India which is comparable with the condition of the Roman slave and the American Negro slave? It would not be unfair to take the same period of time for comparing the condition of the Untouchables with that of the slaves under the Roman Empire. But I am prepared to allow the comparison of the condition of the slaves in the Roman Empire to be made with the condition of the Untouchables of the present day. It is a comparison between the worst of one side and the best of the other, for the present times are supposed to be the golden age for the Untouchables. How does the *de facto* condition of the Untouchables compare with the *de facto* condition of the slaves? How many Untouchables are engaged as the slaves in Rome were, in professions such as those of Librarians, Amanuenses, Shorthand writers? How many Untouchables are engaged, as the slaves in Rome were, in such intellectual occupations as those of rhetoricians, grammarians, philosophers, tutors, doctors and artists? How many Untouchables are engaged, as the slaves in Rome? Can any Hindu dare to give an affirmative answer to anyone of these queries? The Untouchables are completely shut out from any of these avenues in which the slaves found so large a place. This proves how futile is the line of defence adopted by the Hindus to justify untouchability. The pity of the matter is that most people condemn slavery simply because they hold that for one man or class to have by law the power of life and death over another is wrong. They forget that there can be cruel oppression, tyranny, and persecution, with the train of misery, disappointment and desperation even when there is no slavery. Those who will take note of the facts stated above relating to the *de facto* condition of the slaves will admit that it is idle to condemn slavery lightly or hurriedly on the mere *de jure* conception of it. What the law permits is not always evidence of the practices prevalent in society. Many a slave would readily have admitted that they owed everything to slavery, and many did so whether they would have admitted it or not.

Slavery, it must be admitted, is not a free social order. But can untouchability be described as a free social order? The Hindus who came forward to defend untouchability no doubt claim that it is. They, however, forget that there are differences between untouchability and slavery, which makes untouchability a worse type of an unfree social order. Slavery was never obligatory. But untouchability is obligatory. A person is *permitted* to hold another as his slave. There is no compulsion on him if he does not want to. But an Untouchable has no option. Once he is born an Untouchable, he is subject to all the disabilities of an Untouchable. The law of slavery permitted emancipation. Once a slave always a slave was not the fate of the slave. In untouchability there is no escape. Once an Untouchable always an Untouchable.

The other difference is that untouchability is an indirect and therefore the worst form of slavery. A deprivation of a man's freedom by an open and direct way is a preferable form of enslavement. It makes the slave conscious of his enslavement and to become conscious of slavery is the first and most important step in the battle for freedom. But if a man is deprived of his liberty indirectly he has no consciousness of his enslavement. Untouchability is an indirect form of slavery. To tell an Untouchable 'you are free, you are a citizen, you have all the rights of a citizen', and to tighten the rope in such a way as to leave him no opportunity to realise the ideal is a cruel deception. It is enslavement without making the Untouchables conscious of their enslavement. It is slavery though it is untouchability. It is real though it is indirect. It is enduring because it is unconscious. Of the two orders, untouchability is beyond doubt the worse.

Neither slavery nor untouchability is a free social order. But if a distinction is to be made—and there is no doubt that there is distinction between the two—the test is whether education, virtue, happiness, culture, and wealth is possible within slavery or within untouchability. Judged by this test it is beyond controversy that slavery is hundred times better than untouchability. In slavery there is room for education, virtue, happiness, culture, or wealth. In untouchability there is none. Untouchability has none of the advantages of an unfree social order such as slavery. It has all the disadvantages of a free social order. In an unfree social order such as slavery there is the advantage of apprenticeship in a business, craft or art or what Prof. Mures calls 'an initiation into a higher culture'. Neither the crushing of untouchability nor the refusal of personal growth was necessary inherent in slavery, especially slavery as it existed in Roman Empire. It is therefore over hasty to say that slavery is better than untouchability.

This training, this initiation of culture was undoubtedly a great benefit to the slave. Equally it involved considerable cost to the master to train his slave, to initiate him into culture. 'There can have been little supply of slaves educated or trained before enslavement. The alternative was to train them when young slaves in domestic work or in skilled craft, as was indeed done to some extent before the Empire, by Cato, the Elder, for example. The training was done by his owner and his existing staff.... indeed the household of the rich contained special pedagogue for this purpose. Such training took many forms, industry, trade, arts and letters'.

The reason why the master took so much trouble to train the slave and to initiate him in the higher forms of labour and culture was undoubtedly the motive of gain. A skilled slave as an item was more valuable than an unskilled slave. If sold, he would fetch better price, if hired out he would bring in more wages. It was therefore an investment to the owner to train his slave.

In an unfree social order, such as slavery, the duty to maintain the slave in life and the body falls upon the master. The slave was relieved of all responsibility in respect of his food, his clothes and his shelter. All this, the master was bound to provide. This was, of course, no burden because the slave earned more than his keep. But a security for boarding and lodging is not always possible for every freeman, as all wage earners now know to their cost. Work is not always available even to those who are ready to toil and a workman cannot escape the rule according to which he gets no bread if he finds no work. This rule—no work no bread—has no applicability to the slave. It is the duty of the master to find bread and also to find work. If the master fails to find work, the slave does not forfeit his right to bread. The ebbs and tides of business, the booms and depressions are vicissitudes through which all free wage earners have to go. But they do not affect the slave. They may affect his master. But the slave is free from them. He gets his bread, perhaps the same bread, but bread whether it is boom or whether it is depression.

In an unfree social order, such as slavery, the master is bound to take great care of the health and well being of the slave: The slave was property of the master. But this very disadvantage gave the slave an advantage over a freeman. Being property and therefore valuable, the master for sheer self-interest took great care of the health and well-being of the slave In Rome, the slaves were never employed on marshy and malarial land. On such a land only freemen were employed. Cato advises Roman farmers never to employ slaves on marshy and malarial land. This seems strange. But a little examination will show that this was quite natural. Slave was valuable property and as such a prudent man who knows his interest will not expose his valuable possession to the ravages of malaria. The same care need not be taken in the case of freeman because he is not valuable property. This consideration resulted into the great advantage of the slave. He was cared for as no one was.

Untouchability has none of the three advantages of the unfree social order mentioned above. The Untouchable has no entry in the higher arts of civilisation and no way open to a life of culture. He must only sweep. He must do nothing else. Untouchability carries no security as to livelihood. None from the Hindus is responsible for the feeding, housing and clothing of the Untouchable. The health of the Untouchable is the care of nobody. Indeed, the death of an Untouchable is regarded as a good riddance. There is a Hindu proverb, which says 'The Untouchable is dead and the fear of pollution has vanished'.

On the other hand, untouchability has all the disadvantages of a free social order. In a free social order the responsibility for survival in the struggle for existence lies on the individual. This responsibility is one of the greatest disadvantages of a free social order. Whether an individual is able to carry out this responsibility depends upon fair start, equal opportunity and square deal. The Untouchable, while he is a free individual, had neither fair start, nor equal opportunity nor square deal. From this point of view, untouchability is not only worse than slavery but is positively cruel as compared to slavery. In slavery, the master has the obligation to find work for the slave. In a system of free labour workers have to compete with workers for obtaining work. In this scramble for work what chances has the Untouchable for a fair deal? To put it shortly, in this competition with the scales always weighing against him by reason of his social stigma he is the last to be employed and the first to be fired. Untouchability is cruelty as compared to slavery because it throws upon the Untouchables the responsibility for maintaining himself without opening to him fully all the ways of earning a living.

To sum up, the Untouchables unlike the slaves are owned by the Hindus for purposes which further their interests and are disowned by them, when owning them places them under burden. The Untouchables can claim none of the advantages of an unfree social order and are left to bear all the disadvantages of a free social order.

Outside the Fold

What is the position of the Untouchables under the Hindu social order? To give a true idea of their position is the main purpose of this chapter. But it is not easy to strike upon the best means of conveying a realistic and concrete picture of the way the Untouchables live or rather are made to live under the Hindu social order to one who has no conception of it. One way is to draw a model plant so to say of the Hindu social order and show the place given to the Untouchables therein. For this it is necessary to go to a Hindu village. Nothing can serve our purpose better. The Hindu village is a working plant of the Hindu social order. One can see there the Hindu social order in operation in full swing. The average Hindu is always in ecstasy whenever he speaks of the Indian village. He regards it as an ideal form of social organisation to which he believes there is no parallel anywhere in the world. It is claimed to be a special contribution to the theory of social organisation for which India may well be proud of.

How fanatic are the Hindus in their belief in the Indian village as an ideal piece of social organisation may be seen from the angry speeches made by the Hindu members of the Indian Constituent Assembly in support of the contention that the Indian Constitution should recognise the Indian village as its base of the constitutional pyramid of autonomous administrative units with its own legislature, executive and judiciary. From the point of view of the Untouchables, there could not have been a greater calamity. Thank God the Constituent Assembly did not adopt it. Nevertheless the Hindus persist in their belief that the Indian village is an ideal form of social organisation.

This belief of the Hindus is not ancestral belief, nor does it come from the ancient past. It is borrowed from Sir Charles Metcalfe—a civil servant of the East India Company. Metcalfe, who was a revenue officer, in one of his Revenue Papers described the Indian village in the following terms:

> *"The village communities are little republics, having nearly everything they want within themselves and almost independent of any foreign relations. They seem to last when nothing else lasts. Dynasty after dynasty tumbles down, revolution succeeds to revolution; Hindu, Pathan, Moghul, Maratha, Sikh, English, all are masters in turn, but the village communities remain the same. In times of trouble they arm and fortify themselves. An hostile army passes through the country, the village communities collect their cattle within their walls and let the enemy pass unprovoked. If plunder and devastation be directed against them selves, and the forces employed be irresistible, they flee to friendly villages at a distance; but when the storm has passed over, they return and resume their occupations. If a country remains for a series of years the scene of continued pillage and massacre so that the villages cannot be inhabited, the scattered villagers nevertheless return whenever the power of peaceable possession revives. A generation may pass away, but the succeeding generation will return. The sons will take the place of their fathers; the same site for the village, the same position for their houses, the same lands will be reoccupied by the descendants of those who were driven out when the village was repopulated; and it is not a trifling matter that will drive them out, for they will often maintain their post through times of disturbances and convulsion, and acquire strength sufficient to resist pillage and oppression with success. This union of the village communities, each one forming a little state in itself, has, I conceive, contributed more than any other cause to the preservation of the people of India, through all the revolutions and changes which they have referred, and is in a high degree conducive to their happiness and to the enjoyment of a great portion of freedom and independence." Having read this description of an Indian*

village given by a high-placed member of the governing class, the Hindus felt flattered and adopted his view as a welcome compliment. In adopting this view of the Indian village, the Hindus have not done any justice to their intelligence or their understanding. They have merely exhibited the weakness common to all subject people. Since many foreigners are led to accept this idealistic view of the Indian village, it would be better to present a realistic picture of the Society as one finds it in an Indian village.

The Indian village is not a single social unit. It consists of castes. But for our purposes, it is enough to say:

I. The population in the village is divided into two sections—(i) Touchables and (ii) Untouchables.

II. The Touchables form the major community and the Untouchables a minor community.

III. The Touchables live inside the village and the Untouchables live outside the village in separate quarters.

IV. Economically, the Touchables form a strong and powerful community, while the Untouchables are a poor and a dependent community.

V. Socially, the Touchables occupy the position of a ruling race, while the Untouchables occupy the position of a subject race of hereditary bondsmen.

What are the terms of associated life on which the Touchables and Untouchables live in an Indian village? In every village the Touchables have a code which the Untouchables are required to follow. This code lays down the acts of omissions and commissions which the Touchables treat as offences. The following is the list of such offences:

1. The Untouchables must live in separate quarters away from the habitation of the Hindus. It is an offence for the Untouchables to break or evade the rule of segregation.
2. The quarters of the Untouchables must be located towards the South, since the South is the most inauspicious of the four directions. A breach of this rule shall be deemed to be an offence.

3. The Untouchable must observe the rule of distance pollution or shadow of pollution as the case may be. It is an offence to break the rule.
4. It is an offence for a member of the Untouchable community to acquire wealth, such as land or cattle.
5. It is an offence for a member of the Untouchable community to build a house with tiled roof.
6. It is an offence for a member of an Untouchable community to put on a clean dress, wear shoes, put on a watch or gold ornaments.
7. It is an offence for a member of the Untouchable community to give high sounding names to their children. Their names be such as to indicate contempt.
8. It is an offence for a member of the Untouchable community to sit on a chair in the presence of a Hindu.
9. It is an offence for a member of the Untouchable community to ride on a horse or a palanquin through the village.
10. It is an offence for a member of the Untouchable community to take a procession of Untouchables through the village.
11. It is an offence for a member of the Untouchable community not to salute a Hindu.
12. It is an offence for a member of the Untouchable community to speak a cultured language.
13. It is an offence for a member of the Untouchable community, if he happens to come into the village on a sacred day which the Hindus treat as the day of fast and at or about the time of the breaking of fast, to go about speaking, on the ground that their breath is held to foul the air and the food of the Hindus.
14. It is an offence for an Untouchable to wear the outward marks of a Touchable and pass himself as a Touchable.
15. An Untouchable must conform to the status of an inferior and he must wear the marks of his inferiority for the public to know and identify him such as— (a) having a contemptible name. (b) not wearing clean clothes. (c) not having tiled roof. (d) not wearing silver and gold ornaments. A contravention of any of these rules is an

offence. Next come the duties which the Code requires members of the Untouchable community to perform for the Touchables. Under this head the following may be mentioned:

1. A member of an Untouchable community must carry a message of any event in the house of a Hindu such as death or marriage to his relatives living in other villages no matter how distant these villages may be.
2. An Untouchable must work at the house of a Hindu when a marriage is taking place, such as breaking fuel, and going on errands.
3. An Untouchable must accompany a Hindu girl when she is going from her parent's house to her husband's village no matter how distant it is.
4. When the whole village community is engaged in celebrating a general festivity such as Holi or Dushehra, the Untouchables must perform all menial acts which are preliminary to the main observance.
5. On certain festivities, the Untouchables must submit their women to members of the village community to be made the subject of indecent fun. These duties have to be performed without remuneration.

To realise the significance of these duties, it is important to note why they have come into being. Every Hindu in the village regards himself as a superior person above the Untouchables. As an overlord, he feels it absolutely essential to maintain his prestige. This prestige he cannot maintain unless he has at his command a retinue to dance attendance on him. It is in the Untouchable that he finds a ready retinue, which is at his command and for which he does not have to pay. The Untouchables by reason of their helplessness cannot refuse to perform these duties and the Hindu villager does not hesitate to exact them since they are so essential to the maintenance of his prestige.

These offences are not to be found in the Penal Code, enacted by the British Government. Nonetheless so far as the

Untouchables are concerned, they are real. A breach of any of them involves sure punishment for the Untouchables.

Another important thing to note is that the punishment for these offences is always collective. The whole community of Untouchables is liable for punishment though the offence may have been committed by an individual.

How do the Untouchables live? How do they earn their living? Without a knowledge of the ways of earning a livelihood which are open to the Untouchables it would not be possible to have a clear idea of their place in the Hindu Society.

In an agricultural country, agriculture can be the main source of living. But this source of earning a living is generally not open to the Untouchables. This is so for a variety of reasons. In the first place purchase of land is beyond their means. Secondly even if an Untouchable has the money to purchase land he has no opportunity to do so. In most parts the Hindus would resent an Untouchable coming forward to purchase land and thereby trying to become the equal of the Touchable class of Hindus. Such an act of daring on the part of an Untouchable would not only be frowned upon but might easily invite punishment.

In some parts they are disabled by law from purchasing land. For instance in the Province of Punjab there is a law called the Land Alienation Act. This law specifies the communities which can purchase land and the Untouchables are excluded from the list. The result is that in most part the Untouchables are forced to be landless labourers. As labourers they cannot demand reasonable wages. They have to work for the Hindu farmer for such wages as their masters choose to give. On this issue the Hindu farmers can combine to keep the wages to the lowest level possible for it is to their interests to do so. On the other hand the Untouchables have no holding power. They must earn or starve. Nor have they any bargaining power. They must submit to the rate fixed or suffer violence.

The wages paid to the Untouchables are either paid in cash or in corn. In parts of the Uttar Pradesh the corn given to the Untouchables as their wages is called "Gobaraha". "Gobaraha" means privy corn or corn contained in the dung of an animal. In the month of March or April when the crop is fully grown, reaped and dried, it is spread on the threshing floor. Bullocks are made to tread over the corn in order to take the corn out of husk by the pressure of their hooves. While treading over the corn, the bullocks swallow up the corn as well as the straw. As their intake is excessive they find it difficult to digest the corn. Next day, the same corn comes out of their stomach along with their dung: The dung is strained and the corn is separated and given to the Untouchable workmen as their wages which they convert into flour and make into bread.

When the agricultural season is over the Untouchables have no employment and no means of earning a living. In such seasons they subsist by cutting grass and firewood from the jungle and sell it in a nearby town. Even when it is open it depends upon the forest guard. Only if he is bribed he will let them take some grass and firewood from the Government forest. When it is brought to the town they have always to face a buyer's market. The Hindus who are the main body of buyers will always conspire to beat down the wages. Having no power to hold out, the Untouchables have to sell their stuff for whatever is offered to them. Often times they have to walk 10 miles each way from the village to the town and back to sell their stuff.

There is no trade in which they are engaged themselves as a means of earning a livelihood. They have not the capital for it and even if they had, no one would buy from them.

All these sources of earning are obviously precarious and fleeting. There is no security. There is only one secure source of livelihood open to the Untouchables *in* some parts of the country known to me. It is the right—to beg food from the Hindu farmers of the village. Every village has its machinery of administration. The Untouchables of the village are hereditary menials employed in the village administration. As part of their remuneration the whole body of Untouchables get a small parcel of land assigned in the ancient past which is fixed and is never increased and which the Untouchables prefer to leave uncultivated because of its excessive fragmentation. Coupled with this is given to them the right to beg for food.

Shocking as it may seem, this has become a customary right of the Untouchables and even Government takes into account the value of the food obtained by the Untouchables by begging in fixing the remuneration of an Untouchable if he were to be employed in Government job. This right to beg for food from the Touchables is now the principal means of livelihood for 60 millions of Untouchables in India. If anyone were to move in a village after the usual dinner time, he will meet with a swarm of Untouchables moving about the village begging for food and uttering the formula.

This statutory buggery as a means of livelihood for the Untouchables has been reduced to a system. The Untouchable families are attached to different Touchable families in the village as did the serfs and villains to the Lords of the Manors in Medieval Europe. The Untouchable families attached to the Touchable families are at the command of the latter. This relationship has become so personal that one always hears a Touchable speaking of an Untouchable as 'my man' as though he was his slave. This relationship has helped to systematise this matter of begging food by the Untouchables from the Touchable households.

This is the Village Republic of which the Hindus are so proud. What is the position of the Untouchables in this Republic? They are not merely the last but are also the least. He is stamped as an inferior and is held down to that status by all ways and means, which a majority can command. This inferiority is the destiny not merely of an individual but of the whole class. All Untouchables are inferior to all Touchables irrespective of age or qualification. A Touchable youth is above an aged Untouchable and an educated Untouchable must rank below an illiterate Touchable.

The established order is the law made by the Touchables. The Untouchables have nothing to do with it except to obey it and respect it. The Untouchables have no rights against the Touchables. For them there is no equal right, no justice by which that which is due to the Untouchables is allowed to them. Nothing is due to them except what the Touchables are prepared to grant. The Untouchables must not insist on rights. They should pray for mercy and favour and rest content with what is offered.

This established order is a hereditary order both in status as well as in function. Once a Touchable, always a Touchable. Once an Untouchable, always an Untouchable. Once a Brahmin, always a Brahmin. Once a sweeper, always a sweeper. Under it, those who are born high, remain high; those who are born low, remain low. In other words, the established order is based on an inexorable law of karma or destiny, which is fixed once for all and can never be changed. This destiny has no relation to the merits of the individuals living under it. An Untouchable however superior he may be mentally and morally, is below a Touchable in rank, no matter how inferior he may be mentally or morally. A Touchable however poor he may be must always take rank above an Untouchable, however rich he may be.

Such is the picture of the inside life in an Indian village. In this Republic, there is no place for democracy. There is no room for equality. There is no room for liberty and there is no room for fraternity. The Indian village is the very negation of a Republic. If it is a republic, it is a republic of the Touchables, by the Touchables and for the Touchables. The republic is an Empire of the Hindus over the Untouchables. It is a kind of colonialism of the Hindus designed to exploit the Untouchables. The Untouchables have no rights. They are there only to wait, serve and submit. They are there to do or to die. They have no rights because they are outside the village republic and because they are outside the so-called republic, they are outside the Hindu fold. This is a vicious circle. But this is a fact which cannot be gainsaid.

Unfit for Human Association

The Untouchables as explained in the last Chapter are outside the Hindu fold. The question however remains How far removed are they from the Hindus? What respect, what consideration do the Hindus show to them as human beings if not as Hindus? Without an answer to these questions, one cannot get a complete picture of the life of the Untouchables. The answer is there for anyone who cares to note it. The only difficulty is how to present it. There are two ways of presenting it. Either in the form of a statement or by citation of cases. I will adopt the latter. I do not wish to weary the reader with many cases. I will cite only a few, which are quite telling. The first case is from the State of Madras. In the year 1909 an appeal was filed in the Madras High Court by Mr. Venkata Subba Reddy and others all of whom were Hindus against their conviction by the Magistrate under section 339, Indian Penal

Code, for causing obstruction to the complainant and his party who were also caste Hindus. The judgment of the Madras High Court which gives the facts of the case and illustrates the position of the Untouchables vis-a-vis the Hindus in a very striking manner. The judgement is therefore worth quoting. It is as follows:

> *"The Appellants (Venkata Subba Reddy and others) have been convicted of wrongful restraint for having caused certain Pariahs to stand in the public street in the vicinity of a temple with the object of preventing the complainant from conducting a procession from the temple through the street. It is found that the complainant, deterred by fear of the pollution which he would have suffered had he passed near the Pariahs, did not conduct the procession, and that the accused maliciously caused the Pariahs to take up their positions in the street with the sole object of deterring the complainant from going where he had a right to go.*
>
> *We do not think that the accused has committed the offence of wrongful restraint; in our opinion this act did not amount to an obstruction within the meaning of section 339. The Pariahs were no obstruction; in fact there was nothing to prevent the complainant from taking his procession past them and they had a right to be where they were; and it is not suggested that their presence was intended to cause fear of physical injury or any fear that anything would happen to the complainant except the pollution of the procession by their presence.*
>
> *It was not the presence of the Pariahs but the complainant's own disinclination to go near them which prevented him from going where he would; it was his own choice which kept him from leaving the temple as Mr. Kuppuswami Aiyer put it, it was with his own consent that he remained there and there was no fear of injury within the meaning of the Penal Code which would prevent that consent from being a free consent. If it were otherwise, it would follow that a person in the position of the complainant would be justified in complaining of wrongful restraint against any Pariah,*

who having been lawfully in the public street on his own business, refused to move when directed to remove himself to a distance, knowing that if he remained, the complainant would be deterred by fear of pollution from passing near him.

It is clear that there would be no wrongful restraint in such a case and we think, it makes no difference that the Pariahs were posted by the accused.

We therefore set aside the conviction and sentence and direct refund of the fines if paid."

The case is very illuminating. There were in this case two parties. Venkata Subba Reddy was the leader of one party. Both parties were caste Hindus. The quarrel between the parties was over the right to take out a procession. Venkata Subba Reddy wanted to stop his opponents from taking out a procession and did not know how best to do it. It struck him that the effective way would be to get a few Untouchables and ask them to stand on the road and hold fast to it.

The trick succeeded and his opponents could not dare to go in the procession for fear of being polluted. The fact that the Madras High Court gave a judgment to the effect that making the *Pariahs* stand on the road does not constitute obstruction in the legal sense of the term is another matter. The fact remains that the mere presence of the *Pariahs* was enough to drive the Hindus away. What does this mean? It means that the Hindus have an absolute feeling of revulsion towards the Untouchables.

The next case is equally illuminating. It is a case of an Untouchable school teacher in a village in Kathiavar and is reported in the following letter which appeared in the *'Young India'* a journal published by Mr. Gandhi in its issue of 12th December 1929. It expresses the difficulties he had expressed in persuading a Hindu doctor to attend to his wife who had just delivered and how the wife and child died for want of medical attention. The letter says:

"On the 5th of this month a child was born to me. On the 7th, she fell ill and suffered from loose stools. Her vitality seemed to ebb away and her chest became inflamed. Her breathing became difficult and there was

acute pain in the ribs. I went to call doctor—but he said he would not go to the house of a Harijan nor was he prepared to examine the child. Then I went to Nagarseth and Garasia Darbar and pleaded them to help me. The Nagarseth stood surety to the doctor for my paying his fee of two rupees. Then the doctor came but on condition that he would examine them only outside the Harijan colony. I took my wife out of the colony along with her newly born child. Then the doctor gave his thermometer to a Muslim, he gave it to me and I gave it to my wife and then returned it by the same process after it had been applied. It was about eight o'clock in the evening and the doctor on looking at the thermometer in the light of a lamp said that the patient was suffering from pneumonia. Then the doctor went away and sent the medicine. I brought some linseed from the bazaar and used it on the patient. The doctor refused to see her later, although I gave the two rupees fee. The disease is dangerous and God alone will help us.

The lamp of my life has died out. She passed away at about two o'clock this afternoon."

The name of the Untouchable schoolteacher is not given. So also the name of the doctor is not mentioned. This was at the request of the Untouchable teacher who feared reprisals. The facts are indisputable. No explanation is necessary. The doctor, who in spite of being educated refused to apply the thermometer and treat an ailing woman in a critical condition. As a result of his refusal to treat her, the woman died. He felt no qualms of conscience in setting aside the code of conduct, which is binding on his profession. The Hindu would prefer to be inhuman rather than touch an Untouchable. The third case is taken from *"Prakash'* of 23rd August 1932:

"In the village of Jagwal, tahsil Jafarwal on the 6th August, a calf fell into a well. Rammahashaya, a Dom by caste was standing nearby. He at once jumped into the well and caught the calf in his arms. On three or four men coming to help, the calf was safely rescued from the well.

The Hindus of the village, however, raised a hue and cry that their well had been defiled and victimised the poor man. Fortunately, a barrister had come to the scene. He soundly rebuked the men who were tormenting Sadhuram and thus brought them to their senses. Thus, the man's life was saved otherwise no one knows what might have happened."

What is important: saving of the calf by the Untouchable and his polluting the well or the death of the calf and saving the well from being polluted by the Untouchable? From the point of view of the Hindus, it would be better if the calf had died than an Untouchable even for the purpose of saving the calf should have polluted the well. Another case of similar sort is reported in the '*Bombay Samachar*' of 19th December 1936:

"In Kaladi, a village of Calicut, the child of a young woman fell into a well. The woman raised an alarm but none present dared to go down the well. A stranger who was passing by jumped into the well and rescued the child. Later, when the people asked the benefactor who he was, he said, he was an Untouchable. Thereupon instead of being thankful, the man was fully abused and assaulted as he had polluted the well."

How unclean and unfit for association an Untouchable is to a Hindu be evident from the following incident reported in the '*Adi Hindu*' of Lucknow for July 1937: It says:

"An employee of the Madras Holmes Company, who claimed to be one of the high caste persons, passed away recently. When at the cremation ground his pyre was set fire to, his friends and kinsmen threw rice on it. Among these friends unfortunately there was an Untouchable, an Adi-Dravida of Madras. He also joined in the throwing of the rice. At this, the high caste Hindus rebuked him for defiling the pyre. This led on to a heated argument and the upshot was that two men were stabbed in the stomach, one of them died at once upon reaching the hospital and the condition of the other one is said to be critical."

There is one other incident more telling than this. On the 6th of March 1938, a meeting of the Bhangis was held at Kasarwadi (behind Woollen Mills) Dadar, Bombay, under the Chairmanship of Mr. Indulal Yadnik. In this meeting, one Bhangi boy narrated his experience in the following terms: I passed the Vernacular Final Examination in 1933. I have studied English up to the 4th Standard. I applied to the Schools Committee of the Bombay Municipality for employment as a teacher but I failed, as there was no vacancy. Then, I applied to the Backward Classes Officer, Ahmedabad, for the job of a Talati (village Patwari) and I succeeded. On 19th February 1936, I was appointed a Talati in the office of the Mamlatdar of the Borsad Taluka in the Kheda District.

Although my family originally came from Gujarat, I had never been in Gujarat before. This was my first occasion to go there. Similarly, I did not know that untouchability would be observed in Government offices. Besides in my application the fact of my being a Harijan was mentioned and so I expected that my colleagues in the office would know beforehand who I was. That being so, I was surprised to find the attitude of the clerk of the Mamlatdar's office when I presented myself to take charge of the post of the Talati.

The Karkun contemptuously asked, "Who are you?" I replied, "Sir, I am a Harijan"; He said, 'Go away, stand at a distance. How dare you stand so near me. You are in office, if you were outside I would have given you six kicks, what audacity to come here for service! "Thereafter, he asked me to drop on the ground my certificate and the order of appointment as a Talati. He then picked them up. While I was working in the Mamlatdar's office at Borsad I experienced great difficulty in the matter of getting water for drinking. In the verandah of the office there were kept cans containing drinking water. There was a waterman in-charge of these water cans. His duty was to pour out water to clerks in office whenever they needed it.

In the absence of the waterman they could themselves take water out of the cans and drink it. That was impossible in my case. I could not touch the cans for my touch would pollute the water, I had therefore to depend upon the mercy of the waterman. For my use there was kept a small rusty pot. No one would touch it or wash it except myself. It was in this pot that the waterman would dole out water to me. But I could get water only if the waterman was present. This waterman did not like the idea of supplying me with water. Seeing that I was coming for water he would manage to slip away with the result that I had to go without water and the days on which I had no water to drink were by no means few. I had the same difficulties regarding my residence. I was a stranger in Borsad. No caste Hindu would rent a house to me. The Untouchables of Borsad were not ready to give me lodgings for the fear of displeasing the Hindus who did not like my attempt to live as a clerk, a station above me. Far greater difficulties were with regard to food. There was no place or person from where I could get my meals. I used to buy 'Bhajhas' morning and evening, eat them in some solitary place outside the village and come and sleep at night, on the pavement of the verandahs of the Mamlatdar's office. In this way, I passed four days. All this became unbearable to me. Then I went to live at Jentral, my ancestral village. It was six miles from Borsad. Every day I had to walk eleven miles. This I did for a month and a half.

Thereafter the Mamlatdar sent me to a Talati to learn the work. This Talati was-in charge of three villages, Jentral, Khapur and Saijpur. Jentral was his headquarters. I was in Jentral with this Talati for two months. He taught me nothing and I never once entered the village office. The headman of the village was particularly hostile. Once he had said 'you fellow, your father, your brother are sweepers who sweep the village office and you want to sit in the office as our equal? Take cares, better give up this job.'

One day the Talati called me to Saijpur to prepare the population table of the village. From Jentral I went to Saijpur. I found the Headman and the Talati in the village office doing some work. I went, stood near the door of the office and wished them 'good morning' but they took no notice of me. I stood outside for about 15 minutes. I was already tired of life and felt enraged at being thus ignored and insulted. I sat down on a chair that was lying there. Seeing me seated on the chair the Headman and the Talati quietly went away without saying anything to me. A short while after, people began to come and soon a large crowd gathered round me.

This crowd was led by the Librarian of the village library. I could not understand why an educated person should have led this mob. I subsequently learnt that the chair was his. He started abusing me in the worst terms. Addressing the Ravania (village servant) he said 'who allowed this dirty'dog of a Bhangi to sit on the chair?' The Ravania unseated me and took away the chair from me. I sat on the ground. Thereupon the crowd entered the village office and surrounded me. It was a furious crowd raging with anger, some abusing me, some threatening to cut me to pieces with Dharya (a sharp weapon like the sword). I implored them to excuse me and to have mercy upon me. That did not have any effect upon the crowd. I did not know how to save myself. But an idea came to me of writing to the Mamlatdar about the fate that had befallen me and telling him how to dispose of my body in case I was killed by the crowd. Incidentally, it was my hope that if the crowd came to know that I was practically reporting against them to the Mamlatdar they might hold their hands. I asked the Ravania to give me a piece of paper which he did. Then with my fountain pen I wrote the following on it in big bold letters so that everybody could read it:

Be pleased to accept the humble salutations of Parmar Kalidas Shivram. This is to humbly inform you that the hand of death is falling upon me today. It would not have been so if I had listened to the words of my parents. Be so good as to inform my parents of my death. The Librarian read what I wrote and at once asked me to tear it off, which I did. They showered upon me innumerable insults. 'You want us to address you as our Talati? You are a Bhangi and you want to enter the office and sit on the chair? 'I implored for mercy and promised not to repeat this and also promised to give up the job. I was kept there till seven in the evening when the crowd left. Till then the Talati and the Mukhiya had not come. Thereafter I took fifteen days' leave and returned to my parents in Bombay." There is another facet of the social outlook of the Hindus towards the Untouchables, which cannot be neglected. This outlook is best illustrated by a study of the following cases. In the' *Alfzal*" of 8th September 1943:

> *"It was reported from Nasik on 1st September that the Hindus of a village attacked an Achchut family; tied the hands and feet of an elderly woman, placed her on a pile of wood which was subsequently set on fire. All this because they thought she was the cause of the Cholera in the village."*

The Harijan quarters of a village in Kaira District are reported to have been raided by Caste Hindus on suspicion that the Harijans were causing the death of cattle by witchcraft. It is alleged that about 200 villagers armed with sticks raided the Harijan quarters and tying an old woman to a tree, burnt her feet. Another woman is reported to have been belaboured.

The Harijans evacuated the village in panic, but Mr. Chhotabhai Patel, Secretary of the District Harijan Sevak Sangh who was apprized of the incidents has brought back the Harijans to the village and applied to the authorities for their protection.

A similar incident is reported from another village, where Harijans are alleged to have been severely belaboured." The matter did not end there. There was a recurrence of violence in which the whole body of Hindus are reported to have taken part in general assault on the Untouchables. The news appeared in the *Bharat Jyoti* of 22nd September 1946, which is reproduced below:

> *"Five Harijans, including one woman, were injured seriously when a crowd of villagers attacked them with dharias and lathis in a village in Borsad Taluka in Kaira District according to a report received by the Secretary of the Borsad Taluka Harijan Sevak Sangh. The attack was a sequel to the death of about seven buffaloes which the villagers attributed to black magic practised by the Harijans. The injured have been sent to hospital. Police rushed to the spot, and some persons have been arrested. The villagers, it is learnt, are threatening the Harijans that if they make any complaints to the authorities they would be burnt alive. Such incidents often occur in Kaira villages, and the District Magistrate of Kaira has instructed all police and other executive officers to take strong measures against such harassment of Harijans."*

The tale told by these cases is clear and simple. No comment is necessary. To the average Hindu, the Untouchable is not fit even for human association. He is the carrier of evil. He is not a human being. He must be shunned.

Untouchability and Lawlessness

There are many people who must be wondering as to how such an established order so full of inequalities could have survived. What are the forces, which go to support it? The forces which sustain the system the most important is the determination of the Hindus to maintain it at all cost. The Hindus are prepared to use every means to suppress the Untouchables whenever the Untouchables try to upset it even in the slightest degree. The ordinary non-violent Hindu will not hesitate to use the utmost violence against the Untouchables. There is no cruelty, which he will not practice against them to sustain the established order. Not many will readily believe this. But this is a fact. For those who have any doubt on the point, I reproduce below some cases of tyrannies and oppressions practised by the Hindus against the Untouchables as have been reported from time to time in the newspapers:

The following news item appeared in the "*Tej*" of Delhi in its issue of 4th September 1927:

> *"The Shiva Temple of Vykom has been desecrated by the Harijans by their coming too near to the temple. Now the Hindus of that area have decided that the ceremony of purifying the temple should be elaborately performed at great expense before the place is fit for worship again."*

The correspondent of '*Pratap*' reports the following incident which appears in its issue of 2nd September 1932:

> *"Meerut August 1932. On the day of Janmashtami some Harijans tried to gain admittance into Caste Hindu Temple but nothing came except widespread troubles and unrest. This year the local Dalit Association has decided that if the doors of the temples are not opened to them, they will undertake Satyagraha. When the Hindus came to know of this, they started making plans to defeat the moves of the Harijans. At last on the night of Janmashtami, the members of the Harijan community came in the form of a procession and tried to gain access to the temple Gods. The priests, however, refused them permission to enter and said, "You can have audience of the Gods standing outside on the street." Upon this a great crowd gathered at the place. The priests tried to enter the temple and thus a clash took place between the two parties and blows were freely exchanged."*

The Hindus do not allow the Untouchables to enter the Hindu temples. It would be thought that they would allow the Untouchables to have their own temples and install therein the image of God. That is a mistake. The Hindus will not allow even that. It is enough to quote two instances. One is from the "*Pratap*" of 12th February 1923:

> *"In the District of Agra, a Chamar who had seen a Brahmin worshipping the image of Vishnu in his house, began to do the same himself. When the Brahmin came to know of this he was most indignant and with the help of a number of villagers caught hold of the ill-fated Harijan, gave him a sound beating saying, 'How dare you try to win over the God Vishnu'. Finally, they stuffed his mouth with filth and left him. In sheer desperation the Chamar abandoned the Hindu faith and embraced Islam."*

The other is from the *'Hindu'* of 4th July 1939:

> *"A meeting of the Bellary District Harijan Advisory Board was held on 29th June 1939 at the Collector's Bunglow. Mr. A. D. Crombie, CIE., ICS., President of the Committee and Collector presided. With regard to the grievances of the Harijans of Narayanadevarakeri including allegations of extraction of forced labour from them and harassment by moneylenders, the Committee decided to call for official report, with a view to taking action, if necessary. The religious disabilities of the Harijans residing in Kudathini village were brought to the notice of the Committee. It was alleged that though the Harijans constructed a temple in their colony as long as twelve years ago, they could not install the image of God which was also ready in the temple, owing to the objections raised by a section of the Caste Hindus in the place to the Harijans taking out the image in procession in the village before the installation."*

How any attempt to take water from the Hindu well is dealt with by the Hindus can be seen from the following instances. The first one appeared in the *'Pratap'* of 12th February 1923:

> *"Mahashaya Chhedi Lalji has reported that a Chamar was going for idol worship, when on the way he felt thirsty. He cast his own iron pail into a well and drew out some water. Upon this he was rebuked by a high caste Hindu and then soundly beaten and locked up in*

a room. As it happened, I was passing by and when I enquired why this man was being kept under lock and key, the Diwan Saheb replied that this man cast his own pail into our well and wants to profane religion."

That even the Hindu women will not hesitate to take part in the assaults committed by the Hindus against the Untouchables who dare to take water from the Hindu well is a fact. Compare the following report which appeared in the '*Pratap*' of 26th February 1932:

"On 19th February 1932, a very tragic incident took place in the village of Pul Bajwan. This happened when Mahashaya Ramlal went to fetch some water from a well, the same well at which on 13th January 1932 some Rajputs had belaboured Mahashaya Ramlal and his companion. Pandit Bansilal. At that time, a crowd of Rajput women came up armed with all sorts of bats and sticks and gave such a sound beating to the Mahashaya that it is difficult to describe. All his body was covered with blood by the time the Rajput women had done with him. At this time, he is admitted in the hospital of Phuklian."

That even the support of an officer of Government in the exercise of their right to take water from the well will not save the Untouchables from assault is clear from the following incident which appeared in the '*Milap*' of 7th June 1924:

"Some days ago, an officer of the Canal Department came to the village of Rahian in Tehsil Sabha and he ordered some Megha Untouchables to help in drawing out water from a well. At first they refused but the officer rebuked them sternly and forced them to draw water. The next day the Hindus gathered at the well and sent for the Megha through a Chowkidar and asked them why they dared to climb up to the well. One Megha replied that they were obliged to do so and it was no fault of theirs. For this cheek he was attacked by the Hindus with sticks and hands and until the time of writing this, he is lying unconscious. Although the doctor has declared that the injuries are minor ones, a report of attempted murder and unlawful assembly has been filed with the Police. This however has been ignored

and the indifference of the police has created a feeling of great insecurity among the Megha people. The villagers are persecuting the Meghas very much, even their cattle are not allowed to drink water and all wells and ponds have been closed to them."

The Untouchables cannot take water from the Hindu well is not all. They must not build a pucca brick well for themselves even though they may have the money to do so. For having a pucca well for them selves means an attempt to raise themselves to the status of the Hindus which is contrary to the Established Order. The *'Milap'* of 6th June 1934 reports the following incidents: "Lala Ram Prashadji, Secretary of the Achhut Udharak Committee, Punjab, has written to the following effects:

"During this hot season, complaints are being received from everywhere that the supply of water is becoming a great problem. The Depressed Class people, who have no wells of their own sit near the well with their vessels in their hands. If someone is kind enough to pour out some water, well and good, otherwise they sit helpless. In some places, however, no one is allowed to pour out water to these people even for money and if anyone does so, mortal fights ensue. Not only is the use of the village wells forbidden to them, but they are not even allowed to make wells of their own with their own money."

To the same effect is the incident reported in the "*Tej*" of 21st April 1924:

"The Chamars of the village, Opad, numbered about 250. About a month and half ago, they gave up drinking water out of the leather bags of the Muslim water carriers (on the suggestions of the Arya Samaj Pandits?) and now they are in great difficulties about their water supply. The Jats of the village not only refuse to let them draw water out of the village wells but do not even let them make wells of their own. The poor Chamars are living on water from ponds and ditches. Yesterday, Dr. Sukhdevji, Secretary of Dalit Sudhar (Harijan Uplift) Committee came to make investigations in Upad and saw everything with his own eyes. He found the condition of the Chamars abject beyond words and their persecution by the Jats a real fact."

The following is from the *'Times of India'* dated 9th May 1931:

> *"In the Baroda State the Untouchables are supposed to be better treated than in the adjoining British territory, because the State has made laws recognising the equality of the Antyaja with caste people. And yet in Padras Taluka the other day the standing crop of a poor Antyaja woman was fired and she herself brutally assaulted, because she dared to send her little son to the local primary school. Now comes a tale of woe from Chanasma in Kadi Prant where an artisian well has been sunk and built with the labour of the Antayajas who were promised the use of the well. But when the well was ready for use they were first flatly told it was not for them, and when they complained to the Punch the latter generously allowed them to lay a pipe 500 feet long at the end of which they could have a tap all for themselves. Now an unexpected owner of the land at the tap had cropped up, so the pipeline was taken somewhere near to the local tank, but this meant pollution of the tank and therefore of the dirty linen washed there. So the tap was accommodated elsewhere. But did this mean the end of the trouble? No, the enraged caste people have cut the pipeline several times and the Antyajas are without water to drink. How very 'adequate' to use Mr. Gandhi's term, must the Untouchables feel the treatment given to them by their coreligionists."*

Mr. Sanjana in a letter to the *'Times of India'* of the 7th November 1928 reports what Mr. Thakkar saw in the year 1927 regarding the awful plight of the Untouchables in the matter of water.

> *"In Balsad Taluk, Mr. Thakkar saw a Bhangi woman waiting near a well for some merciful 'people' to give her some water. She had waited from morning till noon, and none had given her any. But the most exquisite touch of spirituality is revealed in the manner of giving water to the Bhangis; it cannot be poured direct into their pots—any 'people' doing so would get polluted. Says, Mr. Thakkar, once our teacher Chunibhai had shown the temerity of pouring water direct from his*

bucket into a Bhangi's pot and he had received a stern warning in consequence 'Master this sort of thing won't be (tolerated) here'. A small cistern is built below the slope of the well. Anyone who is moved by pity may pour some water in the cistern. A bamboo pipe just out of the cistern, and the Bhangi women must put her pot under the pipe, and it may get filled in an hour or so. For, adds Mr. Thakkar, it is only the unwanted water remaining over in the bucket of the woman drawing it that is as a rule thrown into the cistern, and that too if she takes pity on the waiting Bhangi woman."

Under the established order, the Untouchables have no right to education and certainly have no right to be admitted to the village school. Those Untouchables who have dared to make a breach in these rules of the Established Order have been severely punished by the Hindus. The following are only a few of the numerous cases that have happened: From the *"Arya Gazette"* of Lahore dated 30th June 1921:

"A Mahashaya wrote an article in the paper 'Young India", *in which he reported that in district surat there is a village called Sisodri. In a very short span of time it has made such progress on the path of nationalism that it could be held up as a model of noncooperation. With all this, however, the old contempt for the Harijan remains. The writer says that in the nationalist school of that place, I saw a Dhed caste child sitting all apart in one corner of I the classroom and proclaiming by his very looks that he was an untouchable. I asked the students why they did not let this boy sit with them and they replied that this could not be until the Harijan left drinking wine and eating meat. The Harijan boy at once said that he had already given these up. The high caste students could say nothing now."*

From the *'Pratap'* of 12th February 1923: "Mahashaya Santramji has reported: It happened recently that a Brahmin teacher was appointed by the Government to go and teach in a village school for Chamar boys. When he came there, the Brahmins, Kshatrias and others boycotted the teacher saying, 'You have come here to teach the Chamars and raise them to our level. Have You?" From the *'Tej'* of 11th April 1924:

"Swami Shradhanandji has written: There was a nationalist school in Khatsayas which I visited towards the end of November 1921. When I enquired how many Harijan children read there, I was told only three and they too, sit outside the classroom in the verandah. In my lecture I objected to this procedure and said that in a nationalist institution, it was only proper that these boys should be allowed to sit inside the classroom. The manager of the school acted on my advice. The next day the benches of the school were all deserted and till this day the Grand building of that nationalist school stands locked out and dreary."

From *"Milap"* dated 18th April 1924:

"Here is an incident from Hoshungabad. The district Council sent a circular letter to the schools that the Harijan children should be educated in the schools. The headmasters began to act on the orders. When one of the schools admitted some Harijan children the Honorary Magistrate took great offence at it and withdrew his children from that school; other guardians also followed suit and all together got a meeting of the school committee convened and resolutions passed in it, that the education of Harijans in the school is against the Public wishes. They said that after coming into contact with Harijans, the Brahmin children change their Janayu (a religious thread) therefore this school committee could not undertake the education of Harijan children."

From *"Pratap"* dated 3rd April 1932:

"Ahmedabad, 1st April 1932: A report has been received from the village of Nawagaon, Baroda State, that ever since the Harijan schools were closed down and permission given to the Harijans to enter the ordinary village schools, the villagers have been subjecting the Harijans to endless persecution. It is reported that the thousand stacks of hay belonging to Harijan farmers, were burnt down, Kerosine oil has been sprinkled into the Harijan wells and attempts made to set fire to their houses. A Harijan boy was assaulted on his way to school and a general boycott of the Harijans has been declared."

The *"Hindustan Times"* in its issue of 26th May 1939 says:

"Several persons are reported to have raided a night school in village Catipore in the district where Kisans and others used to be taught. The teacher was caught hold of by them, and asked to close the school on the ground that the boys of the Untouchables, after acquiring education will begin to assert themselves to treat them on a footing of equality. When the teacher refused to do so he was belaboured and the students were asked to disperse."

The last instance I would like to refer occurred in the year 1935 in *the* village of Kavitha in Dholka Taluka of the Ahmedabad District of the Bombay Presidency. The incident occurred on 8th August 1935. As the Bombay Government had issued orders requiring the admission of the children of the Untouchables in public schools, the Untouchables of village Kavitha thought of taking advantage of the order. What happened to them is reported below:

"On 8-8-1935, the Untouchables of the village Kavitha took four of their children to be admitted in the village school. Much caste Hindus from the village had gathered near the school to witness this. This occasion for admission passed off quietly and nothing untoward happened. From the next day however the caste Hindus of the village withdrew their children from the school as they did not like their children sitting with those of the Untouchables and getting themselves polluted."

"Some time thereafter an Untouchable from the village was assaulted by a Brahmin on 13th August 1935. The male members of the Untouchables of the village had come to Dholka to file a criminal complaint against the Brahmin in the court of the Magistrate. Coming to know that the adult members of the Untouchables were absent the Hindus of the village invaded the quarters of the Untouchables. They were armed with sticks, spears and swords.

Among the invaders was caste Hindu women. They started attacking the old men and women of the Untouchables. Some of the victims fled into the jungle some shut themselves up. These invaders directed their vehemence against those Untouchables who were suspected to have taken a lead in the matter of the admission of their children in the village school. They broke open their doors and not finding them in, they broke the tiles and the rafters of the roofs over their houses.

"Terror-stricken these Untouchables men and women who were assaulted and beaten were anxious about the safety of those of their elders who had gone to Dholka and who were expected back that night. The caste Hindus knowing that the leaders of Untouchables who had gone to Dholka would be returning had concealed themselves behind the bushes and shrubs on the way to the village. Having come to know of this, an old Untouchable woman sneaked out of the village in the dark, met the leaders who were returning and informed them that armed gangs of caste Hindus were hiding themselves to waylay them and that therefore they should not come into the village. They refused to listen fearing that the caste Hindus might do greater mischief in their absence.

At the same time, they were afraid that if they did enter they might be assaulted. They therefore decided to wait outside the village in the field till after midnight. In the meantime, the gang of caste Hindus who were in ambush waited and waited and finally gave up the game and retired. The leaders of the Untouchables entered the village after about 3 a.m. in the night. If they had come earlier and met the murderous gang they would probably have been done to death. On seeing the harm done to person and property they left the village for Ahmedabad before day break, and informed the Secretary of the Harijan Sevak Sangh, a body organised by Mr. Gandhi to look after the welfare of the Untouchables.

But the Secretary was helpless. Not only did the caste Hindus use physical violence, but they conspired to make the life of the Untouchables intolerable. They refused to engage them as labourers; they refused to sell them foodstuffs. They refused to give them facilities for grazing their cattle and they used to commit stray assaults on Untouchable men and women. Not only this, but the caste Hindus in their frenzy poured kerosine oil in the well from which the Untouchables used to get their supply of drinking water. This, they did for days together. The result was that the Untouchables of the village had no water. When things reached this stage the Untouchables thought of filing criminal complaint before a Magistrate which they did on 17th October, making some of the caste Hindus as the accused."

The strange part of the case is the part played by Mr. Gandhi and his henchman, Sardar Vallabhbhai Patel. With all the knowledge of tyranny and oppression practised by the caste Hindus of Kavitha against the Untouchables all that Mr. Gandhi felt like doing was to advise the Untouchables to leave the village. He did not even suggest that the miscreants should be hauled up before a court of law. His henchman Mr. Vallabhbhai Patel, played a part which was still more strange. He had gone to Kavitha to persuade the caste Hindus not to molest the Untouchables.

But they did not even give him a hearing. Yet this very man was opposed to the Untouchables hauling them up in a court of Law and getting them punished. The Untouchables filed the complaint notwithstanding his opposition. But he ultimately forced them to withdraw the complaint on the caste Hindus making some kind of a show of an understanding not to molest, an undertaking, which the Untouchables can never enforce. The result was that the Untouchables suffered and their tyrants escaped with the aid of Mr. Gandhi's friend, Mr. Vallabhbhai Patel.

The Untouchables are claimed by the Hindus as Hindus. But the dead body of an Untouchable cannot be cremated in the Hindu cremation ground. The *"Free Press"* of 7th June, 1946 reports the following:

> *"Citing a recent criminal case in which two Madura Harijans were sentenced to four months rigorous imprisonment for doing an act which was likely to wound the feelings of others, Mr. A. S. Vaidyanatha lyer in a communication to the press draws the attention of the public to the 'cruel suffering which the Harijans have to bear by reason of Untouchability."*

Mr. Vaidyanatha lyer says: 'A Madura Harijan who had lost his eldest child cremated the body in the Madura municipal burning ghat in a shed which is said to be set apart for caste Hindus instead of in the one reserved for Harijans. The Harijan's plea was, he did not know of any such reservation, that it was drizzling and that the former place was better. No caste Hindu raised any objection nor was there any proof that anyone's feelings were wounded. The incident came to the notice of the Madura police who prosecuted the father of the child and another near relation on the ground that such act was likely to wound the feelings of others because the Harijans were Untouchables. Mr. lyer adds, "he brought this case to the notice of the Madras Ministry." The *'Savadhan'* of 22nd April, 1945 says:

> *"On 18th March, 1945, a sweeper died in the village Floda, District Muzaffarnagar. The Sweepers of the village took the dead body to the cremation grounds. This enraged the Tyagi Brahmins of the village who abused the sweepers for their audacity in bringing their dead to the caste Hindu grounds. The sweepers protested that they were Hindus and would cremate the dead. But the Brahmins were not at all amenable to reason and told the sweepers that irrespective of their being Hindus and Muslims they must bury their dead and if they failed to do it they (Brahmins) would themselves bury the dead body. When the poor sweepers were thus threatened and were also afraid of being beaten they buried the dead body."*

This is not all. There is a further point to benoted. The Touchable Hindus dispose of the dead body by cremating it. Just because it is a presumption on the part of the Untouchables to initiate the ways of the Hindus, which are marks of their superior status, the Untouchables must necessarily bury their dead even if they do not wish to do so. An instance of this compulsory burial was reported in the *'Milap'* of 6th June 1924:

> *"The chief cause of the awakening among the Untouchables is the tyranny of the Hindus. I was not aware of this but the reports that I have received from various workers has caused me much pain. From one place I am informed that the Untouchables of that place are not allowed to even burn their dead. This, however it seems has created a new spirit among the sweepers of the place. They have started burying their dead with the head downwards probably to distinguish themselves from others who bury the corpse in a lying position. The Sweepers think that if they also act in imitation of others, it is derogatory."*

The wearing of the sacred thread is evidence of noble birth. The Untouchables with the idea of ennobling themselves thought of wearing the sacred thread. The atrocities committed by the caste Hindus on the Untouchables of the village Ringwari in Garhwal District in U. P. are reported in the *'National Herald'* of 6th June "After leading a fugitive life for well nigh two months as a result of persecution at the hands of the caste Hindus, ten families consisting of 33 Harijans have now been able to return to their-homes in village Ringwari of Chandkot with the help of the district authorities of Garhwal. These Harijans, it may be recalled, had taken full advantage of the social movement started for their uplift by Mahatma Gandhi and the late Swami Shradhanand.

They had taken the sacred thread and made it a part of their duty to perform 'Sandhya'. But this was resented very much by the caste Hindus of Garhwal as according to them it amounted to a virtual invasion of their 'right and privileges'. The resentment found expression in a number of assaults on Harijans and persistent social persecution. They were asked to desist from using 'polies' and 'palkies' in their marriage procession and four of them were compelled at one place to kill a buffalo and eat its flesh.

At Ringwari these atrocities reached a climax, when all the water springs, grazing grounds and other public places were closed to the Harijans who refused to submit to the caste Hindus. In consequence the above mentioned ten families had to leave their villages at dead of night, in order to avoid further persecution." Other instances of similar sort are given below:

1. "Some Arya Samajists managed to raise the caste of some Untouchables and gave them the sign of the caste, namely, the religious thread worn round the neck. But the mass of the Sanatanists could not bear even this because their religion does not allow the Untouchables to wear the thread. This is why thread-wearing Untouchables are daily persecuted by the high caste Hindus."
2. "Bhagat Harichand of Moila, District Mirpur, Jammu State was purified by the Arya Samajists and given the thread to wear. The Hindu Jats of the place began to victimize him and ask him to put off the thread.

Harichand however remained steadfast on his religion. At last one day when the Bhagat Harichand had finished the Gaitri Path, he was caught hold of by the Hindu Jats and severely beaten and his thread broken. The cause of their incensement was this that wheareas before the Shudh, Shudha Meghs had addressed the Jats as 'Gharib Nawaz' (the benefactors of the poor), now they only use 'Namastey'." From the *Arya Gazette* dated 14th September 1929:

"The Hindu Rajputs of the village Ramani, near the town Berhampur, Distt. Gurdaspur, called the Untouchables of their villages from their homes and ordered them to put off the holy thread at once and swear never to put it on again otherwise their lives were in danger. Upon this Untouchables calmly replied 'Maharaj why are you angry with us. Your own brothers, the Arya Samajists have very kindly put these threads round our necks and have ordered us to always protect them for they are the true symbols of the Hindu faith. If you take objection to them, you can tear them off our bodies with your own hands'. Upon this the Rajputs fell upon the poor men with their lathis and kept on thrashing them for a long time. The Untouchables put up with this persecution with great fortitude and refused to resist or protest. But their torments took no pity on their helpless condition and three or four Rajputs actually tore the holy thread off the body of a Harijan named Gori Ram and bruised his body with a hoe in mock imitation of the sign of the thread."

From the *'Milap'* dated 12th October 1929:

"The Rajputs of the village Bahmani have from time past launched a programme against the Untouchables. There is a case going on in the court about the breaking of a holy thread and there is another case too, about an Untouchable woman who was going on to the field to cut the harvest on 7th October 1929 when a Rajput severely thrashed her and caused serious bruises. The woman was brought home on a bed."

What happens to an Untouchable if he remains seated on a cot in the presence of a Hindu can be seen from the following incident reported in *'Jivan'* of July 1938:

"Nanda Ram and Mangali Prasad of village Pachhahera, Police Post Margaon, Tehsil and District Sitapur, invited their friends and relatives for a communal feast. When the guests were sitting on cots and smoking, Thakkur Sooraj Baksh Singh and Harpal Singh, Zamindars of the village, came there, sent for Nanda Ram and Mangali Prasad and asked who the people sitting and smoking were and why they were sitting on cots. Mangali Prasad said that they were his friends and relatives and asked if only Thakkurs could sit on cots. Enraged by this, the Thakkurs beat both the brothers and their men beat the guests severely as a result of which one man and one woman became senseless and others sustained serious injuries."

The Untouchables are Hindus. They are also citizens with the same civic rights. But the Untouchables cannot claim the right of the citizenship if it conflicts with any rules of the Established Order. For instance, no Untouchable can claim lodging in an inn even though it is public. In '*Jivan*' of August 1938, is reported the experience of an Untouchable named Kannhaiya Lal Jatav of Fetegarh:

"When I went to stay in Dharmashala near Allahabad Junction on 15th August 1938 at 10 p.m. there was no difficulty and I laid down on a cot after paying an advance of Re. 1. But at 11 p.m. when the lodgers went to the Manager of the Dharmashala to note down their addresses, and while noting down my address I put down my caste as Jatav; the Manager got wild and said that the Dharmashala was not meant for the stay of low caste people and asked me to get out at once. I pointed out to him that according to the rules of the Dharmashala, it was meant for Hindus only and there was no ban on Untouchables and asked if I was not a Hindu that he was asking me to leave. I also pleaded that being resident of Farrukabad and not acquainted with anyone in Allahabad there was no place where I could go at 11 p.m. On this, the Manager got furious and repeating the couplet from Ramayan (Sudras illiterate, cattle and women all these deserve to be beaten) said that in spite of being a low-caste he dared to talk about rules and law and will not get out unless he is

beaten. Then suddenly he got my bedding etc., threw out of the Dharmashala and all of them were ready to beat me. In the face of such odds, I at once left the Dharmashala and lay down on a plank of wood in front of a shop facing the Dharmashala and had to pay annas 2 as rent to the shopkeeper for a night. I therefore appeal to my Scheduled Caste brethren to hold meetings everywhere and request Government to construct separate Dharmashalas for our people in every town or to get all the existing Dharmashalas opened for us."

Under the Established Order, the work of lifting and removing dead cattle as well as doing the scavenger's work is beneath the dignity of the Hindus. It must be done by the Untouchables. The Untouchables have also begun to think that it is derogatory to their status and are refusing to do it. The Untouchables, however, are forced by the Hindus to do it against their will. The '*Jivan*' of June 1938 reports: "One day, in May 1938, Bhajju Ram Jatav of village Bipoli, Police post Baria, District Aligarh was sitting in his house at about 11 a.m. when some Brahmins namely Prithik, Hodal, Sita Ram, Devi and Chuni, all of whom had lathis came and tried to force him to lift dead cattle; and when he refused saying that he was not used to that work and asked them to go to some one who does that sort of work, he was mercilessly belaboured with lathis." The same journal in its issue of October 1938 gives the following news item:

"On 24th October 1938, some cattle of a Brahmin of village Lodhari, Tehsil Sadabad, District Muttra, died. The Scheduled Caste people of the village who were asked to lift it refused to do so. This enraged the caste Hindus so much that they have asked the Scheduled Caste people not to go to their fields for ablutions nor to allow their cattle to graze in their (caste Hindus) fields."

The Untouchables must not wear decent and clean clothes and they must not wear gold or silver ornaments. If the Untouchables defy these rules, the Hindus will not hesitate to bring them to book. The Untouchables have been trying to defy these rules, with what consequences will be seen from the following incidents, which have been reported in the newspapers:

"Until 1922, the Untouchable caste of Dalai in Berar District of Bundi, were forbidden to eat wheat. In February 1922, a Chamar woman was put on the Rock in Sakatgarh, Jaipur, simply because she was wearing silver ornaments on her feet. The reason given was this that only men of the high castes were allowed to wear silver or to eat wheat. The low caste people should not dare to aspire to these things. So far we had been thinking that such antiquated ideas were supposed to have had probably died out by this time."

The *'Times of India'* in its issue of 4th January 1928 reports the tyranny and oppression practised upon the Balais who form an Untouchable community in Central India for their daringness to wear clean clothes and golden ornaments. Says the 'Times': In May (1927) high caste Hindus *viz.*, Kalotas Rajputs and Brahmins including the Patils and Patwaris of villages Kanana, Bicholee Hafsi, Bicholi Mardana and of about 15 other villages in the Indore district informed the Balais of their respective villages that if they wished to live among them, they must conform to the following rules:

1. Balais must not wear gold lace bordered pugrees;
2. They must not wear dhoties with coloured or fancy borders;
3. They must convey intimation of the death of any Hindu to relatives of the deceased—no matter how far away these relatives may be living;
4. In all Hindu marriages, the Balais must play music before the processions, and during the marriages;
5. The Balai women must not wear fancy gowns for jackets;
6. Balai women must attend all cases of confinement of Hindu women;
7. The Balais must render services without demanding remuneration, and must accept whatever a Hindu is pleased to give;
8. If the Balais do not agree to abide by these terms, they must clear out of the villages.

The Balais refused to comply; and the Hindu element proceeded against them. Balais were not allowed to get water from the village wells; they were not allowed to let their cattle to graze. Balais were prohibited from passing through land owned by a Hindu; so that if the field of a Balai was surrounded by fields owned by Hindus, the Balai could have no access to his own field. The Hindus also let their cattle graze down the fields of Balais. The Balais submitted petitions to the Darbar of Indore against these persecutions, but as they could get no timely relief, and the oppression continued, hundreds of Balais with their wives and children, were obliged to abandon their homes in which their ancestors lived for generations, and to migrate to adjoining states, *viz.* to villages in Dhar, Dewas, Bangali, Bhopal, Gwalior and other states.

Only a few days ago the Hindus of Reoti village barely 8 miles to the North of Indore city ordered the Balais to sign a stamped agreement in accordance with the rules framed against the Balais by the Hindus of other villages. The Balais refused to comply, It, is alleged that some of them were beaten by the Hindus; and one Balai was fastened to a post, and was told that he would be let go, on agreeing to sign the agreement. He signed the agreement, and was released ". The next is from the *'Arya Gazette'* dated 21st January, 1928:

> *"Up till now the tales of woe that were usually related of the persecution of the Harijans were mostly from the Madras province, but now thanks to the treatment of the Maharana of the Simla Hills, one has not to go so far to search for these stories. In the Simla district, their dwells a caste called 'Collie' whose members are very handsome and hard working. The Hindus of that area consider them to be Untouchables although they do not engage in any such work which should render them objectionable in the eyes of the Hindu religion. The members of this caste are not only powerful and well built but intelligent also. Almost all the songs that the dwellers of the Simla Hills sing are composed by the 'Collies'. These people labour all day long and venerate the Brahmins excessively but still they cannot so much as pass near the house of a Brahmin. Their children cannot read in schools and 'Pathashalas' (religious monastic schools). Their women folk cannot wear gold ornaments. It has even been reported that some Collies have gone to the Punjab and earned some money with*

which they have bought gold rings and earrings. When however they have brought these back to their homes, they have been cast into the jail and not freed until the ornaments had passed into the pockets of the State Officers."

The following letter appeared in the *'Pratap'* of 23rd June 1926: "Swami Ramanandji Sanyasi writes:

On the 23rd of March 1926, in the evening a Chamar came to me who had recently managed to escape from the clutches of the Jats. He related to me a moving tale of the sufferings that his caste had to put up with in the village of Kheri near Faridabad in the District of Gurgaon. On the morning of 24th March I reached Faridabad in the District of Gurgaon, so as to investigate the state of affairs myself. The result of my enquiries is briefly as follows:

"On the 5th of March the marriage took place of the daughter of a Chamar called Gorkhi. The financial condition of the Chamar was comparatively good and he entertained his guests in the same way as people of the high castes do. Moreover, before handing away his daughter, he gave her three gold ornaments. This news spread amongst the Jats and was widely discussed. It was decided finally that the high castes had been insulted by the fact that the lower castes have started viewing with them. Till the 20th of March nothing untoward happened but on the morning of the 21st the Jats called a meeting of the Panchayat (village council) to consider the matter. Just at that moment a party of the Chamars of which the greater portion was composed of boys, girls and women was setting out for Faridabad on its daily duty. The party had just gone out of the village as far as the Dharmashala when the Jats attacked it. All the men of the party were belaboured and the women were thrashed with shoes. The backs of some were broken and of some the arms. Not only this, even their implements were robbed. A Muslim happened to pass along that way and the Jats took hold of him also and robbed him of his big gold earrings as well as of twenty-eight rupees. On the 22nd of March some groups of the Jats went into the fields of the Chamar and played

havoc with them. The crop thus destroyed was estimated at about a thousand rupees. At that time, Nanwa, the son of Kori, was working in the fields. The Jats gave him also a thorough beating. On the 22nd of March again a party of the Jats sallied forth armed with flaming torches dipped in Kerosene oil, with the intention of setting fire to the houses of the Chamars but later came away. On the 23rd of March at midnight a house was set on fire belonging to the grandfather of that married girl who has been mentioned above. The house is now a heap of ashes. It contained sixteen skins ready to be made into shoes and worth 90 rupees. They also got burnt up together with the other household goods. The general situation now is that the Jats have surrounded the town and no Chamar is allowed to go out. The Baniyas also, out of fear of the Jats, have refused to sell anything to the Chamars. For three days the Chamars as well as their cattle have been starving."

The following is a more recent occurrence. It has happened in Malabar. The facts of the case are revealed by the following resolution passed at the first Chirakal Taluka Harijan Conference held at Cherukunn in Malabar on 5th June 1945 with Shri K. Kannan, M.L.A., presiding:

"This Conference invites the urgent attention of the Government and the public to the increasing cases of inhuman oppressions of the Scheduled Castes of Malabar by Hindus, Muslims and Christians, particularly to the severest type of oppression now going on, almost with impunity, in the Nattika Firka, Ponnani Taluk, where something like a regular Harijan hunting is taking place every day as a result of the Harijans trying to wear gold ornaments and use clean clothes and umbrellas. In addition to numerous cases of assaults a Harijan marriage party was waylaid and assaulted and the shirts of men and the sarees of women removed by force and a Harijan student mercilessly beaten in Vadanpilly on 27th May 1945. This Conference while congratulating the progressive Thiya youths of the place under the enlightened leadership of Messrs. C. S. Gopalan, M. S. Sankaranarayan and P. C. Ramakrishna

Vydier for their magnificient efforts to help the Harijans, most emphatically protests against the callous indifference of the local authorities, particularly/of the Police Department in that the ill-treated Harijans did not get any timely protection from them.

This conference desires to state that almost in all cases of the above-said oppressions, the aggrieved Harijans have received neither protection nor justice from the police. There are instances where poor Harijans were even beaten by the Police for their coming forward to give evidence in such cases. In so far as these events have reduced the Harijans of Malabar to a very miserable plight and the situation, if left alone, is likely to develop into a crisis endangering the lives of all progressive Harijans who are trying to break the shackles of caste and economic exploitation of the vested interests in Malbar. This Conference most earnestly appeals to the Government of India, the Hon'ble Dr. B. R. Ambedkar and all the enlightened people in the country to see that the Harijans are allowed to live in this land as free citizens of a democratic country unmolested by any people and promptly protected by the administration whenever they are oppressed by others."

The Untouchables must not eat rich food even if they can afford it.

It is an offence for the Untouchables to live above their station in life. The *'Pratap'* of 26th February 1928 relates the following occurrence:

"In the State of Jodhpur at a place Chandayal, you will still see men who do not think that the Harijans have even the right to eat Halva. One of the Untouchable castes is that of Sargaroes. Sometime back on the occasion of the Marriage ceremony of two or three girls, Halva was prepared for the members of the marriage party. For this purpose, maida (white flour) was brought from the Thakur Sahib. At mealtime, the marriage party came for meals but just at that time the Kanwar Sahib of Chandawala sent orders to the Saragaroes that they could not eat Halva. Some cringing sycophants negotiated a compromise in this way that the Kanwar

Sahib be presented with Rs. 200 and then permission will be given to eat Halva. At this the Sargaroes got infuriated and refused to pay the money."

To lead a marriage procession through the main streets of the village is the right of every caste Hindu. It is also in evidence that the community, which enjoys this right, is accepted as a respectable community. The Untouchables have no such right. But they have been seeking to establish such a right by taking their marriage procession through the main streets of the village with the object of establishing their social status. The following incidents show how the Hindus have dealt with this claim. From the *'Adi-Hindu'* dated July 1927:

"Bangalore, 27th May 1927: Seven Brahmins were sentenced to pay a fine of hundred rupees each, by the First Class Magistrate. These men had wantonly attacked a procession of the well-known Pariah Untouchable caste when it was passing along the Mallkot Road where only Brahmins live."

From the *'Pratap'* dated 25th October 1931: "In the village of Hargaon, district Garhwal when the high caste Hindus heard that a marriage party of the Untouchables was coming and the bridegroom was sitting in a palanquin they sallied forth in great numbers and surrounded the party and gave it a severe beating. In intense cold they held up the marriage party and kept it without food for 24 hours. The members of the party were inhumanly treated and were only rescued from this difficult situation by the coming of the Police."

From the *'Satya Samwad'* Lahore dated 3rd November 1931: "A marriage party was passing near Delhi, carrying the bridegroom in a palanquin. The high caste Hindus took offence at this for they thought it to be an insult to them. They held up the party for two days and gave it nothing either to eat or drink. At last the police came and chased away these tyrants and rescued the marriage party."

The *'Jivan'* a Hindu journal for June 1938 reports,

1. "In village Sevra, the Golas (Purva Thakurs) who boast of being Congressites, have so mercilessly beaten with spears and lathis the unarmed Jatavs of that village that five of them were lying wounded in the hospital

with arms and ribs broken. Bansi has sustained fracture of the skull bone and is still unconscious in the hospital. All this happened because when a marriage party came to the village the bridegroom was wearing a glittering crown (Pukka Mohar) which offended the Thakurs, who wanted to attack the marriage party; but desisted because of the party's superior strength and were therefore content with only insulting the marriage party within the Zamindari at that time."

2. "In village Dorra, Tehsil Fatechand, District Agra, a marriage party came to the house of Moti Ram Jatav from village Rampur. The bridegroom was wearing a glittering crown and the party also brought band music and fireworks. The Caste Hindus objected to the party proceeding with the music band playing and displaying fireworks. Moti Ram protested against this and said that they were also as good human beings as any others. On this, the caste Hindus caught hold of Moti Ram and gave him a severe beating and also attacked the marriage party. A sum of Rs. 15-1-0 tied in Moti Ram's turban was also removed."
3. "While a marriage party was on its way to the house of Prem Singh and Girvar Singh, Jatavs of village Khurva, Police post Sakini, District Aligarh, it was prevented by the caste Hindus from proceeding further unless the music band stopped playing, and the procession was threatened to be killed and looted if the music was not stopped. Caste Hindus were also enraged for refusal by the Jatavs to do 'Begar" and for the audacity to have music band playing with a marriage party. On the marriage party's refusal to stop music, the caste Hindus were so much enraged that they threw brickbats and stones at the party."

The *'Hindustan Times'* of the 24th of March 1945 reports the following incident relating to the same subject:

"A Shilpakar marriage party of the village of Dhanuri in Lands down sub-division carrying the bridegroom in a 'palki' was proceeding to the bride's house in the village of Mall Dhangu. A man introducing himself as an agent of the Patwari of Mall Dhangu advised the

party to go through an out of the way route to avoid disturbance by caste Hindus. The party, accordingly, took a forest path and when they were at a lonely spot a whistle brought out about 200 caste Hindus who, it is alleged, attacked the party and carried away the 'palki". The Shilpakar party reached the bride's house two days later and the marriage was, it is reported, performed in the presence of the Sub-divisional Magistrate and a police party brought by him. The Patwari has been suspended in this connection."

The *Civil and Military Gazette of Lahore* in its issue of 24th June 1945 reports:

"A party of Rajputs, armed with axes, lathis and daggers, attacked yesterday Harijans of a village in Gwalior State, killing one and inflicting serious injuries on four. The Rajputs and the Harijans of the village were on hostile terms for some time past ever since the Harijans took out a procession to celebrate the birth of an heir apparent to the Gwalior Darbar. The Rajputs strongly protested against it, as according to them, Harijans were not entitled to the privileges of such celebrations. Last month, a proclamation was issued by the Maharaja giving equal rights to the Harijans."

Here are a few cases to show how the Hindus treat with violence any attempt on the part of the Untouchables to imitate the ways and manners of the Hindus and to have a little pride in themselves. The following is from the *"Bombay Samachar"* of 4th November 1936:

"At Uttapalam (in Malabar) an Ezhava by caste named Sivaraman, aged 17, went to the shop of a caste Hindu to buy salt and asked in the Malayalam language for 'uppu'. In Malabar, according to custom, caste Hindus alone can use the word 'uppu' for salt; being only a Harijan he ought to have used the word 'pulichatan'. Consequently, the high caste grocer was very angry and is alleged to have thrashed Sivaraman so severely that the latter died."

The following instances are collected from the *'Samata':*

(1) "At Kathi (District Poona) the people have begun to

persecute the Untouchables because the latter have begun saying 'Ram, Ram and Namaskar'. Be it known to the un-intimated that these are salutations which only the higher castes have the right to employ; the Mahars, etc. must say 'Johar' or 'Paya Lagu' (I touch your feet) to the people.

(2) The Untouchables of Tanoo (District Poona) tried to behave 'like Touchable Hindu people'; the result of this impudent encroachment is that many of them have had to leave the village and some have migrated to Bavda.

(3) At Valapur (District of Sholapur) the Mahars are persecuted because they have dared to refuse to address Touchables as 'Saheb' and to say 'Paya Lagu' ('I touch your feet') in salutation.

(4) At Jambad (District Sholapur) the Untouchables refused to make 'Nautch' and 'Tamasha' for the diversion of their Touchable lords. Therefore these Untouchables were thrashed, their huts were burnt down or pulled down, and they were driven out of the village limits.

(5) At Bavda (District Poona) some Untouchables exhorted their fellow-outcastes to give up eating the leavings of higher caste people, dead animals, etc., and to refuse to do the dirty work of the people. The elders of the village have told these Mahars with new fanglad notions that it is their 'Dharma' to eat what they have always been eating and do what they have been doing. Those Mahars who do not follow their ancient and eternal 'Dharma' have been thrashed by the people and threatened with expulsion from the village."

The Hindu treats the Untouchables as being born to serve the Hindu community. It being his duty to serve, the Untouchables cannot refuse to serve the Hindu whenever the latter call upon to do so. The Hindus of the village hold the belief that they can commandeer the labour of the Untouchables. The system is known as '*Begar*', or forced labour. A few instances will show that dire consequences follow from the refusal of the Untouchables to submit to the system. The '*Jivan*' of December 1938 report the following incidents: "On 29th November 1938, the Jatavs of village Kohana, district Muttra were seriously tortured by the Jats and Brahmins for refusing Begar.

The Thakkurs and the Brahmins of this village used to extract Begar from the Jatavs and to harass them. The latter decided not to do Begar and do only that work for which wages were paid. Recently, a bullock died in the village and the Thakkurs and other caste Hindus tried to force the Jatavs to lift it, but they said that they could do that only if they were paid. This enraged the caste Hindus so much that they asked a sweeper to fill the Jatavs' well with excreta and make them not to go to their fields for ablutions and decided to tease them in every way. When the Jatavs prevented the Sweeper from putting excreta in their well, he called the Jats, Thakkurs and Brahmins who were all ready for an attack. They attacked the Jatavs with lathis and seriously belaboured them and also set fire to their houses as a result of which six houses were burnt to ashes and 18 Jatavs were wounded seriously and a lot of their household property was taken away by the rowdies." The same *Journal* in its issue of February 1939 reports:

> *"The Jats of village Abhaipura, tehsil Kirvali, district Agra, are used to extract Begar (Forced labour) from the poor Scheduled Caste people and beat them on demanding wages. Some three months back Sukhi Jat forced Sukh Ram, Ghanshyam and Humka, Jatavs to do work for them and did not pay any wages. These persons are so much fed up with such high-handedness that they have left the villages and lived with their relatives in other villages, while their utensils and other household goods have been taken away by the Jats and concealed in some barn."*

The '*Savadhan*' in its issue of 3rd June 1945 reports the following incident:

> *"Mehraji Kori, a Scheduled Caste woman has filed a complaint in the court of Mr. Mahboob Alam, City Magistrate under Sections 376, 341 and 354-A against Brahma Singh, Sulaiman and Aftab, constables of Jubi Police post. It is alleged that at about 10-30 p.m. on 2nd May 1945 these three constables, Sumar, Kahar, Kallu Bibis son and some others came and searched her house and then took her to the police station and kept her there for the whole night. In the early hours of the morning these constables took her to a small room bolted it and*

then all three of them violated her modesty one by one. Then she was removed to another small room where charcoal and pieces of paper were filled in her private part and they put their private organs in her mouth. Her clothes were torn and saturated with blood. The following day her mother was forced to do begar work for the whole day and then both of them were left off at 10 p.m.

Murala, wife of Maharaji's husband's younger brother has also filed a similar complaint. She has alleged that the same constables took her to the police post the same night and returned her to her house. On the way she was caught by Madari Teli, near Kumar Tola, to the ruins of a house and her modesty violated. Messrs. Munna Lal, Bhushan and Ram Bharose, advocates are appearing for the complainant."

In the *'Hindustan Times'* of 15th April 1945 occurs the following news item:

"For refusal to do forced labour, it is alleged, a large number of Harijans in the village of Dukheri in Ambala District were recently assaulted by a party of Rajputs. A man and a woman, both Harijans, were killed. It is also alleged that a large number of houses belonging to Harijans were set on fire. Telegrams have been sent to the Commissioner and the Deputy Inspector General of Police to inquire into the matter."

From these instances, it will be clear to anyone that the Hindus do not hesitate to use violence to hold down the Untouchables and maintain the established order and even to commit, murder. Mr. Lajpat Rai in his book'.Unhappy India' in which he tried to reply to and refute the charges levelled by Miss Mayo in her 'Mother India' gives a lengthy and lucid description of the lynching of the Negroes in the United States and the atrocities committed upon them by the members of the Ku Klux Klan and asks:

"What however is very relevant to her to ask is: is the unjustifiable and cruel attitude of the Brahmins towards the Pariah *more unjustifiable and more cruel than that of the Klansmen of America towards the Negroes?"*

> *"What are the caste cruelties of India put by the side of what the whiteman has done to the non-white people?"*

Lala Lajpatrai, if he had cared to investigate could have found that the cruelties and atrocities practised by the Hindus against the Untouchables were no less than those practised by the Americans upon the Negroes. If these atrocities are not so well known to the world as are those practised upon the Negro, it is not because they do not exist. They are not known because there is no Hindu, who will not do his best to conceal truth in order to hide his shame, Some might think that this description of the Established Order and the rules made thereunder are matters of ancient past. This is a complete mistake. The Established Order subsists even today and the rules are as operative today as they were when they were made. This will be evident from the two following statements on the condition of the Untouchables which have appeared in the *'Hindustan Times'*. The first appeared in the issue of 8th March 1945. The first one is written by one Kesarilaiji Bordia, Headmaster of a school called Vidya Bhuwan in Udaipur. It reads as follows:

Many are the disabilities under which the Harijans in Mewar live. They cannot enter temples, nor can they draw water from public wells. They cannot join the caste Hindus in festivals and processions. They have to take out their Rath Yatra or Doll procession through a different route and on a different day. And they cannot ride through the village. Even silver ornaments, let alone gold ones on their person are resented by the caste Hindus. The result is, they have to content themselves with tin and brass articles. Age-old usage prevents them from using butter or gur in wedding feasts. In Schools and other public places, Harijan boys cannot sit with the children of caste Hindus. They are asked to absent themselves on the inspection day in order to save the Inspector from embarrassment.

A memorandum has been submitted to the State Government. If the Government chooses to declare in unequivocal terms the disapproval of these disabilities, the hands of non-official bodies which are fighting untouchability will be strengthened." The second is in the form of a statement issued by the President of the *Harijan Sevak Sangh* and refers to the condition of the Untouchables in the State of Mewar. It reads as under: The Mewar Harijan Sevak Sangh has sent a Memorandum to the Mewar Government drawing their attention to the various disabilities of Harijans in the State and their consequent hardships. The Memorandum brings out how civil liberties of Harijans are curtailed in several ways by the orthodoxy and prejudices of caste Hindus. I enumerate below some of the unjust practices, which still persist in the State and for the rectification of which the State has taken no effective measures. They are as follows:

1. Harijans have no liberty in the selection of clothes to wear. The form of dress must follow the age-long pattern; personal tastes and desires have no place in the choice of the dress.
2. At wedding feasts they have no choice in the selection of food materials. Even on payment they cannot use costly articles.
3. They cannot ride the village on a horse.
4. They are not allowed accommodation in public vehicles.
5. On religious festivals they cannot take out procession of their idols except through specified routes.
6. They have no access to wells and temples."

"Three years ago in company with Thakkur Bapa, I travelled all over the State and placed before the Government and public my impressions of the conditions obtaining there and pleaded for reform. On perusal of the above mentioned memorandum and other reports sent to me, I find that the past few years have hardly brought any change and conditions are more or less static. It is heart breaking to find that passage of time cuts no ice with us. The result is that there is hardly any change in our age-long practices and prejudices. This perversity which blinds us to the tyranny and injustices of our ways also makes us impervious to the incalculable harm we have already suffered as a result of it. Even if the ignorant prejudice of the common man is unshaken the enlightened Governments of the twentieth century ought to be more alive to their responsibilities."

The dates of these communications are important. They are of the year 1945. None can say that this Hindu Established

Order is a thing of the ancient past. The fact that these latest accounts refer to the Indian States should not be understood to mean that the established Order has vanished from British India. The chapters to follow will present enough evidence to show that the same Established Order is very much alive in British India.

In the *"Times of India"* of 31st August 1950 occurs the following news item:

The following facts of a case revealed in the hearing of an appeal in the Allahabad High Court, are illustrative of the socio-economic conditions of lower castes in the rural areas: Chiranji, a dhobi of the village of Sarras in the District of Etah, went out as a military employee in the last war and remained out of his village for four or five years. When he was discharged, he returned to his home. He stopped washing clothes and used to go about in the village in his military uniform. This coupled with the fact that he refused to wash clothes even for the men of the Raja of Sarras the sole zamindar in the village, was resented by the villagers.

On December 31, 1947, when the dhobi was washing his clothes, four villagers, including the Raja's servants, approached him and asked him to wash their clothes which he refused. The villagers took Chiranji to the Raja's house and gave him a beating.

His mother and mother's sister went there to intercede on his behalf but they too were assaulted. The attackers then went away leaving Chiranji in the custody of one Ram Singh; finding him alone, Chiranji was alleged to have slapped him and run away. Ram Singh and other servants of the Raja chased him to his house where he had taken shelter. The villagers insisted upon his opening the door but when there was no response, his house was set on fire. A number of other huts were also reduced to ashes.

The dhobi lodged a complaint with the Police who disbelieved his story and wanted to prosecute him for a false report. He then filed a complaint in a Magistrate's Court. The accused were convicted and sentenced to three years' imprisonment, each. The High Court upheld the sentences imposed by the Magistrate. The following news item has appeared in the '*Indian*

News Chronicle' dated 31st August 1950. Inhuman Treatment towards Harijans in Pepsu: Depressed Classes League's Memorandum to Government.

Patiala, August 1950: "The unprovoked thrashing of the Backward Class people, inhuman insults heaped upon their women folk, indiscriminate detachment of the Harijans from the lands, the virtual confinement of the Harijans and their cattle in their mud houses for days together without any fault is a long tale of suffering whose echoes are rising in proportion to the diminishing echoes of crime in general," says a memorandum presented by the PEPSU Provincial Depressed Classes League to the State Government.

> *"While crime in PEPSU is on the decrease due to the vigorous efforts of the police," the memorandum adds, "it is a pity that the sector of the Backward Class should be deprived of the protection from the unsociable elements". The Backward Classes economically handicapped as they are, find it very difficult to ventilate their day-to-day grievances to the authorities concerned who could immediately come to their rescue, and are perforce, compelled to submit to their lot, to the encouragement of the aggressor, and thus the wail of disgust against the present state of affairs grows still louder which in its turn is made stock of by the interested parties."*

The Provincial Depressed Classes League further quoted an instance to show how much inhuman treatment was being meted out to Harijans in PEPSU. Chand Singh a Harijan of village Katu, district Bernala, was made to go round the village on the back of donkey with face blackened for the fault of having drunk water at the well of a high caste zamindar. "In the changed atmosphere of free India, the members of the Scheduled Castes in the PEPSU are daily finding themselves put in a tight corner as a result of the unprecedented repression let loose upon them by the members of high castes.'"

The Provincial Depressed Classes League has further suggested formation of district and central special commissions in the State with wide powers to deal with the complaints on Harijans on the spot and afford them other facilities. Concluding, the League has urged upon the State Government that pending an all-India enactment in this connection, it may, temporarily be provided that the Harijans have equal rights in the village common, to ease the situation from further deterioration.

Why Lawlessness is Lawful?

The foregoing discussion must have made clear two things, which must be borne in mind. One is the sharp division between the touchables and untouchables, the other is the deep antagonism between the two.

Every village has two parts, the quarters of the touchables and the quarters of the untouchables. Geographically the two are separate. There is always appreciable distance between the two. At any rate there is no contiguity or proximity between them. The untouchables quarters have a distinct name such as Maharwada, Mangwada, Chamrotti, Khatkana, etc. *De jure* for the purposes of Revenue Administration or Postal Communication, the quarters of the untouchables are included in the village. But *de-facto* it is separate from the village. When the Hindu resident of a village speaks of the village he means to include in it only the caste Hindu residents and the locality occupied by them. Similarly when the untouchable speaks of the village he means to exclude from it the untouchables and the quarters they occupy. Thus in every village the touchables and untouchables form two separate groups. There is nothing common between them. They do not constitute a folk. This is the first thing which must be noted.

The second thing to note with regard to this division of the village into two groups is that these groups are real corporations which no one included within them can escape. As has been well said the American or European belongs to groups of various kinds, but he "joins" most of them. He of course is born into a family, but he does not stay in it all his life unless he pleases. He may choose his own occupation, residence, wife, political party, and is responsible generally speaking for no one's acts but his own. He is an "individual" in a much fuller sense because all his relationships are settled by himself for himself. The touchables or untouchables are in no sense individuals because all or nearly all of his relationship are fixed when he is born in a certain group. His occupation, his dwelling, his gods and his politics are all determined for him by the group to which he belongs. When the touchables and untouchables meet they meet not as man to man, individual to individual but as members of groups or as nationals of two different States.

This fact has an important effect upon the mutual relationship between the touchables and untouchables in a village. The relationship resembles the relationship between different clans in primitive society. In primitive society the member of the clan has a claim, but the stranger has no standing. He may be treated kindly, as a guest, but he cannot demand "justice" at the hands of any clan but his own. The dealing of clan with clan is a matter of war or negotiation, not of law; and the clan less man is an 'outlaw', in fact as well as in name and lawlessness against the strangers is therefore lawful. The untouchable not being a member of the group of touchables is a stranger. He is not a kindred. He is an outlaw. He cannot claim justice. He cannot claim rights which the touchable is bound to respect.

The third thing to note is that the relationship between the two, the touchables and the untouchables, has been fixed. It has become a matter of status. This status has unmistakably given the untouchables a position of inferiority vis-a-vis the touchables. This inferiority is embodied in a Code of Social conduct to which the untouchables must conform. What kind of a code it is, has already been stated. The untouchable is not willing to conform to that Code. He is not prepared to render unto Ceasar what belongs to Ceasar. The untouchable wants to have his relationship with the touchables by contract. The touchable wants the untouchables to live in accordance with the rules of status and not rise above it. Thus the two halves of the village, the touchables and the untouchables are now struggling for resettling what the touchable thinks is settled forever. The conflict is centred round one question—What is to be the basis of this relationship? Shall it be contract or shall it be status?

This raises some very interesting questions. How did the untouchables come to have the status of the lowliest and the low? Why has the Hindu cultivated this hostility and contempt for the untouchables? Why does the Hindu indulge in lawlessness in suppressing the untouchables as though such lawlessness is lawful? To give an adequate answer to these questions one has to go to the law of the Hindus. Without a working knowledge of the rules of the Hindu Law, it would be impossible to give any satisfactory answer to this question. For our purpose, it is not necessary to cover the whole field of Hindu Law in all its branches. It is enough to know that branch of the Hindu law which may be called the law of persons—or to put it in nontechnical language—that part of the Hindu law which deals with differences of right, duty or capacity which result from differences of status.

It is therefore proposed to give a catalogue of the rules of the Hindu Law which relate to the law of persons. These rules are collected from the Law Books of Manu, Yajnavalkya, Narada, Vishnu, Katyayana, etc., who are some of the principal lawgivers recognised by the Hindus as persons having authority to lay down the law.

A mere reproduction of the rules however interesting cannot be helpful in enabling a person who goes through them to have an idea of the basic conceptions which underlie the Hindu Law of Persons. For that purpose mere reproduction of the rules will not do. Some order is evidently necessary. What is therefore done is to group these rules under certain heads. The whole thing is cast in the form of a digest divided into sections, each section being an assembly of rules dealing with one definite matter.

Different Classes: Their Origin and Their Duties

1. This (Universe) existed in the shape of Darkness, unperceived destitute of distinctive marks, untenable by reasoning, unknowable, wholly immersed, as it were in a deep sleep.
2. Then the divine self-existent (Svayambhu, himself) indiscernible (but) making (all) this, the great elements and the rest, discernible, appeared with irresistible (creative) power, dispelling the darkness.
3. But for the sake of the prosperity of the worlds, he caused the Brahmana, the Kshatriya, the Vaishya, and the Sudra to proceed from his mouth, his arms, his thighs and his feet.
4. But in order to protect this Universe He, the most resplendent one, assigned separate (duties and)

occupations to those who sprang from his mouth, arms, thighs and feet.

5. To the Brahmans he assigned teaching and studying (the veda), sacrificing (performing sacrificial ceremonies) for their own benefit and for others, giving and accepting (of alms).
6. The Kshatriya he commanded to protect the people, to bestow gifts, to offer sacrifices, to study (the Veda), and to abstain from attaching himself to sensual pleasures.
7. The Vaishya to tend cattle, to bestow gifts, to offer sacrifices, to study (the Veda), to trade, to lend money and to cultivate the land.
8. One occupation only the lord prescribed to the Sudra, to serve meekly even these (other) three castes.
9. A student, an apprentice, a hired servant, and fourthly, an official: these must be regarded as labourers. Slaves are those who are born in the house and the rest.
10. The Sages have distinguished five sorts of attendants according to law. Among these are four sorts of labourers (mentioned above). The slaves (are the fifth category, of which there are) fifteen species.
11. One born at (his master's) house; one purchased; one received (by gift); one obtained by inheritance; one maintained during a general famine; one pledged by his rightful owner.
12. One released from a heavy debt; one made captive in a fight; one won through a wager; one who has come forward declaring 'I am thin' an apostate from asceticism; one enslaved for a stipulated period.
13. One who has become a slave in order to get a maintenance; one enslaved on account of his connection with a female slave; and oneself sold. These are fifteen classes of slaves as declared in law.
14. Among these the four named first cannot be released from bondage, except by the favour of their owners. Their bondage is hereditary.
15. The Sages have declared that the state of dependence is common to all these; but that their respective position and an income depends on their particular caste & occupation.

Equality before Law

1. When two persons abuse each other, their punishment shall be equal if they are equals in caste; if one is inferior to the other, his punishment shall be double; for a superior, half (of the ordinary punishment) is ordained.
2. When persons equal in caste and qualities abuse one another, the punishment ordained for them in the system of law is thirteen Panas and a half.
3. For a Brahman abusing a Kshatriya, the fine shall be half a hundred (Fifty Panas); for abusing a Vaishya, half of fifty (twenty-five Panas); for abusing a Sudra, twelve & a half.
4. This punishment has been declared for (abusing) a virtuous Sudra who has committed no wrong; no offence is imputable to a Brahman for abusing (a Sudra) devoid of virtue.
5. A Vaishya shall be fined a hundred (Panas) for reviling a Kshatriya, a Kshatriya reviling a Vaishya shall have to pay half of that amount as a fine.
6. In the case of a Kshatriya reviling a Sudra, the fine shall be twenty Panas; in the case of a Vaishya, the double amount is declared to be the proper fine by persons learned in law.
7. A Sudra shall be compelled to pay the first fine for abusing a Vaishya; the middling fine (for abusing) a Kshatriya; the highest fine (for abusing) a Brahman.
8. A Kshatriya having defamed a Brahmana shall be fined one hundred (panas); a Vaishya one hundred and fifty or two hundred; a Sudra shall suffer corporal punishment.
9. A Brahmana shall be fined fifty (panas) for defaming a Kshatriya; in (the case of) a Vaishya the fine shall be twenty-five panas; in (the case of) a Sudra twelve.
10. A once born man (a Sudra), who insults a twice born man with gross invective, shall have his tongue cut out; for he is of low origin.
11. If he mentions the names and castes (Jati) of the (twice

born) with contumely an iron nail, ten fingers long, shall be thrust red hot into his mouth.

12. If he arrogantly teaches Brahmans their duty, the King shall cause hot oil to be poured into his mouth and into his ears.
13. For mutual abuse by a Brahmana and a Kshatriya a fine must be imposed by a discerning (King), on the Brahmana the lowest amercement, but on the Kshatriya the middle most.
14. With whatever limb a man of a low caste does hurt to (a man of three) highest (castes) even that limb shall be cut off; that is the teaching of Manu.
15. He (low caste man) who raises his hand or a stick, shall have his hand cut off; he who in anger kicks with his foot, shall have his foot cut off.
16. A low caste man who tries to place himself on the same seat with a man of a high caste, shall be branded on his hip and be banished, or (the King) shall cause his buttock to be gashed.
17. If out of arrogance he spits (on a superior) the King shall cause both his lips to be cut off, if he urinates (on him), the penis; if he breaks wind (against him) the anus.
18. If he lays hold of the hair (of a superior), let the (King) unhesitatingly cut off his hands, likewise (if he takes him by the feet) the beard, the neck or the scrotum.

Status, Dignity and Position of each Class

1. Man is stated to be purer above the navel (than below); hence the self-existent (Swayambhu) has declared the purest (part) of him to be his mouth.
2. As the Brahmana sprang from the mouth, as he was the first-born and as he possesses the Veda, he is by right the lord of his whole creation.
3. For the self-existent (Swayambhu) having performed austerities, produced him first from his own mouth, in order that the offerings might be conveyed to the gods and manes and that this universe might be preserved.

4. What created being can surpass him, through whose mouth the gods continually consume the sacrificial viands and the manes, the offerings of the dead.
5. Of created beings the most excellent are said to be those who are animated; of the animated, those who subsist by intelligence; of the intelligent mankind, and of men the Brahmanas.
6. A Brahmana coming into existence is born as the highest on earth, the lord of all created things.
7. Whatever exists in the world is the property of the Brahmana; on account of the excellence of his origin the Brahmana is indeed, entitled to all.
8. A Brahmana be he ignorant or learned is a great divinity, just as the fire, whether carried forth (for the performance of a burnt oblation) or not carried forth, is a great divinity.
9. Thus though Brahmans employ themselves in all (sorts of) mean occupations, they must be honoured in every way; for (each of) them is a great divinity.
10. But let (the father perform or) cause to be performed the Namadheya (the right of naming the child) on the tenth or twelfth (day after birth), or on a lucky lunar day, in a lucky Muhurta, under an auspicious constellation.
11. Let (the first part of) a Brahman's name (denote something) auspicious, a Kshatriya's be connected with power, and a Vaishya's with wealth, but a Sudra's (express something) contemptible.
12. (The second part of) a Brahmana's (name) shall be (a word) implying happiness, of a Kshatriya's (a word) implying protection, of a Vaishya's (a term) expressive of thriving and of a Sudra's (an expression) denoting service.
13. Let him (a Brahmana) not dwell in a country where the rulers are Sudras, nor in one which is surrounded by unrighteous men, nor in one which has become subject to heretics, nor in one swarming with men of the lowest castes.
14. When the King cannot himself decide the causes (of

litigants) then he should appoint thereto a Brahmana learned in the various Shastras.

15. Where a Brahmana (endowed with the qualities enumerated) cannot be had (the King) should appoint a Kshatriya or a Vaishya, proficient in the Sacred law, but the (the King) should carefully avoid a Sudra as a Judge,
16. Whatever is done by others (as Judges) than these must be regarded as done wrongly, even if they be officers (of the King) and even if by chance the decision is according to the Sacred texts.
17. A Brahmana who subsists only by the name of his caste (Jati), or one who merely calls himself a Brahmana (though his origin be uncertain), may, at the King's pleasure interpret the law to him, but never a Sudra.
18. The Kingdom of that Monarch, who looks on while a Sudra settles the law, will sink (low), like a cow in a morass.
19. A Brahmana who knows the law need not bring any (offence) to the notice of the King, by his own power alone he can punish those men who injure him.
20. His own power is greater than the power of the King; the Brahmana therefore, may punish his foes by his own power alone.
21. The Brahmana is declared (to be) the creator (of the world), the punisher, the teacher, (and hence) a benefactor (of all created beings); to him let no man say anything unpropitious, nor use any harsh words.

Inter-relationship between the Classes I

1. In the inverse order of the four castes slavery is not ordained.
2. Members of three Varnas can become slaves but a Brahman can never become a slave. Slavery in the case of the (three) Varnas *viz.*, Kshatriyas, Vaishyas and Sudras is in their direct order and not in their inverse order. A Sudra could be the slave of any master of the four castes, a Vaishya of any master of the first three castes but not of a Sudra Master, a Kshatriya could be

the slave of a Brahman or Kshatriya Master but not of a Vaishya or Sudra Master.

3. Even one of the same caste (*i.e.* a Brahman) should not make a Brahmana work as a Slave..... A man who is Kshatriya, Vaishya or Sudra may occasionally do the work of slave for a man of the same caste (as his own) but a Brahman should never be made to do the work of a slave.
4. For the first marriage of twice born men (wives) of equal caste are recommended; but for those who through desire proceed (to marry again) the following females (chosen) according to the (direct) order (of the castes), are most approved.
5. It is declared that a Sudra woman alone (can be) the wife of a Sudra, she and one of his own caste (the wives) of a Vaishya, those two and one of his own caste (the wives) of a Kshatriya, those three and one of his own caste (the wives) of a Brahmana.
6. If twice born men wed women of their own and of other (lower castes), the seniority, honour and habitation of those (wives) must be (settled) according to the order of the castes (Varna).
7. Among all (twice born men) the wife of equal caste alone, not a wife of a different caste by any means, shall personally attend her husband and assist him in his daily sacred rights.
8. A Sudra who has inter-course with a woman of a twice born caste, guarded or unguarded (shall be punished in the following manner); if she was unguarded, he loses the part (offending) and all his property; if she was guarded, everything (even his life).
9. (For inter-course with a guarded Brahmani) a Vaishya shall forfeit all his property after imprisonment for a year; a Kshatriya shall be fined one thousand (panas) and be shaved with the urine (of an ass).
10. If a Vaishya or a Kshatriya has connection with an unguarded Brahmani, let him fine the Vaishya five hundred (panas) and the Kshatriya one thousand.
11. If a Vaishya approaches a guarded female of the Kshatriya caste, or a Kshatriya a (guarded) Vaishya

woman, they both deserve the same punishment as in the case of an unguarded Brahmana female.

12. A Brahmand shall be compelled to pay a fine of one thousand (panas) if he has intercourse with guarded (females of) those two (castes); for (offending with) a (guarded) Sudra female a fine of one thousand (panas shall be inflicted) on a Kshatriya or a Vaishya.
13. For (intercourse with) an unguarded Kshatriya (female) a fine of five hundred (panas shall fall) on a Vaishya; but (for the same offence) a Kshatriya shall be shaved with the urine (of a donkey) or (pay) the same fine.
14. A Brahmana who approaches unguarded females (of the) Kshatriya or Vaishya (castes), or a Sudra female, shall be fined five hundred (panas); but (for intercourse with) a female (of the) lowest (castes), one thousand.
15. But let (a householder) offer, in accordance with the rule, to a guest who has come (of his own accord) a seat and water, as well as food, garnished (with seasoning) according to his ability.
16. But a Kshatriya (who comes) to the house of a Brahman is not called a guest (atithi), nor a Vaishya, nor a Sudra, nor a personal friend, nor a relative, nor the teacher.
17. But if a Kshatriya comes to the house of a Brahman in the manner of a guest, (the householder) may feed him according to his desire, after the Brahmans have eaten.
18. Even a Vaishya and a Sudra who have approached his house in the manner of quests, he may allow to eat with his servants, showing (thereby) his compassionate disposition.

Duties—Privileges—Immunities—Disabilities

1. Brahmans who are intent on the means (of gaining union with) Brahman and firm in (discharging) their duties, shall live by duly performing the following six acts, (which are enumerated) in their (proper) order.
2. Teaching, studying, sacrificing for him self, sacrificing for others, making gifts and receiving them are the six acts (prescribed) for a Brahmana.

3. But among the six acts (ordained) for him three are his means of subsistence, (*viz.*) sacrificing for others, teaching and accepting gifts from pure men.
4. (Passing) from the Brahman to the Kshatriya, three acts (incumbent on the former) are forbidden (*viz.*,) teaching, sacrificing for others, and thereby, the acceptance of gifts.
5. The same are likewise forbidden to a Vaishya that is a settled rule; for Manu, the lord of creatures (Prajapati), has not prescribed them for (men of) those two (castes).
6. To carry arms for striking and for throwing (is prescribed) for Kshatriyas as a means of subsistence; to trade, (to rear) cattle, and agriculture for Vaishyas; but their duties are liberality, the study of the Veda and the performance of sacrifices.
7. Among the several occupations the most commendable are, teaching the Veda for a Brahamana, protecting the people for a Kshatriya and trade for a Vaishya.
8. The service of Brahmanas alone is declared (to be) an excellent occupation for a Sudra; for whatever else besides this he may perform will bear him no fruit.
9. But a Brahmana unable to subsist by his peculiar occupations just mentioned, may live according to the law applicable to the Kshatriyas; for the latter is "next to him in rank.
10. If it be asked "How shall it be, if he cannot maintain himself by either (of these occupations? the answer is) he may adopt a Vaishya's mode of life, employing himself in agriculture and rearing cattle.
11. A Kshatriya who has fallen into distress may subsist by these means (open to the Vaishya).
12. A Vaishya who is unable to subsist by his own duties, may even maintain himself by a Sudra's mode of life, avoiding (however) acts forbidden (to him), and he should give it up, when he is able to do so.
13. But a Sudra being unable to find service with the twice-born and threatened with the loss of his sons and wife (through hunger), may maintain himself by handicrafts.

14. A Kshatriya must never arrogantly adopt the mode of life (prescribed for his) betters (that is for the Brahmanas).
15. (The King) should order a Vaishya to trade, to lend money, to cultivate the land, to lend cattle and the Sudra to serve the twice born castes.
16. (The King) should carefully compel Vaishyas and Sudras to perform the work (prescribed) for them; for if these two (castes) swerved from their duties, they would throw this (whole) world into confusion.
17. A blind man, an idiot, (a cripple) who moves with the help of a board, a man full seventy years old, and he who confers benefits on Srotriyas, shall not be compelled by any (king) to pay a tax.
18. Though dying (with want) a King must not levy a tax on Srotriyas, and no Srotriya residing in his kingdom must perish from hunger.
19. Let the King make the common inhabitants of his realm who live by traffic, pay annually some trifle, which is called a tax.
20. Mechanics and artisans, as well as Sudras who subsist by manual labour, he (the king) may cause to work (for himself) one (day) in each month.
21. Tonsure (of the head) is ordained for a Brahmana (instead of capital punishment); but men of other castes shall suffer capital punishment.
22. Let him (the King) never slay a Brahmana though he have committed all (possible) crimes; let him banish such an (offender) leaving all his property (to him) and (his body) unhurt.
23. No greater crime is known on the earth than slaying a Brahmana: a King, therefore, must not even conceive in his mind the thought of killing a Brahmana.
24. When a learned Brahmana has found treasure deposited in former (times), he may take even the whole (of it); for he is master for everything.
25. When the King finds treasutre of old concealed in the ground, let him give one half to the Brahmanas and place the (other) half in his treasury.

Mode of Life

1. (A Sudra who is) pure, the servant of his betters, gentle in his speech, and free from pride, and always seeks a refuge with Brahmanas, attains (in the next life) a higher caste.
2. But let a Sudra serve Brahmanas, either for the sake of heaven, or with a view to both (this life and the next); for he who is called the servant of a Brahmana thereby gains all his ends.
3. If a Sudra (unable to subsist by serving Brahmanas) seeks a livelihood, he may serve Kshatriyas, or he may also seek to maintain himself by attending on a wealthy Vaishya.
4. They must allot to him out of their own family (property) a suitable maintenance, after considering his ability, his industry, and the number of those whom he is bound to support.
5. The remnants of their food must be given to him, as well as, their old clothes, the refuse of their grain and their old household furniture.
6. No collection of wealth must be made by a Sudra, even though he be able (to do it); for a Sudra who has acquired wealth, gives pain to the Brahamana.
7. Sudras who live according to the law, shall each month shave (their heads); their mode of purification (shall be) the same as that of Vaishyas and their food the fragments of an Aryan's meal. As has been said the society for which the ancient lawgivers laid down their ordinances consisted of two parts—one part consisted of those who were comprised within the system of Chaturvarna. The other part consisted of those who were without the pale of Chaturvarna. They are spoken of in Manu as Bahyas, *i.e.,* outside the pale of Chaturvarna. They are spoken of as low castes. The origin of these low castes is a subject with which I am not concerned for the moment. It is enough to say that according to these ancient law givers of Hindus these low castes are the result of the progeny of intermarriages between those four classes—the Brahmanas-

Kshatriyas-Vaishyas-Sudras—who are included within the system of Chaturvarna. How far this is true will be examined at another time. We are primarily concerned with social relationship and not with origin. So far the ordinances relating to those who were within the Chaturvarna have been given. It now remains to give the ordinances which relate to those who were outside the Chaturvarna or who were called the low castes. The ordinances which regulate the life of the low castes are strange to say very few. Few though they be they give them such a short shrift that one does not find any necessity for more detailed code of ordinances.

They are as follows:

1. All those tribes in this world, which are excluded from (the community of) those born from the mouth, the arms, the thighs, and the feet (of Brahman), are called Dasyus, whether they speak the language of the Mlenchhas (barbarians) or that of the Aryans.
2. Near well-known trees and burial ground, on mountains and in groves, let these (tribes) dwell, known (by certain marks), and subsisting by their peculiar occupations.
3. But the dwelling of the Chandalas and Shwapakas shall be outside the village, they must be made Apapatras and their wealth (shall be) dogs and donkeys.
4. Their dress (shall be) the garments of the dead, (they shall eat) their food from broken dishes, black iron (shall be) their ornaments, they must always wander from place to place.
5. A man who fulfils a religious duty, shall not seek intercourse with them; their transactions (shall be) among themselves, and their marriages with their equals.
6. Their food shall be given to them by others (than an Aryan giver) in a broken dish; at night they shall not walk about in villages and in towns.
7. By day they must go about for the purpose of their work, distinguished by marks at the King's command, and they shall carry out the corpses (of persons) who have no relatives, that is a settled rule.

8. By the King's order they shall always execute the Criminals in accordance with the law, and they shall take for themselves the clothes, the beds and the ornaments of (such) criminals.
9. He who has had connection with a woman of one of the lowest castes shall be put to death.
10. If one who (being a member of the Chandala or some other low caste) must not be touched, intentionally defiles by his touch one who (as a member of a twice born caste) may be touched (by other twice born persons only) he shall be put to death.

2

Ambedkar on Theories of the Origin of Untouchability

Racial Difference as the Origin of Untouchability

As has been said the field is quite unexplored. No student of Sociology has paid any attention to it. Writers, other than Sociologists, who have written about India and her people have been content with merely recording the custom of Untouchability with varying degrees of disapprobation and leaving it at that. So far as my researches go, I have come across only one author who has attempted to explain how Untouchability has come about. It is Mr. Stanley Rice. According to Mr. Rice.

There is a strong probability that the outcasts were the survivors of the conquered peoples, who, as caste tended to coincide with occupation, became the drum-beating, leather-working, and farm labouring classes to which as serfs they had been relegated from early times. *They were not the races* conquered by the Aryans; the *Paraiyans belonged to the aborigines who were conquered by the Dravidians* and being of a different race they were not admitted to the totem of similar clans with which marriage is always intimately connected, since that would have led to free intercourse and the gradual degradation of race. But this prohibition cannot have been absolute; there are always exceptions.

In the course of the centuries, some forty or more, the inevitable miscegenation may very well have obliterated the racial distinctions between aboriginal and early Dravidian.

These people have been admitted to a sort of lowly participation in the Hindu system in the atmosphere of which they have lived for so long, for Hinduism is at once the most tolerant and intolerant of creeds. It does not proselytize; you cannot become a Hindu as you can become a Mussalman, and those within the fold are liable to the most rigid restrictions. But it has always been ready to embrace aboriginal tribes who are willing to submit to its laws, though it may assign to them a very lowly place and they have always been kept at a distance and have been excluded from the temples. It would seem, therefore, that anthropological arguments are in any case not conclusive when we consider these factors which must have profoundly modified the original racial characteristics and must have changed their outlook.

Thus the Dravidians applied to the Paraiyans the same test which the Aryans are assumed to have applied to the conquered inhabitants. They reduced them to the position of serfs and assigned to them those duties which it was thought beneath their own dignity to perform. Nor was marriage the only consideration. The disabilities of the Paraiyans were due also-and to an even greater degree-to the mystical qualities inherent in Tabu. To admit such a man to the totem family was not only contrary to the social order; it would bring upon the clan the anger of their particular god.

But to admit him to the worship of the god within the sacred precincts of a temple was to call down authentic fire from Heaven, whereby they would be consumed. It would be sacrilege of the same kind as the offering of unconsecrated or unorthodox fire by Korah, Dathan and Abhiram. But though debarred from taking an active part in worship, the Paraiyans might yet do the menial services connected with it, provided that they did not entail the pollution of the sacred building. In Christian terminology the Paraiyan, although he could neither officiate at the altar, nor preach a sermon nor even be one of the congregation, might still ring the bell-on one condition. He could not regard himself as of the communion; he was, in fact, excommunicate.

And as such, he was ceremonially unclean. No washing with water, no cleansing ceremony, could remove that stain which was indelibly fixed by the operation of Tabu. To touch him, to have any dealings with him save as it were, at arm's length, was by a sort of contagious magic a defilement. You could employ him to till your field because that entailed no contact of any kind, beyond giving an order, you need have no further communication with him. The seal of pollution was set on his forehead; it was inherent in him as surely as the blood in his veins. And so from being the vile, degraded fellow which Indian opinion had made him, he became viler and more degraded from the kinds of occupation left open to him."

The theory of Mr. Rice really divides itself into two parts. For, according to him, the origin of untouchability is to be found in two circumstances—Race and Occupation. Obviously, they require separate consideration. This Chapter will be devoted to an examination of his theory of racial difference as the origin of untouchability.

The racial theory of Mr. Rice contains two elements:

(1) That the Untouchables are non-Aryan, non-Dravidian aboriginals; and

(2) That they were conquered and subjugated by the Dravidians.

This theory raises the whole question of the invasions of India by foreign invaders, the conquests made by them and the social and cultural institutions that have resulted therefrom. According to Mr. Rice, there have been two invasions of India. First is the invasion of India by the Dravidians. They conquered the non-Dravidian aborigines, the ancestors of the Untouchables, and made them Untouchables. The second invasion is the invasion of India by the Aryans.

The Aryans conquered the Dravidians. He does not say how the conquering Aryans treated the conquered Dravidians. If pressed for an answer he might say they made them Sudras. So that we get a chain. The Dravidians invaded India and conquered the aborigines and made them Untouchables. After Dravidians came the Aryans. The Aryans conquered the Dravidians and made them Sudras. The theory is too mechanical, a mere speculation and too simple to explain a complicated set of facts relating to the origin of the Sudras and the Untouchables. When students of ancient Indian history delve into the ancient past they do often come across four names, the Aryans, Dravidians, Dasas and Nagas. What do these names indicate? This question has never been considered. Are these names Aryans, Dravidians, Dasas and Nagas the names of different races or are they merely different names for a people of the same race? The general assumption is that they are different races. It is an assumption on which theories like that of Mr. Rice, which seek to explain the social structure of the Hindu Society, particularly its class basis, are built. Before such a theory is accepted it is necessary to examine its foundations.

Starting with the Aryans it is beyond dispute that they were not a single homogeneous people. That they were divided into two sections is beyond dispute. It is also beyond dispute that the two had different cultures. One of them may be called Rig Vedic Aryans and the other the Atharva Vedic Aryans. Their cultural cleavage appears to be complete. The Rig Vedic Aryans believed in Yajna. The Atharva Vedic Aryans believed the Magis. Their mythologies were different. The Rig Vedic Aryans believed in the Deluge and the creation of their race from Manu. The Atharva Vedic Aryans did not believe in Deluge but believed in the creation of their race from Brahma or Prajapati. Their literary developments also lay along different paths.

The Rig Vedic Aryans produced Brahmanas, Sutras and Aranyakas. The Atharva Vedic Aryans produced the Upanishads. Their cultural conflict was so great that the Rig Vedic Aryans would not for a long time admit the sanctity of the Atharva Veda nor of the Upanishads and when they did recognize it they called it Vedanta which contrary to the current meaning of the word—namely, essence of the Vedas—originally meant something outside the boundary of the Vedas and, therefore, not so sacred as the Vedas and regarded its study as Anuloma. Whether these two sections of Aryans were two different races we do not know. We do not know whether the word Aryan is a term indicative of race. Historians have therefore made a mistake in proceeding on the assumption that the Aryans were a separate race.

A greater mistake lies in differentiating the Dasas from the Nagas. The Dasas are the same as Nagas. Dasas is merely another name for Nagas. It is not difficult to understand how the Nagas came to be called Dasas in the Vedic literature. Dasa is a Sanskritized form of the Indo-Iranian word Dahaka. Dahaka was the name of the king of the Nagas. Consequently, the Aryans called the Nagas after the name of their king Dahaka, which in its Sanskrit form became Dasa a generic name applied to all the Nagas.

Who were the Nagas? Undoubtedly they were non-Aryans. A careful study of the Vedic literature reveals a spirit of conflict, of a dualism, and a race for superiority between two distinct types of culture and thought. In the Rig Veda, we are first introduced to the Snake-god in the form of Ahi Vitra, the enemy of the Aryan god Indra. Naga, the name under which the Snake-god was to become so famous in later days, does not appear in early Vedic literature. Even when it does for the first time in the Satapatha Brahmana (X1.2,7,12), it is not clear whether a great snake or a great elephant is meant. But this does not conceal the nature of Ahi Vitra, since he is described always in Rig Veda as the serpent who lay around or hidden in waters, and as holding a full control over the waters of heaven and earth alike.

It is also evident from the hymns that refer to Ahi Vitra, that he received no worship from the Aryan tribes and was only regarded as an evil spirit of considerable power who must be fought down.

The mention of the Nagas in the Rig Veda shows that the Nagas were a very ancient people. It must also be remembered that the Nagas were in no way an aboriginal or uncivilised people. History shows a very close association by intermarriage between the Naga people with the Royal families of India. The Devagiri record of the Kadamba king Krisnavarma connects the beginning of the Kadamba-kula with the Nagas. The Royakota grant of 9th Century A.D. mentions the marriage of Asvathama with a Nagi and the foundation of the Pallava line by Skandasishya, the issue of this marriage. Virakurcha, who according to another Pallava inscription dated in the 9th century A.D. was the ruler of the dynasty, is also mentioned in the same inscription as having married a Nagi and obtained from her the insignia of royalty.

The marriage of Gautamiputra, the son of the Vakataka king Pravarasena, with the daughter of the Bharasiva king

Bhava Naga, is a historical fact. So is the marriage of Chandragupta II with princess Kuvera Naga 'of Naga Kula A Tamil poet asserts that Kokkilli, an early Chola king, had married a Naga princess. Rajendra Chola is also credited to have won 'by his radiant beauty the hand of the noble daughter of Naga race. The Navasahasanka Charita describes the marriage of the Paramara king Sindhuraja (who seems to have reigned towards the early part of the 10th Century A. D.) with the Naga princess Sasiprabha, with such exhaustive details in so matter-of-fact-a-manner as to make us almost feel certain that there must have been some historical basis for this assertion From the Harsha inscription of V. S. 1030-973 A.D. we know that Guvaka I, who was the sixth king in the genealogy upwards from Vigraharaja Chahamana and thus might be supposed to have been ruling towards the middle of the 9th Century was "famous as a hero in the assemblies of the Nagas and other princes." Sanatikara of the Bhaumn dynasty of Orissa, one of whose dates was most probably 921 A.D., is mentioned in an inscription of his son as having married Tribhuana Mahadevi of the Naga family

Not only did the Naga people occupy a high cultural level but history shows that they ruled a good part of India. That Maharashtra is the home of the Nagas goes without saying. Its people and its kings were Nagas

That Andhradesa and its neighbourhood were under the Nagas during the early centuries of the Christian era is suggested by evidence from more sources than one. The Satavahanas, and their successors, the Chutu Kula Satakarnis drew their blood more or less from the Naga stock. As Dr. H.C. Roy Chaudhri has pointed out, the Dvatrima satpukalitta represents Salivahana, the mythological representative of the Satavahana dynasty, as of mixed Brahmana and the Naga origin This is amply attested to by the typical Naga names which occur in their dynastic lists. That the Naga grew to be very powerful towards the end of the Satavahana rule is also proved by a number of facts. A chief called Skandanaga is found ruling the Bellary district, in the reign of Pulumavi, the last king of the main Satavahana line. Secondly, Naga Mulanika the daughter of a Chutu king, is mentioned as making a gift of a Naga, together with her son, who is called Sivakanda-

Naga-Sri. All the known kings of this line bear the same name and thus prove a close association with the Nagas. Thirdly, the name of Uragapura, the capital of Soringoi, suggests not an isolated reign of one Naga king but a Naga Settlement in that locality of tolerably long duration.

From Buddhist tradition of Ceylon and Siam we also know that there was a Naga country called Majerika near the Diamond Sands, *i.e.* Karachi.

Then during the third and early part of the 4th Century A.D. Northern India also was ruled by a number of Naga kings is clearly proved by Puranic as well as numismaric and epigraphic evidence. Three independent groups of Vidisa, Campavati or Padmavati and Mathura are distinctly mentioned in such a way as to leave little doubt of their importance. The name Bhava Naga, the only known king of the Bharasiva dynasty, also seems to connect him with the Nagas. It is not possible to enter here into a discussion of the coins of the second group, or the question of indentification of Achyuta Ganapati Naga or Nagasena of Allahabad Pillar inscription with these Puranic Naga kings Of all the Nagas referred to in ancient Indian History, the North Indian Naga houses of the 4th century A.D. stand out as the most prominent and historically the most tangible. We do not know whether Nagabhatta and his son Maharaja Mohesvara Naga of the Lahore Copper Seal belonged to any of these three groups or formed a separate Naga family by themselves. But all this sufficiently justifies the conclusion of Dr. C. C. Roy Chaudhari that the Kushana kingdom of Northern India disappeared in the 4th Century A.D. having been conquered by the Nagas. These Nagas must have been ruling over different portions of Uttarapatha till they were themselves swept away before the conquering arms of Samudragupta.

As late as the time of Skandagupta, however we find one Sarvanaga as the governer of Antarvedi In the neighbourhood of Saurashtra and Bharukaccha especially, the Nagas seem to have held a prominent position down to the 6th Century A.D. From the Junagadh inscription Skandagupta appears to have dealt severely with a Naga rebellion In 570 A.D. Dadda I Gurjara uprooted the Nagas who have been identified with the jungle tribes ruled over by Brihul laka of Broach

Dhruvasena 11's grant of G.S. 334 (645 A.D.) also mentions as Dutaka the Pramatri Srinaga.

The next important revival of the Nagas particularly in Central India seems to date about the 9th Century A.D. In 800 A.D. Maharaja Tivaradeva of Sripura in Kosala most probably defeated a Naga tribe. Sometime after this period, we also note two references to Nagas in the inscription of Bengal.

The Ramganj record of Mahamandalika Isvara Ghosha introduces us to a Ghosha Naga family of Dhekkari, which was to be assigned to 11th century A.D. The Bhuvanesvara Prasasti of Bhatta Bhavadeva, the minister of Harivarmadeva in 12th century A.D. also refers to destruction of Naga kings by him. The Ramacharita mentions the conquest of Utkala, the kingdom of Bhava-Bhushana-Santati, by Ramapala, but it is not clear whether in this case the Nagas or the Chandras were meant. The greater probability would however lie in favour of the former, since they were the more well known.

It was in the period 10th-12th Century A.D. that the different branches of the Sendraka, Sinda, or Chindaka family, which called themselves lords of Bhogavati and Nagavarnsi gradually spread themselves over different portions of Central India, particularly Baster. The Nagattaras of Begur, too, appear in an inscription of the 10th Century A.D. as having fought against king Viramahendra, on behalf of the W. Ganga king Ereyappa and being distinguished for bravery in the fight. If the evidence of Navashasanka Charita is accepted, then the Naga king, whose daughter Sasiprabha was married to Sindhuraja Paramara, must also have been ruling in Ratnavad on the Narmada at about this period.

Who are the Dravidians? Are they different from the Nagas? Chare they two different names for a people of the same race? The popular view is that the Dravidians and Nagas are names of two different races. This statement is bound to shock many people. Nonetheless, it is a fact that the term Dravidians and Nagas are merely two different names for the same people. It is not to be denied that very few will be prepared to admit the proposition that the Dravidians and Nagas are merely two different names for the same people and fewer that the Dravidians as Nagas occupied not merely South India but that they occupied the whole of India-South as well as North.

Nonetheless, these are historical truths. Let us see what the authorities have to say on the subject. This is what Mr. Dikshitiar, a well-known South Indian scholar, has to say on the subject in his Paper on South India in the Ramayana:

> *"The Nagas, another tribe-semi-divine in character, with their totems as serpent, spread throughout India, from Taksasila in the North-West to Assam in the North-East and to Ceylon and South India in the South. At one time they must have been powerful. Contemporaneous with the Yakwas or perhaps subsequent to their fall as a political entity, the Nagas rose to prominence in South India. Not only parts of Ceylon but ancient Malabar were the territories occupied by the ancient Nagas......... In the Tamil classics of the early centuries after Christ, we hear frequent references to Naganadu......... Remnants of Naga worship are still lingering in Malabar, and the temple in Nagercoil in South Travancore is dedicated to Naga worship even today. All that can be said about them is that they were a sea-faring tribe. Their womenfolk were renowned for their beauty. Apparently the Nagas had become* merged *with the Cheras who rose to power and prominence at the commencement of the Christian Era."*

Further light is thrown on the subject by C. F. Oldham who has made a deep study of it. According to Mr. Oldham:

The Dravidian people have been divided, from ancient times, into Cheras, Cholas and Pandyas. Chera, or Sera (in old Tamil Sarai) is the Dravidian equivalent for Naga; Cheramandala, Nagadwipa, or the Naga country. This seems to point distinctly to the Ashura origin of the Dravidians of the South. But in addition to this there still exists, widely spread over the Ganges valley, a people who call themselves Cherus or Seoris, and who claim descent from the serpent gods The Cherus are of very ancient race; they are believed to have once held a great portion of the valley of the Ganges, which, as we have already seen, was occupied in very early times by Naga tribes. The Cherus appear to have been gradually ousted from their lands, during the troublous times of the Mohammedan invasions, and they are now poor and almost landless. There can be little doubt that these people are kinsmen of the Dravidian Cheras.

The Cherus have several peculiar customs and amongst them one which seems to connect them with the Lichhavis, as well as with the Newars of Nepal. This is the election of a raja for every five or six houses, and his investiture, in due form, with the tilak or royal frontal mark. Both Lichavis and Newars had many customs in common with the Dravidians of the South. Each venerated the serpent, Karkotaka Naga being to Nepal what Nila Naga was to Kashmir. A Naga, too, was the tutelary deity of Vaisali, the Lichavi capital. The marital relations of Newars and Lichavis closely resembled those of the Tamil people, and go far to show a common origin.

Property amongst the Newars descended in the female line, as it (Mice did amongst the Arattas, Bahikas or Takhas of the Punjab, whose sisters' sons, and not their own, were their heirs This is still a Dravidian custom. In short, a recent Dravidian writer, Mr. Balakrishna Nair, says that his people 'appear to be, in nearly every particular, the kinsfolk of the Newars. Besides all this, however, there are other links connecting the Naga people of the South with those of the north of India. In an inscription discovered by Colonel Tod at Kanswah near the river Chambal, a Raja, called Salindra, 'of the race of Sarya, a tribe renowned amongst the tribes of the mighty' is said to be ruler of Takhya.

This was evidently the Takhya or Takha kingdom of the Punjab, which was visited by Hiouen-Tsiang, and which has been already referred to. It seems, therefore, that the Naga people of Takhya were known also by the name of Sarya. Again, in the outer Himalaya, between the Sudej and Beas Valleys, is a tract of country called Sara, or Seoraj. In this district the Naga demigods are the chief deities worshipped. There is another Seoraj in the Upper Chinab Valley, and this too is occupied by a Naga worshipping people.

The name Saraj, or Seoraj, appears to be the same as the Sarya of Colonel Tod's inscription and as Scori, which is the alternative name of the Cherus of the Ganges Valley. It also seems to be identical with Sarai, which we have already seen, is the old Tamil name for the Chera or Naga. Apparently, therefore, the Saryas or Takhya, the Saraj people of the Sutlej Valley, the Scons or Cherus of the valley of the Ganges, and the Cheras, Seras, or Kerakis at Southern India, are but different branches of the same Naga-worshipping people. It may be noted, too, that in some of the Himalayan dialects, Kira or Kiri means a serpent This name, from which was perhaps derived the term Kirate so often applied to the people of the Himalayas, is found in the Rajatarangini, where it is applied to a people in or near Kashmir. The Kiras are mentioned by Varaha Mihira, and in a copper plate published by Prof. Kielhom.

An inscription at the Baijnath temple in the Kangra valley gives Kiragrams as the then name of the place This, in the local dialect, would mean the village of serpents. The Naga is still a popular deity at Baijnath, and throughout the neighbouring country. The term Kira is thus an equivalent for Naga, and it can scarcely be doubted that the serpent-worshipping Kiras of the Himalayas were closely related to the Dravidian Keras, Cheras or Keralas of the South.

Similarity of name is not always to be trusted, but here we have something more. These people, whose designation is thus apparently the same, are all of Solar race; they all venerate the hooded serpent; and they all worship, as ancestors, the Naga demigods. From the foregoing it would seem tolerably certain that the Dravidians of Southern India were of the same stock as the Nagas or Ashuras of the North.

It is thus clear that the Nagas and Dravidians are one and the same people. Even with this much of proof, people may not be found ready to accept the thesis. The chief difficulty in the way of accepting it lies in the designation of the people of South India by the name Dravidian. It is natural for them to ask why the term Dravidian has come to be restricted to the people of South India if they are really Nagas. Critics are bound to ask: If the Dravidians and the Nagas are the same people, why is the name Nagas not used to designate people of South India also. This is no doubt a puzzle. But it is a puzzle which is not beyond solution. It can be solved if certain facts are borne in mind. The first thing to be borne in mind is the situation regarding language. Today the language of the Southern India differs from that of the people of Northern India. Was this always so? On this question the observations of Mr. Oldham are worth attention.

It is evident that the old Sanskrit grammarians considered the language of the Dravidian countries to be connected with the vernaculars of northern India; and that, in their opinion, it was especially related to the speech of those people who, as we have seen, were apparently descendants of the Ashura tribes. Thus, in the 'Shahasha Chandrika', Lakshmidhara says that the Paisachi language is spoken in the Paisachi countries of Pandya, Kckaya, Vahlika, Sahya, Nepala, Kuntala, Sudesha, Bhota, Gandhara, Haiva and Kanoj; and that these are the Paisachi countries. Of all the vernacular dialects, the paisachi is said to have contained the smallest infusion of Sanskrit.

That the Ashuras originally spoke a language which differed from that of the Aryas seems evident. Several passages are quoted by Prof. Muir, from the Rig Veda, in which the word 'mridavach' is applied to the speech of the Ashuras (R.vi.74, 2; v. vi.3; v.vii.6). Of these passages. Professor Muir observes: "The word mridavach, which I have translated "injuriously speaking", is explained by Sayana as meaning "one whose organs of speech are destroyed". The original meaning of the expression was, doubtless that the language of the Ashuras was more or less unintelligible to the Aryas. The same explanation will apply to another passage in the Rig Veda, where it is said: 'May we (by propitiating Indra) conquer the ill speaking man.'

From the Satapatha Brahmana we find that 'the Ashuras, being deprived of speech, were undone, crying. 'He lava', 'He lava'. Such was the unintelligible speech which they uttered. And he who speaks thus is a Miecha. Hence, let no Brahman speak barbarous language, since such is the speech of Ashuras.

We learn from Manu, that 'those tribes who are outside of the classes produced from the mouth, arms, thighs and feet of Brahman, whether they speak the language of the Miechas or of the Aryas, are called Dasyus., In the time of Manu; therefore, the Aryan language and that of the Miechas or Ashuras were both in use. At the period described in the Mahabharata, however, the Ashura language must have almost died out amongst the Aryanized tribes; as Vidura addressed Yudhishthira in the Miecha tongue, so as to be unintelligible to all except Yudhishthira.

At a later period than this, however, the grammarian Rama Tarkavagisa refers to 'those who speak like Nagas.' It would seem, therefore, that the unregenerate Ashuras retained the language, as well as the religion and customs, of their forefathers long after their converted brethren had discarded them. It was evidently amongst these unregenerate tribes that the Paisachi dialects were in use; and amongst these tribes, as we have just seen, were the Dravidian Pandyas

This view, that the Tamil and cognate tongues were founded upon the ancient Ashura speech, is very strongly confirmed by the fact that the language of the Brahuis, a tribe on the borders of Sindh, has been found to be very closely allied to them. Indeed, Dr. Caldwell says: 'The Brahui (language) enables us to trace the Dravidian race, beyond the Indus, to the southern confines of Central Asia. This country, as I have already pointed out, was the home of the Ashuras or Nagas, to which race apparently belonged the founders of the Dravidian kingdoms.'

Taking into consideration all the evidence which has been brought forward, the only possible conclusion seems to be, that the Dravidians, of the south of India, were of the same stock as the Ashuras or Nagas of the North. The second thing to be borne in mind is that the word 'Dravida' is not an original word. It is the Sanskritized form of the word Tamil'.

The original word Tamil' when imported into Sanskrit became *Damita* and later on *Damilla* became Dravida. The word Dravida is the name of the language of the people and does not denote the race of the people. The third thing to remember is that Tamil or Dravida was not merely the language of South India but before the Aryans came it was the language of the whole of India and was spoken from Kashmere to Cape Camorin. In fact, it was the language of the Nagas throughout India. The next thing to note is the contact between the Aryan and the Nagas and the effect it produced on the Nagas and their language. Strange as it may appear the effect of this contact on the Nagas of North India was quite different from the effect it produced on the Nagas of South India. The Nagas in North India gave up Tamil which was their mother tongue and adopted Sanskrit in its place.

The Nagas in South India retained Tamil as their mother tongue and did not adopt Sanskrit the language of the Aryans. If this difference is borne in mind it will help to explain why the name Dravida came to be applied only for the people of South India. The necessity for the application of the name

Dravida to the Nagas of Northern India had ceased because they had ceased to speak the Dravida language. But so far as the Nagas of South India are concerned not only the propriety of calling them Dravida had remained in view of their adherence to the Dravida language but the necessity of calling them Dravida had become very urgent in view of their being the only people speaking the Dravida language after the Nagas of the North had ceased to use it. This is the real reason why the people of South India have come to be called Dravidians.

The special application of the use of the word Dravida for the people of South India must not, therefore, obscure the fact that the Nagas and Dravidas are the one and the same people. They are only two different names for the same people. Nagas was a racial or cultural name and Dravida was their linguistic name.Thus the Dasas are the same as the Nagas and the Nagas are the same as the Dravidians. In other words what we can say about the races of India is that there have been at the most only two races in the field, the Aryans and the Nagas. Obviously the theory of Mr. Rice must fall to the ground. For it postulates three races in action when as a matter of fact we see that there are only two.

Granting however that there was a third aboriginal race living in India before the advent of the Dravidians, can it be said that these pre-Dravidian aboriginals were the ancestors of the present day Untouchables of India? There are two tests we can apply to find the truth. One is the anthropometric test and the other is the ethnological. Considered in the light of the anthropometric characteristics of the Indian people Prof. Ghurye has something very striking to say in his volume on 'Caste and Race in India' from which the following is an extract:

Taking the Brahmin of the United Provinces as the typical representative of the ancient Aryans we shall start comparisons with him. If we turn to the table of differential indices we find that he shows a smaller differential index as compared with the Chuhra and the Khatri of the Punjab than with any caste from the United Provinces except the Chhatri. The differential index between the Khatri and the Chuhra is the only slightly less than that between the Brahmin of the United Provinces and the Chuhra of the Punjab. This means that the Brahmin of the United Provinces has closer physical affinities with the

Chuhra and the Khatri of the Punjab than with any caste from his own province except the very high caste of the Chhatri...... The reality of this close affinity between the United Provinces Brahmin and the Punjab Chuhra is more clearly brought out if we look at the table of differential indices between the United Provinces Brahmin and the Brahmins of other regions. Even the differential index between the United Provinces Brahmin and the Bihar Brahmins, who from what we know about the history of spread of the Aryan culture, is expected to be very nearly allied to the former, is just as high as that between the United Provinces Brahmin and the Chuhra........ On historical ground we expect Bihar to approximate to the United Provinces. On referring to the table we find that the Kurmi comes near to the Brahmin, and the Chamar and the Dom stand much differentiated from him.

But the Chamar in this case is not as much distinct from the Brahmin as the United Provinces Chamar is from the United Provinces Brahmin.. The table for Bengal shows that the Chandal who stands sixth in the scheme of a social precedence and whose touch pollutes, is not much differentiated from the Brahmin, from whom the Kayasthas, second in rank, can hardly be said to be distinguished. In Bombay the Deshastha Brahmin bears as closer affinity to the Son-Koli, a fisherman caste, as to his own compeer, the Chitpavan Brahmin. The Mahar, the Untouchable of the Maratha region, come next together with the Kunbi, the peasant. Then follow in order the Shenvi Brahmin, the Nagar Brahmin and the high caste Maratha. These results are rather old. Stated in a generalised form they mean that there is no correspondence between social gradation and physical differentiation in Bombay.

Finally we come to Madras. Here we must treat the different linguistic areas separately for the schemes of social precedence in the various areas are different. According to the average given by Risely and by E. Thurston the order of castes is as follows: Kapu, Sale, Malla, Golla, Madiga, Fogata and Komati.

According to their social status they are ranked as below: Brahmin, Komati, Golla, Kapu and others and Sale, Fagota and others. Mala Madiga occupy the lowest rank being the Pariahs of the Telugu country. In the Canarese the nasal index gives the following order: Kamatak Smarts, Brahmin, Bant,

Billiva, Mandya Brahmin, Vakkaliga, Ganiga, Linga Banajiga, Panchala, Kurha, Holeya, Deshastha Brahmift, Toreya and Bedar.

In the scheme of social precedence the castes are as under: Brahmin, Bant and Vakkaliga, Toreya, etc., Kuruba and Ganiga, Badaga and Krumba and Solaga, Billiva, Beda Holeya.

The significance of the comparison is enhanced when we remember that the nasal index of the Holeya, the Untouchables of the Canarese region is 75.1 that of the highest of the Brahmin being 71.5 while those of the jungle Krumba and the Solaga, who when Hinduised occupy the rank allotted to them in the list, are 86.1 and 85.1 respectively.

The Tamil castes may be arranged according to their nasal index as follows: Ambattan, Vellai, Ediayan, Agamudaiyan, Tamil Brahmin, Palli, Malaiyali, Shanan and Parayan. The Nasal indices of four typical Malayalam castes are: Tiyan, 75; Nambudri 75.5; Nayar 76.7; Charuman 77.2. The order of social precedence among these is: Nambudri, Nayar, Tiyan and Charuman. The nasal index of the Kanikar, a jungle tribe of Tranvancore is 8.46. Thus, the Charuman (an Unapproachable) belonging to the same race as the Brahmin rather than to Kanikar."

To omit from the above extract what is said about other communities and to draw attention to what relates to the Untouchables only, it is clear that the nasal index of the Chuhra (the Untouchables) of the Punjab is the same as the nasal index of the Brahmin of the United Provinces; the nasal index of the Chamar (the Untouchables) of Bihar is not very much distinct from the Brahmin of Bihar; the nasal index of the Holeya (an Untouchable) of the Carese is far higher than that of the Brahmin of Kamatak and that the nasal index of the Cheruman (an Unapproachable lower than the Pariah) of the Tamil belongs to the same race as the Brahmin of the Tamil Nad. If anthropometry is a science which can be depended upon to determine the race of a people, then the result obtained by the application of anthropometry to the various strata of Hindu society disprove that the Untouchables belong to a race different from the Aryans and the Dravidians. The measurements establish that the Brahmin and the Untouchables belong to the same race.

From this it follows that if the Brahmins are Aryans the Untouchables are also Aryans. If the Brahmins are Dravidians the Untouchables are also Dravidians. If the Brahmins are Nagas, the Untouchables are also Nagas. Such being the facts, the theory propounded by Mr. Rice must be said to be based on a false foundation.

The racial theory of Untouchability not only runs counter to the results of anthropometry, but it also finds very little support from such facts as we know about the ethnology of India. That the people of India were once organized on tribal basis is quite well known, and although the tribes have become castes the tribal organisation still remains intact. Each tribe was divided into clans and the clans were composed of groups of families. Each group of families had a totem which was some object, animate or inanimate. Those who had a common totem formed an exogamous group popularly known as Gotra or Kula. Families having a common gotra were not allowed to intermarry for they were supposed to be descended from the same ancestor having the same blood running in their veins. Having regard to this fact an examination of the distribution of the totems among the different castes and communities should serve as good a test for determining race as anthropometry has been.

Unfortunately, the study of the totems and their distribution among different communities has been completely neglected by students of sociology. This neglect is largely due to the current view propagated by the Census Commissioners that real unit of the Hindu social system and the basis of the fabric of Hindu society is the sub-caste founded on the rule of endogamy. Nothing can be a greater mistake than this. The unit of Hindu society is not the sub-caste but the family founded on the rule of exogamy. In this sense the Hindu family is fundamentally a tribal organisation and not a social organisation as the sub-caste is. The Hindu family is primarily guided in the matter of marriage by consideration of *Kul* and *Gotra* and only secondarily by considerations of caste and sub-caste. *Kul* and *Gotra* are Hindu equivalents of the totem of the Primitive Society. This shows that the Hindu society is still tribal in its organisation with the family at its base observing the rules of exogamy based on *Kul* and *Gotra.* Castes and sub-castes are social organisations which are superimposed over the tribal organisation and the rule of endogamy enjoined by them does not do away with the rule of exogamy enjoined by the tribal organisations of *Kul* and *Gotra.*

The importance of recognizing the fact that it is the family which is fundamental and not the sub-caste is obvious. It would lead to the study of the names of *Kul* and *Gotra* prevalent among Hindu families. Such a study would be a great help in determining the racial composition of the people of India. If the same *Kul* and *Gotra* were found to exist in different castes and communities it would be possible to say that the castes though socially different were racially one. Two such studies have been made, one in Maharashtra by Risley and another in the Punjab by Mr. Rose and the result flatly contradict the theory that the Untouchables are racially different from the Aryans or the Dravidians.

The main bulk of the population in Maharashtra consists of Marathas. The Mahars are the Untouchables of Maharashtra. The anthropological investigation shows that both have the same *Kul.*. Indeed the identity is so great that there is hardly a *Kul* among the Marathas which is not to be found among the Mahars and there is no *Kul* among the Mahars which is not to be found among the Marathas. Similarly, in the Punjab one main stock of people consists of Jats. The Mazabi Sikhs are Untouchables most of them being Chamars by caste. Anthropological investigation shows that the two have the same *Gotras.* Given these facts how can it be argued that the Untouchables belong to a different race? As I have said if totem, kul, and gotra, have any significance it means that those who have the same totem must have been kindred. If they were kindred they could not be persons of different race.

The racial theory of the origin of Untouchability must, therefore, be abandoned.

Occupational Origin of Untouchability

We may now turn to the occupational theory of the origin of Untouchability. According to Mr. Rice, the origin of Untouchability is to be found in the unclean and filthy occupations of the Untouchables. The theory is a very plausible one. But there are certain difficulties in the way of its being accepted as a true explanation of the origin of Untouchability.

The filthy and unclean occupations which the Untouchables perform are common to all human societies. In every human Society there are people who perform these occupations. Why were such people not treated as Untouchables in other parts of the world?

The second question is: Did the Dravidians have a nausea against such callings or against persons engaged in them? On this point, there is no evidence. But we have evidence about the Aryans. That evidence shows that the Aryans were like other people and their notions of purity and impurity did not fundamentally differ from those of other ancient people. One has only to consider the following texts from Narada Smriti to show that the Aryans did not at all mind engaging themselves in filthy occupations. In Chapter V Narada is dealing with the subject matter of breach of contract of service. In this Chapter, there occur the following verses:

1. The sages have distinguished five sorts of attendants according to law. Among these are four sorts of labourers; the slaves (are the fifth category of which there are) fifteen species.
2. A student, an apprentice, a hired servant, and fourthly an official.
3. The sages have declared that the state of dependence is common to all these but their respective position and income depends on their particular caste and occupations.
4. Know that there are two sorts of occupations; pure work and impure work; impure work is that done by the slaves. Pure work is that done by labourers.
5. Sweeping the gateway, the privy, the road and the place for rubbish; shampooing the secret parts of the body; gathering and putting away the leaving of food, ordure and urine.
6. And lastly, rubbing the master's limbs when desired; this should be regarded as impure work. All other work besides this is pure.
7. Thus have the four classes of servants doing pure work been enumerated. All the others who do dirty work are slaves, of whom there are fifteen kinds

It is clear that impure work was done by the slaves and that the impure work included scavenging. The question that arises is: Who were these slaves? Were they Aryans or non-Aryans? That slavery existed among the Aryans admits of no doubt. An Aryan could be a slave of an Aryan. No matter to what Varna an Aryan belonged he could be a slave. A Kshatriya could be a slave. So could a Vaishya. Even a Brahmin was not immune from the law of slavery. It is when *Chaturvarna* came to be recognized as a law of the land that a change was made in the system of slavery. What this change was can be seen from the following extract from the Narada Smriti:

> *"39. In the inverse order of the (four) castes slavery is not ordained, except where a man violated the duties peculiar to his caste. Slavery (in that respect) is analogous to the condition of a wife".*

Yajnavalkya also says that:

> *"183(2) Slavery is in the descending order of the Vamas and not in the ascending order"*

This is explained by Vijnaneswara in his Mitakshara, a Commentary on Yajnavalkya Smriti in the following terms:

> *"Of the Varna such as the Brahmin and the rest, a state of slavery shall exist in the descending order (Anulomeyna). Thus, of a Brahmin, a Kshatriya, and the rest may become a slave; of a Kshatriya, the Vaishya and the Sudra; and of a Vaishya, a Sudra; this state of slavery shall operate in the descending order."*

The change was a mere reorganisation of slavery and the basis of the principles of graded inequality which is the soul of Chaturvarna. To put it in a concrete form, the new law declared that a Brahmin could have a Brahmin, Kshatriya, Vaishya and a Sudra as his slave. A Kshatriya could have Kshatriya, a Vaishya and a Sudra as his slave. A Vaishya could have a Vaishya and a Sudra as his slave. A Sudra could have a Sudra only. With all this, the law of slavery remained and all Aryans whether they were Brahmins, Kshatriyas, Vaishyas or Sudras if they become slaves were subject to it.

Having regard to the duties prescribed for the slaves, this change in the law of slavery does not matter at all. It still means that a Brahmin if he was a slave, a Kshatriya if he was a slave, a Vaishya if he was a slave, did the work of a scavenger. Only a Brahmin would not do scavenging in the house of a Kshatriya, Vaishya or a Sudra. But he would do scavenging in the house of a Brahmin. Similarly, a Kshatriya would do scavenging in the house of a Brahmin and the Kshatriya. Only he would not do in the house of a Vaishya or Sudra and a Vaishya would do scavenging in the house of a Brahmin, Kshatriya and Vaishya. Only he would not do it in the house of a Sudra. It is, therefore, obvious that the Brahmins, Kshatriyas and Vaishyas who are admittedly the Aryans did the work of scavengers which is the filthiest of filthy occupations. If scavenging was not loathsome to an Aryan how can it be said that engaging in filthy occupations was the cause of Untouchability. The theory of filthy occupation as an explanation of Untouchability is, therefore, not tenable.

New Theories of the Origin of Untouchability

Contempt for Buddhists as the Root of Untouchability

The Census Reports for India published by the Census Commissioner at the interval of every ten years from 1870 onwards contain a wealth of information nowhere else to be found regarding the social and religious life of the people of India. Before the Census of 1910 the Census Commissioner had a column called "Population by Religion". Under this heading the population was shown (1) Muslims, (2) Hindus, (3) Christians, etc. The Census Report for the year 1910 marked a new departure from the prevailing practice. For the first time it divided the Hindus under three separate categories, (i) Hindus, (ii) Animists and Tribal, and (iii) the Depressed Classes or Untouchables. This new classification has been continued ever since.

This departure from the practice of the previous Census Commissioners raises three questions. First is what led the Commissioner for the Census of 1910 to introduce this new classification. The second is what was the criteria adopted as a basis for this classification. The third is what are the reasons for the growth of certain practices which justify the division of Hindus into three separate categories mentioned above.

The answer to the first question will be found in the address presented in 1909 by the Muslim Community under leadership of H.H. The Aga Khan to the then Viceroy, Lord Minto, in which they asked for a separate and adequate representation for the Muslim community in the legislature, executive and the public services.

In the address there occurs the following passage:

> *"The Mohamedans of India number, according to the census taken in the year 1901 over sixty-two millions or between one-fifth and one-fourth of the total population of His Majesty's Indian dominions,* and if a reduction be made for the uncivilised portions of the community enumerated under the heads of animist and other minor religions, as well as for those classes who are ordinarily classified as Hindus but properly speaking are not Hindus at all, the proportion of Mohamedans to the Hindu Majority becomes much larger *We therefore desire to submit that under any system of representation extended or limited a community in itself more numerous than the entire population of any first class European power except Russia may justly lay claim to adequate recognition as an important factor in the State."*
>
> *"We venture, indeed, with Your Excellency's permission to go a step further, and urge that the position accorded to the Mohammedan community in any kind of representation direct or indirect, and in all other ways effecting their status and influence should be commensurate, not merely with their numerical strength but also with their political importance and the value of the contribution which they make to the defence of the empire, and we also hope that Your Excellency will in this connection be pleased to give due consideration to the position which they occupied in India a little more than hundred years ago and of which the traditions have naturally not faded from their minds."*

The portion in italics has a special significance. It was introduced in the address to suggest that in comprising the numerical strength of the Muslims with that of the Hindus the population of the animists, tribals and the Untouchables should be excluded. The reason for this new classification of 'Hindus' adopted by the Census Commissioner in 1910 lies in this demand of the Muslim community for separate representation on augmented scale. At any rate this is how the Hindus understood this demand.

Interesting as it is, the first question as to why the Census Commissioner made this departure in the system of classification is of less importance than the second question. What is important is to know the basis adopted by the Census Commissioner for separating the different classes of Hindus into (1) those who were hundred per cent Hindus and (2) those who were not.

The basis adopted by the Census Commissioner for separation is to be found in the circular issued by the Census Commissioner in which he laid down certain tests for the purpose of distinguishing these two classes. Among those who were not hundred percent Hindus were included castes and tribes which:

(1) Deny the supremacy of the Brahmins.

(2) Do not receive the Mantra from a Brahmin or other recognized Hindu Guru.

(3) Deny the authority of the Vedas.

(4) Do not worship the Hindu gods.

(5) Are not served by good Brahmins as family priests.

(6) Have no Brahmin priests at all.

(7) Are denied access to the interior of the Hindu temples.

(8) Cause pollution (a) by touch, or (b) within a certain distance.

(9) Bury their dead.

(10) Eat beef and do no reverence to the cow.

Out of these ten tests some divide the Hindus from the Animists and the Tribal. The rest divide the Hindus from the Untouchables. Those that divide the Untouchables from the Hindus are (2), (5), (6), (7), and (10). It is with them that we are chiefly concerned.

For the sake of clarity it is better to divide these tests into parts and consider them separately. This Chapter will be devoted only to the consideration of (2), (5), and (6).

The replies received by the Census Commissioner to questions embodied in tests (2), (5) and (6) reveal (1) that the Untouchables do not receive the Mantra from a Brahmin; (2)

that the Untouchables are not served by good Brahmin priests at all; and (3) that Untouchables have their own priests reared from themselves. On these facts the Census Commissioners of all Provinces are unanimous.

Of the three questions the third is the most important. Unfortunately the Census Commissioner did not realise this. For in making his inquiries he failed to go to the root of the matter to find out: Why were the Untouchables not receiving the Mantra from the Brahmin? Why Brahmins did not serve the Untouchables as their family priests? Why do the Untouchables prefer to have their own priests? It is the 'why of these facts which is more important than the existence of these facts. It is the 'why' of these facts which must be investigated. For the clue to the origin of Untouchability lies hidden behind it.

Before entering upon this investigation, it must be pointed out that the inquiries by the Census Commissioner were in a sense one-sided. They showed that the Brahmins shunned the Untouchables. They did not bring to light the fact that the Untouchables also shunned the Brahmins. Nonetheless, it is a fact. People are so much accustomed to thinking that the Brahmin is the superior of the Untouchables and the Untouchable accepts himself as his inferior; that this statement that the Untouchables look upon the Brahmin as an impure penvon is sure to come to them as a matter of great surprise. The fact has however been noted by many writers who have observed and examined the social customs of the Untouchables. To remove any doubt on the point, attention is drawn to the following extracts from their writings.

The fact was noticed by Abbe Dubois who says: "Even to this day a Pariah is not allowed to pass a Brahmin Street in a village, though nobody can prevent, or prevents, his approaching or passing by a Brahmin's house in towns. The Pariahs, on their part will under no circumstances, allow a Brahmin to pass through their *paracherries* (collection of Pariah huts) as they firmly believe it will lead to their ruin".

Mr. Hemingsway, the Editor of the Gazetteer of the Tanjore District says: "These casts (Parayan and Pallan or Chakkiliyan castes of Tanjore District) strongly object to the entrance of a Brahmin into their quarters believing that harm will result to them therefrom". Speaking of the Holeyas of the Hasan District of Mysore, Captain J.S.F. Mackenzie says:- "Every village has its Holigiri as the quarters inhabited by the Holiars, formerly agrestic serfs, is called outside the village boundary hedge. This, I thought was because they were considered as impure race, whose touch carries defilement with it."

Such is the reason generally given by the Brahmins who refuse to receive anything directly from the hands of a Holiar, and yet the Brahmins consider great luck will wait upon them if they can manage to pass through the Holigiri without being molested. To this Holiars have a strong objection, and, should a Brahmin attempt to enter their quarters, they turn out in a body and slipper him, in former times, it is said, to death. Members of the other castes may come as far as the door, but they must not enter the house, for that would bring the Holiar bad luck. If, by chance, a person happens to get in, the owner takes care to tear the intruder's cloth, tie up some salt in one corner of it, and turn him out. This is supposed to neutralise all the good luck which might have accrued to the trespasser, and avert any evil which ought to have befallen the owner of the house.

What is the explanation of this strange phenomenon? The explanation must of course fit in with the situation as it stood at the start, *i.e.,* when the Untouchables were not Untouchables but were only Broken Men. We must ask why the Brahmins refused to officiate at the religious ceremonies of the Broken Men? Is it the case that the Brahmins refused to officiate? Or is it that the Broken Men refused to invite them? Why did the Brahmin regard Broken Men as impure? Why did the Broken Men regard the Brahmins as impure? What is the basis of this antipathy?

This antipathy can be explained on one hypothesis. It is that the Broken Men were Buddhists. As such they did not revere the Brahmins, did not employ them as their priests and regarded them as impure. The Brahmin on the other hand disliked the Broken Men because they were Buddhists and preached against them contempt and hatred with the result that the Broken Men came to be regarded as Untouchables.

We have no direct evidence that the Broken Men were Buddhists. No evidence is as a matter of fact necessary when the majority of Hindus were Buddhists. We may take it that they were.

That there existed hatred and abhorrence against the Buddhists in the mind of the Hindus and that this feeling was created by the Brahmins is not without support.

Nilkant in his *Prayaschit Mayukha* quotes a verse from Manu which says: "If a person touches a Buddhist or a flower of Pachupat, Lokayata, Nastika and Mahapataki, he shall purify himself by a bath."

The same doctrine is preached by Apararka in his Smriti. Vradha Harit goes further and declares entry into the Buddhist Temple as sin requiring a purificatory bath for removing the impurity.

How widespread had become this spirit of hatred and contempt against the followers of Buddha can be observed from the scenes depicted in Sanskrit dramas. The most striking illustration of this attitude towards the Buddhists is to be found in the Mricchakatika. In Act VII of that Drama the hero Charudatta and his friend Maitreya are shown waiting for Vasantasena in the park outside the city. She fails to turn up and Charudatta decides to leave the park. As they are leaving, they seethe Buddhist monk by name Samvahaka. On seeing him, Charudatta says: "Friend Maitreya, I am anxious to meet Vasantsena... Come, let us go. (After walking a little) Ah! here's aninauspicious sight, a Buddhist monk coming towards us. (After a little reflection) well, let him come this way, we shall follow this other path. (Exit.)

In Act VIII the monk is in the Park of Sakara, the King's brother-in-law, washing his clothes in a pool. Sakara accompanied by Vita turns up and threatens to kill the monk. The following conversation between them is revealing:

Sakara-Stay, you wicked monk.

Monk-Ah! Here's the king's brother-in-law! Because some monk has offended him, he now beats up any monk he happens to met.

Sakara-Stay, I will now break your head as one breaks a radish in a tavern. *(Beats him).*

Vita-Friend, it is not proper to beat a monk who has put on the saffron-robes, being disgusted with the world.

Monk-*(Welcomes)* Be pleased, lay brother.

Sakara-Friend, see. He is abusing me.

Vita-What does he say?

Sakara-He calls me lay brother *(upasaka)*. Am I a barber?

Vita-Oh! He is really praising you as a devotee of the Buddha.

Sakara-Why has he come here?

Monk-To wash these clothes.

Sakara-Ah! you wicked monk. Even I myself do not bathe in this pool; I shall kill you with one stroke."

After a lot of beating, the monk is allowed to go. Here is a Buddhist Monk in the midst of the Hindu crowd. He is shunned and avoided. The feeling of disgust against him is so great that the people even shun the road the monk is travelling. The feeling of repulsion is so intense that the entry of the Buddhist was enough to cause the exit of the Hindus. The Buddhist monk is on a par with the Brahmin. A Brahmin is immune from death-penalty. He is even free from corporal punishment. But the Buddhist monk is beaten and assaulted without remorse, without compunction as though there was nothing wrong in it.

If we accept that the Broken Men were the followers of Buddhism and did not care to return to Brahmanism when it became triumphant over Buddhism as easily as other did, we have an explanation for both the questions. It explains why the Untouchables regard the Brahmins as inauspicious, do not employ them as their priest and do not even allow them to enter into their quarters. It also explains why the Broken Men came to be regarded as Untouchables. The Broken Men hated the Brahmins because the Brahmins were the enemies of Buddhism and the Brahmins imposed untouchability upon the Broken Men because they would not leave Buddhism. On this reasoning it is possible to conclude that one of the roots of untouchability lies in the hatred and contempt which the Brahmins created against those who were Buddhist.

Can the hatred between Buddhism and Brahmanism be taken to be the sole cause why Broken Men became Untouchables? Obviously, it cannot be. The hatred and contempt preached by the Brahmins was directed against Buddhists in general and not against the Broken Men in particular. Since untouchability stuck to Broken Men only, it is obvious that there was some additional circumstance which has played its part in fastening untouchability upon the Broken Men. What that circumstance could have been? We must next direct our effort in the direction of ascertaining it.

Beef Eating as the Root of Untouchability

We now take up test No. 10 referred to in the circular issued by the Census Commissioner and to which reference has already been made in the this book. The test refers to beef-eating.

The Census Returns show that the meat of the dead cow forms the chief item of food consumed by communities which are generally classified as untouchable communities. No Hindu community, however low, will touch cow's flesh. On the other hand, there is no community which is really an Untouchable community which has not something to do with the dead cow. Some eat her flesh, some remove the skin, some manufacture articles out of her skin and bones.

From the survey of the Census Commissioner, it is well established that Untouchables eat beef. The question however is: Has beef-eating any relation to the origin of Untouchability? Or is it merely an incident in the economic life of the Untouchables? Can we say that the Broken Men came to be treated as Untouchables because they ate beef? There need be no hesitation in returning an affirmative answer to this question. No other answer is consistent with facts as we know them.

In the first place, we have the fact that the Untouchables or the main communities which compose them eat the dead cow and those who eat the dead cow are tainted with untouchability and no others. The co-relation between untouchability and the use of the dead cow is so great and so close that the thesis that it is the root of untouchability seems to be incontrovertible. In the second place if there is anything that separates the Untouchables from the Hindus, it is beef-eating. Even a superficial view of the food taboos of the Hindus will show that there are two taboos regarding food which serve as dividing lines. There is one taboo against meat-eating. It divides Hindus into vegetarians and flesh eaters. There is another taboo which is against beef eating. It divides Hindus into those who eat cow's flesh and those who do not. From the point of view of untouchability the first dividing line is of no importance. But the second is. For it completely marks off the Touchables from the Untouchables. The Touchables whether they are vegetarians or flesh-eaters are united in their objection to eat cow's flesh. As against them stand the Untouchables who eat cow's flesh without compunction and as a matter of course and habit.

In this context it is not far-fetched to suggest that those who have a nausea against beef-eating should treat those who eat beef as Untouchables.

There is really no necessity to enter upon any speculation as to whether beef-eating was or was not the principal reason for the rise of Untouchability. This new theory receives support from the Hindu Shastras. The Veda Vyas Smriti contains the following verse which specifies the communities which are included in the category of Antyajas and the reasons why they were so included :

L.12-13 "The *Charmakars* (Cobbler), the *Bhatta* (Soldier), the *Bhilla,* the *Rajaka* (washerman), the *Puskara,* the *Nata* (actor), the *Vrata,* the *Meda,* the *Chandala,* the *Dasa,* the *Svapaka,* and the *Kolika*-these are known as Antyajas as well as others who eat cow's flesh."

Generally speaking the Smritikars never care to explain the why and the how of their dogmas. But this case is exception. For in this case, Veda Vyas does explain the cause of untouchability. The clause "as well as others who eat cow's flesh" is very important. It shows that the Smritikars knew that the origin of untouchability is to be found in the eating of beef. The dictum of Veda Vyas must close the argument. It comes, so to say, straight from the horse's mouth and what is important is that it is also rational for it accords with facts as we know them.

The new approach in the search for the origin of Untouchability has brought to the surface two sources of the origin of Untouchability. One is the general atmosphere of scorn and contempt spread by the Brahmins against those who were Buddhists and the second is the habit of beef-eating kept on by the Broken Men. As has been said the first circumstance could not be sufficient to account for stigma of Untouchability attaching itself to the Broken Men. For the scorn and contempt for Buddhists spread by the Brahmins was too general and affected all Buddhists and not merely the Broken Men. The reason why Broken Men only became Untouchables was because in addition to being Buddhists they retained their habit of beef-eating which gave additional ground for offence to the Brahmins to carry their new-found love and reverence to the cow to its logical conclusion. We may therefore conclude that the Broken Men were exposed to scorn and contempt on the ground that they were Buddhists the main cause of their Untouchability was beef-eating.

The theory of beef-eating as the cause of untouchability also gives rise to many questions. Critics are sure to ask: What is the cause of the nausea which the Hindus have against beef-eating? Were the Hindus always opposed to beef-eating? If not, why did they develop such a nausea against it? Were the Untouchables given to beef-eating from the very start? Why did they not give up beef-eating when it was abandoned by the Hindus? Were the Untouchables always Untouchables? If there was a time when the Untouchables were not Untouchables even though they ate beef why should beef-eating give rise to Untouchability at a later-stage? If the Hindus were eating beef, when did they give it up? If Untouchability is a reflex of the nausea of the Hindus against beef-eating, how long after the Hindus had given up beef-eating did Untouchability come into being? These questions must be answered. Without an answer to these questions, the theory will remain under cloud. It will be considered as plausible but may not be accepted as conclusive. Having put forth the theory, I am bound to answer these questions. I propose to take up the following heads:

(1) Did the Hindus never eat beef?
(2) What led the Hindus to give up be heating?
(3) What led the Brahmins to become vegetarians?
(4) Why did beef-eating give rise to Untouchability? and
(5) When was Untouchability born?

Did the Hindus Never Eat Beef?

To the question whether the Hindus ever ate beef, every Touchable Hindu, whether he is a Brahmin or a non-Brahmin, will say 'no, never'. In a certain sense, he is right. From times no Hindu has eaten beef. If this is all that the Touchable Hindu wants to convey by his answer there need be no quarrel over it. But when the learned Brahmins argue that the Hindus not only never ate beef but they always held the cow to be sacred and were always opposed to the killing of the cow, it is impossible to accept their view.

What is the evidence in support of the construction that the Hindus never ate beef and were opposed to the killing of the cow?

There are two series of references in the Rig Veda on which reliance is placed. In one of these, the cow is spoken of as *Aghnya.* They are Rig Veda 1.164, 27; IV.1.6; V 82-8; V11.69. 71; X.87. *Aghnya* means 'one who does not deserve to be killed'. From this, it is' argued that this was a prohibition against the killing of the cow and that since the Vedas are the final authority in the matter of religion, it is concluded that the Aryans could not have killed the cows, much less could they have eaten beef. In another series of references the cow is spoken of as sacred. They are Rig Veda V1.28.1.8. and VIII, 101. 15. In these verses the cow is addressed as Mother of Rudras, the Daughter of Vasus, the Sister of the Adityas and the Centre of Nectar. Another reference on the subject is in Rig Veda VIII. 101. 16 where the cow is called Devi (Goddess).

Raliance is also placed on certain passages in the Brahmanas and Sutras.

There are two passages in the Satapatha Brahmana which relate to animal sacrifice and beef-eating. One is at 111.1.2.21 and reads as follows:

> *"He (the Adhvaryu) then makes him enter the hall. Let him not eat (the flesh) of either the cow or the ox, for the cowand the ox doubtless support everything here on earth. The gods spake, 'verily, the cow and the ox support everything here; come, let us bestow on the cow and the ox whatever vigour belonged to other species (of animals); and therefore the cow and the ox eat most Hence were one to eat (the flesh) of an ox or a cow, there would be, as it were, an eating of everything, or, as it were, a going to the end (or, to destruction)... Let him therefore not eat (the flesh) of the cow and the ox."*

The other passage is at 1, 2, 3, 6. It speaks against animal sacrifice and on ethical grounds.

A similar statement is contained in the Apastambha Dharma Sutra at 1, 5, 17, 29. Apastambha lays a general embargo on the eating of cow's flesh.

Such is the evidence in support of the contention that the Hindus never ate beef. What conclusion can be drawn from this evidence?

So far as the evidence from the Rig Veda is concerned the conclusion is based on a misreading and misunderstanding of the texts. The adjective *Aghnya* applied to the cow in the Rig Veda means a cow that was yielding milk and therefore not fit for being killed. That the cow is venerated in the Rig Veda is of course true. But this regard and venerations of the cow are only to be expected from an agricultural community like the Indo-Aryans. This application of the utility of the cow did not prevent the Aryan from killing the cow for purposes of food. Indeed the cow was killed because the cow was regarded as sacred. As observed by Mr. Kane: "It was not that the cow was not sacred in Vedic times, it was because of her sacredness that it is ordained in the Vajasaneyi Samhita that beef should be eaten."

That the Aryans of the Rig Veda did kill cows for purposes of food and ate beef is abundantly clear from the Rig Veda itself. In Rig Veda (X. 86.14) Indra says:-"They cook for one 15 plus twenty oxen". The Rig Veda (X.91.14) says that for Agni were sacrificed horses, bulls, oxen, barren cows and rams. From the Rig Veda (X.72.6) it appears that the cow was killed with a sword or axe.

As to the testimony of the Satapatha Brahmana, can it be said to be conclusive? Obviously, it cannot be. For there are passages in the other Brahmanas which give a different opinion.

To give only one instance. Among the Kamyashtis set forth in the Taittiriya Brahmana, not only the sacrifice of oxen and cows are laid down, but we are even told what kind and description of oxen and cows are to be offered to what deities. Thus, a dwarf ox is to be chosen for sacrifice to Vishnu; a drooping horned bull with a blaze on the forehead to Indra as the destroyer of Vritra; a black cow to Pushan; a red cow to

Rudra; and so on. The Taittiriya Brahmana notes another sacrifice called *Panchasaradiya-seva,* the most important element of which was the immolation of seventeen five-year old humpless, dwraf-bulls, and as many dwarf heifers under three year-old.

As against the statement of the Apastamba Dharma Sutra, the following points may be noted.

First is the contrary statement contained in that Very Sutra. At 15, 14, 29, the Sutra says:

> *"The cow and the bull are sacred and therefore should be eaten". The second is the prescription of Madhuparka contained in the Grahya Sutras. Among the Aryans the etiquette for receiving important guests had become settled into custom and had become a ceremony. The most important offering was Madhuparka. A detailed descriptions regarding Madhuparka are to be found in the various Grahya Sutras. According to most of the Grahya Sutras there are six persons who have a right to be served with Madhuparka namely; (1) Ritwija or the Brahmin called to perform a sacrifice, (2) Acharya, the teacher, (3) The bridegroom (4) The King (5) The Snatak, the student who has just finished his studies at the Gurukul and (6) Any person who is dear to the host. Some add Atithi to this list. Except in the case of Ritvija, King and Acharya, Madhuparka is to be offered to the rest once in a year. To the Ritvija, King and Acharya it is to be offered each time they come.*

What was this Madhuparka made of? There is divergence about the substances mixed in offering Madhuparka. Asv.gr and Ap.gr. (13.10) prescribe a mixture of honey and curds or clarified butter and curds. Others like Par.gr. (13) prescribe a mixture of three (curds, honey and butter). Ap.gr. (13.11-12) states the view of some that those three may be mixed or five (those three with fried *yava* grain and barley). Hir.gr.L, 12, 10-12 give the option of mixing three of five (curds, honey, ghee, water and ground grain). The Kausika Sutra (92) speaks of nine kinds of mixtures, *viz., Brahma* (honey and curds). *Aindra* (of payasa), *Saurnya* (curds and ghee), *Pausna* (ghee and mantha), *Sarasvata* (milk and ghee), *Mausala* (wine and ghee, this being used only in Sautramanai and Rajasuya sacrifices),

Parivrajaka (sesame oil and oil cake). The Madhava gr.l.9.22 says that the Veda declares that the Madhuparka must not be without flesh and so it recommends that if the cow is let loose, goat's meat or payasa (rice cooked in milk) may be offered; the Hir.gr. 1.13, 14 says that other meat should be offered; Baud.gr. (1.2,51-54) says that when the cow is let off, the flesh of a goat or ram may be offered or some forest flesh (of a deer, etc.) may be offered, as there can be no Madhuparka without flesh or if one is unable to offer flesh one may cook ground grains.

Thus the essential element in Madhuparka is flesh and particularly cow's flesh. The killing of cow for the guest had grown to such an extent that the guest came to be called 'Goghna' which means the killer of the cow. To avoid this slaughter of the cows the Ashvateyana Grahya Sutra (1.24.25) suggests that the cow should be let loose when the guest comes so as to escape the rule of etiquette.

Thirdly, reference may be made to the ritual relating to disposal of the dead to counter the testimony of the Apastamba Dharma Sutra. The Sutra says:

1. He should then put the following (sacrificial) implements (on the dead body)
2. Into the right hand the (spoon called) Guhu.
3. Into the left the (other spoon called) Upabhrit.
4. On his right side the wooden sacrificial sword called *Sphya,* on his left side the Agnihotrahavani (*i.e.*, the laddle with which the Agnihotra oblations are sacrified).
5. On his chest the (big sacrificial laddle called) Dhruva. On his head the dishes. On his teeth the pressing stones.
6. On the two sides of his nose, the two smaller sacrificial laddles called *Sruvas.*
7. Or, if there is only one (Sruva), breaking it (in two pieces).
8. On his two ears the two Prasitraharanas (i.e., the vessels into which the portion of the sacrificial food belonging to the Brahmin) is put
9. Or, if there is only one (Prasitraharana), breaking it (in two pieces).

10. On his belly the (vessel called) Patri.
11. And the cup into which the cutoff portion (of the sacrificial food) are put.
12. On his secret parts the (staff called) Samy.
13. On his thighs two kindling woods.
14. On his legs the mortar and the pestle.
15. On his feet the two baskets.
16. Or, if there is only one (basket), breaking it in two pieces.
17. Those of the implements which have a hollow (into which liquids can be poured) are filled with sprinkled butter.
18. The son (of the deceased person) should take the under and the upper millstone for himself.
19. And the implements made of copper, iron and earthenware.
20. Taking out the omentum of the she-animal he should cover therewith the head and the mouth (of the dead person) with the verse, 'But on the armour (which will protect thee) against Agni, by that which comes from the cows.' (Rig Veda. X. 16.7).
21. Taking out the kidneys of the animal he should lay them into the hands (of the dead body) with the verse, escape the two hounds, the sons of Sarma (Rig Veda X 14.10) the right kidney into the right hand and the left into the left hand.
22. The heart of the animals he puts on the heart of the deceased.
23. And two lumps of flour or rice according to some teachers.
24. Only if there are no kidneys according to some teachers.
25. Having distributed the whole (animal), limb by limb (placing its different limbs on the corresponding limbs of the deceased) and having covered it with its hide, he recites when the Pranita water is carried forward (the verse), 'Agni do not overturn this cup,' (Rig Veda, X. 16.8).

26. Bending his left knee he should sacrifice Yugya oblation into the Dakshina fire with the formulas 'To Agni Svaha, to Kama Svaha, to the world Svaha, to Anumati Svaha'.
27. A fifth (oblation) on the chest of the deceased with the formula 'from this one verily thou hast been born. May he now be born out of thee. To the heaven worlds Svaha.'"

From the above passage quoted from the Ashvalayan Grahya Sutra it is clear that among the ancient Indo-Aryans when a person died, an animal had to be killed and the parts of the animal were placed on the appropriate parts of the dead body before the dead body was burned.

Such is the state of the evidence on the subject of cow-killing and beef-eating. Which part of it is to be accepted as true? The correct view is that the testimony of the Satapatha Brahmana and the Apastamba Dharma Sutra in so far as it supports the view that Hindus were against cow-killing and beef-eating, are merely exhortations against the excesses of cow-killing and not prohibitions against cow-killing. Indeed the exhortations prove that cow-killing and eating of beef had become a common practice. That notwithstanding these exhortations cow-killing and beef-eating continued. That most often they fell on deaf ears is proved by the conduct of Yajnavalkya, the great Rishi of the Aryans. The first passage quoted above from the Satapatha Brahmana was really addressed to Yajnavalkya as an exhortation. How did Yajnavalkya respond? After listening to the exhortation this is what Yajnavalkya said:-'" I, for one, eat it, provided that it is tender"

That the Hindus at one time did kill cows and did eat beef is proved abundantly by the description of the Yajnas given in the Buddhist Sutras which relate to periods much later than the Vedas and the Brahmanas. The scale on which the slaughter of cows and animals took place was colossal. It is not possible to give a total of such slaughter on all accounts committed by the Brahmins in the name of religion. Some idea of the extent of this slaughter can however be had from references to it in the Buddhist literature. As an illustration reference may be made to the Kutadanta Sutra in which Buddha preached against the performance of animal sacrifices to Brahmin Kutadanta.

Buddha, though speaking in a tone of sarcastic travesty, gives a good idea of the practices and rituals of the Vedic sacrifices when he said:

> *"And further, O Brahmin, at that sacrifice neither were any oxen slain, neither goats, nor fowls, nor fatted pigs, nor were any kind of living creatures put to death. No trees were cut down to be used as posts, no Darbha grasses mown to stress around the sacrificial spot. And the slaves and messengers and workmen there employed were driven neither by rods nor fear, nor carried on their work weeping with tears upon their faces."*

Kutadanta on the other hand in thanking Buddha for his conversion gives an idea of the magnitude of the slaughter of animals which took place at such sacrifices when he says:

> *"I, even I be take myself to the venerable Gautama as my guide, to the Doctrine and the Order. May the venerable One accept me as a disciple, as one who, from this day forth, as long as life endures, has taken him as his guide. And I myself, O, Gautama, will have the seven hundred bulls, and the seven hundred steers, and the seven hundred heifers, and the seven hundred goats, and the seven hundred rams set free. To them I grant their life. Let them eat grass and drink fresh water and may cool breezes waft around them."*

In the Samyuta Nikaya (111,1-9) we have another description of a Yajna performed by Pasenadi, king of Kosala. It is said that five hundred bulls, five hundred calves and many heifers, goats and rams were led to the pillar to be sacrificed.

With this evidence no one can doubt that there was a time when Hindus-both Brahmins and non-Brahmins ate not only flesh but also beef.

Why did Non-Brahmins Give up Beef-eating?

The food habits of the different classes of Hindus have been as fixed and stratified as their cults. Just as Hindus can be classified on their basis of their cults so also they can be classified on the basis of their habits of food. On the basis of their cults, Hindus are either *Saivites* (followers of Shiva) or *Vaishnavites* (followers of Vishnu). Similarly, Hindus are either

Mansahari (those who eat flesh) or *Shakahari* (those who are vegetarians).

For ordinary purposes the division of Hindus into two classes *Mansahari* and *Shakahari* may be enough. But it must be admitted that it is not exhaustive and does not take account of all the classes which exist in Hindu society. For an exhaustive classification, the class of Hindus called *Mansahari* shall have to be further divided into two sub-classes: (i) Those who eat flesh but do not eat cow's flesh; and (ii) Those who eat flesh including cow's flesh; In other words, on the basis of food taboos, Hindu society falls into three classes: (i) Those who are vegetarians; (ii) Those who eat flesh but do not eat cow's flesh; and (iii) Those who eat flesh including cow's flesh. Corresponding to this classification, we have in Hindu society three classes: (1) Brahmins; (2) Non-Brahmins; and (3) The Untouchables. This division though not in accord with the fourfold division of society called Chaturvarnya, yet it is in accord with facts as they exist. For, in the Brahmins we have a class which is vegetarian, in the non-Brahmins the class which eats flesh but does not eat cow's flesh and in the Untouchables a class which eats flesh including cow's flesh.

This threefold division is therefore substantial and is in accord with facts. Anyone who stops to turn over this classification in his mind is bound to be struck by the position of the Non-Brahmins. One can quite understand vegetarianism. One can quite understand meat-eating. But it is difficult to understand why a person who is a flesh-eater should object to one kind of flesh namely cow's flesh. This is an anomaly which call for explanation. Why did the Non-Brahmin give up beef-eating? For this purpose it is necessary to examine laws on the subject. The relevant legislation must be found either in the Law of Ashoka or the Law of Manu.

To begin with Ashoka. The edicts of Ashoka which have reference to this matter are Rock Edict No.I and Pillar Edict Nos.II and V. Rock Edict No.1 reads as follows:

> *"This pious Edict has been written by command of His Sacred and Gracious Majesty) the King. Here (in the capital) no animal may be slaughtered for sacrifice, nor may the holiday feast be held, because His Sacred and Gracious Majesty, the king sees much offence in the*

holiday feasts, although in certain places holiday feasts arc excellent in the sight of His Sacred and Gracious Majesty the king."

"Formerly, in the kitchen of His Sacred and Gracious Majesty the King, each day many hundred thousands of living creatures were slaughtered to make curries. But now, when this pious edict is being written, only three living creatures are slaughtered (daily) for curry, to wit, two peacocks and one antelope: the antelope, however, not invariably. Even those three living creatures henceforth shall not be slaughtered."

Pillar Edict No.II was in the following terms:

"Thus saith His Sacred and Gracious Majesty, the King:- "The Law of Piety is excellent. But wherein consists the Law of Piety? In these things, to wit, little piety, many good deeds, compassion, liberality, truthfulness and purity. The gift of spiritual insight I have given in manifold ways: whilst on two-footed and four-footed beings, on birds and the denizens of the waters, I have conferred various favours-even unto the boon of life; and many other good deeds have I done. For this purpose, have I caused this pious edict to be written, that men may walk after its teaching, and that it may long endure; and he who will follow its teaching will do well."

Pillar Edict V says:

Thus said His Sacred and Gracious Majesty, the king.

When I had been consecrated twenty-six years the following species were declared *exempt from slaughter,* namely:

Parrots, starlings adjutants, Brahmany ducks, geese, *pandirnukhas, gelatas,* bats, queen-ants, female tortoises, boneless fish, *vedaveyakas, gangapuputakas,* skate, (river) tortoise, porcupines, tree-squinrels, *barasingha* stag, Brahmany bulls, monkeys, rhinoceros, grey doves village pigeons, and *all fourfooted animals which are not utilised or eaten.*

She-goats, ewes, cows, that is to say, those either with young or in milk, are exempt from slaughter as well as their offspring up to six months of age. The caponing of cocks must not be done. Chaff must not be burned along with the living things in it Forests must not be burned either for mischief or so as to destroy living creatures. The living must not be fed with the living. At each of the three seasonal full moons, and at the full moon of the month Tishya (December-January) for three days in each case, namely, the fourteenth and fifteenth days of the first fortnight, and the first day of the second fortnight, as well as on the first days throughout the year, fish is exempt from killing and may not be sold. On the same days, in elephant-preserves or fishponds no other classes of animals may be destroyed.

On the eighth, fourteenth and fifteenth days of each fortnight, as well as on the Tishya and Punarvasa days and festival days, the castration of bulls must not be performed, nor may he-goats, rams, boars and other animals liable to castration be castrated. On the Tishya and Punarvasa days, on the seasonal full moon days, and during the fortnights of the seasonal full moons the branding of horses and oxen must not be done.

During the time upto the twenty-sixth anniversary of my consecration twenty-five jail deliveries have been effected."

So much for the legislation of Ashoka.

Let us turn to Manu. His Laws contain the following provisions regarding meat-eating:-

V.11. Let him avoid all carnivorous birds and those living in villages, and one hoofed animals which are not specially permitted (to be eaten), and the Tithbha (Parra) Jacana.

V.12. The sparrow, the Plava, the Hamsa, the Brahmani duck, the village-cock, the Sarasa crane, the Raggudal, the woodpecker, the parrot, and the starling.

V.13. Those which feed striking with their beaks, web-footed birds, the Koyashti, those which scratch with their toes, those which dive and live on fish, meat from a slaughterhouse and dried meat.

V.14. The Baka and the Balaka crane, the raven, the Khangartaka (animals) that eat fish, village-pigs, and all kinds of fishes.

V.15. He who eats the flesh of any (animals) is called the eater of the flesh of that (particular) creature, he who eats fish is an eater of every (kind of) flesh; let him therefore avoid fish.

V.16. (But the fish called) Pathine and (that called) Rohita may be eaten, if used for offering to the gods or to the manes; (one may eat) likewise Ragivas, Simhatundas, and Sasalkas on all occasions.

V.17. Let him not eat solitary or unknown beasts and birds though they may fall under (the categories of) eatable creatures, not any five-toed (animals).

V.18. The porcupine, the hedgehog, the iguana, the rhinoceros, the tortoise, and the hare they declare to be eatable; likewise those (domestic animals) that have teeth in one jaw excepting camels."

Here is survey of the legislation both by Ashoka and by Manu on the slaughter of animals. We are of course principally concerned with the cow. Examining the legislation of Ashoka the question is: Did he prohibit the killing of the cow? On this issue there seem to be a difference of opinion. Prof. Vincent Smith is of opinion that Ashoka did not prohibit the killing of the cow. Commenting on the legislation of Ashoka on the subject, Prof. Smith says:

"It is noteworthy that Ashoka's rules do not forbid the slaughter of cow, which, apparently, continued to be lawful."

Prof. Radhakumud Mookerji joins issue with Prof. Smith and says that Ashoka did prohibit the slaughter of the cow. Prof. Mookerji relies upon the reference in Pillar Edict V to the rule of exemption which was made applicable to all four-footed animals and argues that under this rule cow was exempted from killing. This is not a correct reading of the statement in the Edict. The Statement in the Edict is a qualified statement.

It does not refer to all four-footed animals but only to four-footed animals, *which are not utilised or eaten.* 'A cow cannot be said to be a four-footed animal which was not utilised or eaten. Prof. Vincent Smith seems to be correct in saying that Ashoka did not prohibit the slaughter of the cow. Prof. Mookerji tries to get out of the difficulty by saying that at the time of Ashoka the cow was not eaten and therefore came within the prohibition. His statement is simply absurd for the cow was an animal which was very much eaten by all classes.

It is quite unnecessary to resort as does Prof. Mookerji to a forced construction of the Edict and to make Ashoka prohibit the slaughter of the cow as though it was his duty to do so.

Ashoka had no particular interest in the cow and owed no special duty to protect her against killing. Ashoka was interested in the sanctity of all life human as well as animal.

He felt his duty to prohibit the taking of life where taking of life was not necessary. That is why he prohibited slaughtering animal for sacrifice which he regarded as unnecessary and of animals which are not utilised nor eaten which again would be want on and unnecessary. That he did not prohibit the slaughter of the cow in specie may well be taken as a fact which for having regard to the Buddhist attitude in the matter cannot be used against Ashoka as a ground for casting blame.

Coming to Manu there is no doubt that he too did not prohibit the slaughter of the cow. On the other hand he made the eating of cow's flesh on certain occasions obligatory.

Why then did the non-Brahmins give up eating beef? There appears to be no apparent reason for this departure on their part. But there must be some reason behind it. The reason I like to suggest is that it was due to their desire to imitate the Brahmins that the non-Brahmins gave up beef-eating. This may be a novel theory but it is not an impossible theory.

As the French author, Gabriel Tarde has explained that culture within a society spreads by imitation of the ways and manners of the superior classes by the inferior classes. This imitation is so regular in its flow that its working is as mechanical as the working of a natural law.

Gabriel Tarde speaks of the laws of imitation. One of these laws is that the lower classes always imitate the higher classes. This is a matter of such common knowledge that hardly any individual can be found to question its validity.

That the spread of the cow-worship among and cessation of beef-eating by the non-Brahmins has taken place by reason of the habit of the non-Brahmins to imitate the Brahmins who were undoubtedly their superiors is beyond dispute. Of course there was an extensive propaganda in favour of cow-worship by the Brahmins.

The Gayatri Purana is a piece of this propaganda. But initially it is the result of the natural law of imitation. This, of course, raises another question: Why did the Brahmins give up beef-eating?

What Made the Brahmins become Vegetarians?

The non-Brahmins have evidently undergone a revolution. From being beefeaters to have become non-beef-eaters was indeed a revolution. But if the non-Brahmins underwent one revolution, the Brahmins had undergone two. They gave up beef-eating which was one revolution. To have given up meat-eating altogether and become vegetarians was another revolution.

That this was a revolution is beyond question. For as has been shown in the this books there was a time when the Brahmins were the greatest beefeaters. Although the non-Brahmins did eat beef they could not have had it every day. The cow was a costly animal and the non-Brahmins could ill afford to slaughter it just for food. He only did it on special occasion when his religious duty or personal interest to propitiate a deity compelled him to do. But the case with the Brahmin was different. He was a priest. In a period overridden by ritualism there was hardly a day on which there was no cow sacrifice to which the Brahmin was not invited by some non-Brahmin. For the Brahmin every day was a beef-steak day. The Brahmins were therefore the greatest beefeaters. The Yajna of the Brahmins was nothing but the killing of innocent animals carried on in the name of religion with pomp and ceremony with an attempt to enshroud it in mystery with a view to conceal their appetite for beef. Some idea of this mystery pomp and ceremony can be had from the directions contained in the Atreya Brahamana touching the killing of animals in a Yajna.

The actual killing of the animal is preceded by certain initiatory Rites accompanied by incantations too long and too many to be detailed here. It is enough to give an idea of the main features of the Sacrifice. The sacrifice commences with the erection of the Sacrificial post called the Yupa to which the animal is tied before it is slaughtered. After setting out why the Yupa is necessary the Atreya Brahamana proceeds to state what it stands for. It says:

> *"This Yupa is a weapon. Its point must have eight edges. For a weapon (or iron club) has eight edges. Whenever he strikes with it an enemy or adversary, he kills him. (This weapon serves) to put down him (every one) who is to be put down by him (the sacrificer). The Yupa is*

> *a weapon which stands erected (being ready) to slay an enemy. Thence an enemy (of the sacrificer) who might be present (at the sacrifice) comes of all ill after having seen the Yupa of such or such one."*

The selection of the wood to be used for the Yupa is made to vary with the purposes which the sacrificer wishes to achieve by the sacrifice. The Atreya Brahamana says:

> *"He who desires heaven, ought to make his Yupa of Khadira wood. For the gods conquered the celestial world by means of a Yupa, made of Khadira wood. In the same way the sacrificer conquers the celestial world by means of a Yupa, made of Khadira wood."*

He who desires food and wishes to grow fat ought to make his Yupa of Bilva wood. For the Bilva tree bears fruits every year; it is the symbol of fertility; for it increases (every year) in size from the roots up to the branches, therefore it is a symbol of fatness. He who having such a knowledge makes his Yupa of Bilva wood, makes fat his children and cattle.

As regards the Yupa made of Bilva wood (it is further to be remarked), that they call light' Bilva. He who has such a knowledge becomes a light' among his own people, the most distinguished among his own people. He who desires beauty and sacred knowledge ought to make his Yupa of Palasa wood. For the Palasa is among the trees of beauty and sacred knowledge. He who having such a knowledge makes his Yupa of Palasa wood, becomes beautiful and acquires sacred knowledge.

As regards the Yupa made of Palasa wood (there is further to be remarked), that the Palasa is the womb of all trees. Thence they speak on account of the palasam (foliage) of this or that tree (*i.e.* they call the foliage of every tree palasam). He who has such a knowledge obtains (the gratification of) any desire, he might have regarding all trees (*i.e.* he obtains from all trees any thing he might wish for).

This is followed by the ceremony of anointing the sacrificial post.

> *"The Adhvaryu says (to the Hotar): "We anoint the sacrificial post (Yupa); repeat the mantra (required)". The Hotar then repeats the verse: "Amjanti tvam*

adhvare" (3, 8, 1) i.e." The priests anoint thee, O tree! with celestial honey (butter); provide (us) with wealth if thou standest here erected, or if thou art lying on thy mother (earth)." The "celestial honey" is the melted butter (with which the priests anoint the Yupa). (The second half verse from) "provide us" &c. means: "thou mayest stand or lie, provide us with wealth."

(The Hotar then repeats:) jato jayate sudinatve" &c. (3, 8, 5) *i.e.*, "After having been born, he (the Yupa) is growing (to serve) in the prime of his life the sacrifice of mortal men. The wise are busy in decorating (him, the Yupa) with skill. He, as an eloquent messenger of the gods, lifts his voice (that it might be heard by the gods)." He (the Yupa) is called jata, *i.e.*, born, because he is born by this (by the recital of the first quarter of this verse). (By the word) vardhamana, *i.e.*, growing, they make him (the Yupa) grow in this manner. (By the words:) punanti (*i.e.* to clean, decorate), they clean him in this manner. (By the words:) "he as an eloquent messenger, &c." he announces the Yupa (the fact of his existence) to the gods.

The Hotar then concludes (the ceremony of anointing the sacrificial post) with the verse "yuva suvasah parivitah" (3, 8, 4), *i.e.* "the youth decorated with ribands, has arrived; he is finer (than all trees) which ever grew; the wise priests raise him up under recital of well-framed thoughts of their mind." The youth decorated with ribands, is the vital air (the soul), which is covered by the limbs of the body. (By the words;) "he is finer," &c. he means that he (the Yupa) is becoming finer (more excellent, beautiful) by this (mantra)." The next ceremony is the carrying of fire round the sacrificial animal. The Attreya Brahmana gives the following directions on this point. It says:

"When the fire is carried round (the animal) the Adhvaryu says to the Hotar: repeat (thy mantras)'. The Hotar then repeats this triplet of verses, addressed to Agni, and composed in the Gayatri metre: Agnir Hota no adhvare (4.15.1-3) i.e. (1) Agni, our priest, is carried round about like a horse, he who is among gods, the god of sacrifices, (2) Like a charioteer Agni passes thrice by the sacrifice; to the gods he carries the offering, (3) The master of food, the seer of Agni, went round the offering; he bestows riches on the sacrificer."

When the fire is carried round (the animal) then he makes him (Agni) prosper by means of his own deity and his own metre. 'As a horse he is carried' means: they carry him as if he were a horse, round about. Like a charioteer Agni passes thrice by the sacrifice means; he goes round the sacrifice like a charioteer (swiftly). He is called *vajapati* (master of food) because he is the master of (different kinds of) food.

The Advaryu says: give Hotar! the additional order for despatching offerings to the gods.

The Hotar then says: (to the slaughterers): Ye divine slaughtereres, commence (your work), as well as ye who are human! that is to say, he orders all the slaughterers among gods as well as among men (to commence).

Bring hither the instruments for killing, ye who are ordering the sacrifice, in behalf of the two masters of the sacrifice.

The animal is the offering, the sacrificer the master of the offering. Thus he (the Hotar) makes prosper the sacrificer by means of his (the sacrifcer's) own offering. Thence they truly say: for whatever deity the animal is killed, that one is the master of the offering.

If the animal is to be offered to one deity only, the priest should say: *Medhapataye* 'to the master of the sacrifice (singular)', if to two deities, then he should use the dual 'to both masters of the offering', and if to several deities, then he should use the plural, 'to the masters' of the offering'. This is the established custom.

Bring ye for him fire! For the animal when carried (to the slaughter) saw death before it. Not wishing to go to the gods, the gods said to it: Come we will bring thee to heaven! The animal consented and said: One of you should walk before me. They consented. Agni then walked before it, and it followed after Agni. Thence they say, every animal belongs to Agni, for it followed after him. Thence they carry before the animal fire (Agni).

Spread the (sacred) grass! the animal lives on herbs. He (the Hotar) thus provides the animal with its entire soul (the herbs being supposed to form part of it).

After the ceremony of carrying fire round the animal comes the delivery of the animal to the priests for sacrifice. Who should offer the animal for sacrifice? On this point the direction of the Atreya Brahmana is:

> "The mother, the father, the brother, sister, friend, and companions should give this (animal) up (for being slaughtered)! *When these words are pronouced, they seize the animal which is (regarded as) entirely given up by its relations (parents, &c.)*"

On reading this direction one wonders why almost everybody is required to join in offering the animal for sacrifice. The reason is simple. There were altogether seventeen Brahmin priests who were entitled to take part in performing the sacrifice. Naturally enough they wanted the whole carcass to themselves. Indeed they could not give enough to each of the seventeen priests unless they had the whole carcass to distribute. Legally the Brahmins could not claim the whole carcass unless everybody who could not claim any right over the animal had been divested of it. Hence the direction requiring even the companion of the sacrificer to take part in offering the animal.

Then comes the ceremony of actually killing the animal. The Atreya Brahmana gives the details of the mode and manner of killing the animal. Its directions are:

> *"Turn its feet northwards! Make its eye to go to the sun, dismiss its breath to the wind, its life to the air, its hearing to the directions, its body to the earth. In this way he (the Hotar) places it (connects it) with these worlds. Take off the skin entire (without cutting it). Before operating the naval, tear* out omentum. Stop its breathing within *(by stopping its mouth). Thus he (the Hotar) puts its breath in the animals.* Make of its breast a piece like an eagle, of its arms *(two pieces like)* two hatchets, of its forearms *(two pieces like)* two spikes, of its shoulders *(two pieces like)* two Kashyapas, its loins should be unbroken *(entire); (make of)* its thighs *(two pieces like)* two shields, of the two kneepans *(two pieces like)* two oleander leaves; take out its twenty-six ribs according to their order; preserve every limb of it in its integrity. *Thus he benefits all its limbs."*

There remain two ceremonies to complete the sacrificial killing of the animal. One is to absolve the Brahmin priests who played the butcher's part. Theoretically they are guilty of murder for the animal is only a substitute for the sacrificer. To absolve them from the consequences of murder, the Hotar is directed by the Atreya Brahmana to observe the following injunction:

Do not cut the entrails which resemble on owl (when taking out the omentum), nor should among your children, O *slaughterers! or among their offspring any one be found who might cut them.* By speaking these words he presents these entrails to the slaughterers among the gods as well as to those among men.

The Hotar shall then say thrice: O *Adhrigu* (and ye others), *kill* (the animal), *do it well;* kill it, O *Adhrigu.*

After the animal has been killed, (he should say thrice:) *Far may it* (the consequences of murder) be (from us). For Adhrigu among the gods is he who silences (the animal) and the *Apapa* (away, away!) is he who puts it down. By speaking those words he surrenders the animal to those who silence it (by stopping its mouth) and to those who butcher it

The Hotar then mutters (he makes, *Japa)',* "O slaughterers! may all good you might do abide by us! and all mischief you might do go elsewhere!" The Hotar Gives by (this) speech the order (for killing the animal), for Agni had given the order for killing (the animal) with the same words when he was the Hotar of the gods.

By those words (the *Japa* mentioned) the Hotar removes (all evil consequences) from those who suffocate the animal and those who butter it, in all that they might transgress the rule by cutting one piece too soon, the other too late, or by cutting a too large, or a too small piece. The Hotar enjoying this happiness clears himself (from all guilt) and attains the full length of his life (and it serves the sacrificer) for obtaining his full life. He who has such a knowledge, attains the full length of his life." The Attreya Brahmana next deals with the question of disposing of the parts of the dead animal. In this connection its direction is:

"Dig a ditch in the earth to hide its excrement. The excrement consist of vegetable food; for the earth is the place for the herbs. Thus the Hotar puts them (the excrements) finally in their proper places. Present the

evil spirits with the blood! For the gods having deprived (once) the evil spirits of their share in the Haviryajnas (such as the Pull and New Moon offerings) apportioned to them the husk and smallest grains, and after having them turned out of the great sacrifice (such as the Soma and animal sacrifices), presented to them the blood. Thence the Hotar pronounces the words: present the evil spirits with the blood! By giving them this share he deprives the evil spirits of any other share in the sacrifice. They say: one should not address the evil spirits in the sacrifice, and evil spirits whichever they might be (Rakshasa, Ashuras etc.): for the sacrifice is to be without (the) evil spirits (not to be disturbed by them). But others say: one should address them; for (he who deprives any one, "entitled to a share of this share, will be punished (by him whom he deprives); and if he himself does not suffer the penalty, then his son, and if his son be spared, then his grandson tviu suffer it, and thus he resents on him (the son or grandson) what he wanted to resent on you."

"However, if the Hotar addresses them, he should do so with a low voice. For both, the low voice and the evil spirits, are, as it were, hidden. If he addresses them with a loud voice, then such one speaks in the voice of the evil spirits, and is capable of producing Rakshasa sounds (a horrible, terrific voice). The voice in which the haughty man and *the drunkard speak is that* of *the evil spirits (Rakshasas). He who has such a knowledge will neither himself become haughty nor will such a man be among his offspring."*

Then follows the last and the concluding ceremony that of offering parts of the body of the animal to the gods. It is called the Manota. According to the Atreya Brahmana:

"The Adhvaryu says (to the Hotar): recite the verses appropriate to the offering of the parts of the sacrificial animal which are cut off for the Manota. He then repeats the hymn: Thou, O Agni, art the first Manota (6.1)"

There remains the question of sharing the flesh of the animal. On this issue the division was settled by the Atreya Brahmana in the following terms:

"Now follows the division of the different parts of the sacrificial animal (among the priests). We shall describe it. The two jawbones with the tongue are to be given to the Prastotar, the breast in the form of an eagle to the Udgatar, the throat with the palate to the Ptatihartar, the lower part of the right loins to the Hotar: the left to the Brahma; the right thigh to the *Maitravaruna; the left to the Brahmanachhamsi; the right side with the shoulder to the Adhvaryn; the left side to those who accompany the chants; the left shoulder to the Pratipashatar; the lower part of the right arm to the Neshtar; the lower part of the left arm to the Potar; the upper of the right thigh to the Achhavaka; the left to the Agnidhara; the upper part of the fight arm to the Atreya; the left to the Sadasya; the back bone and the urinal bladder to the Grihapati (sacrificer); the right feet to the Grihapati who gives a feasting: the left feet to the wife of that Grihapati who gives a feasting; the upper lip is common to both (the Grihapati and his wife), which is to be divided by the Grihapati. They offer the tail of the animal to wives, but they should give it to a Brahmana; the fleshy processes (manikah) on the neck and three gristles* (fakasah) *to the Gravastut; three other gristles and one-half of the fleshy part (on the back* (vaikartta) *to the Unnetar; the other half of the fleshy part on the neck and the left lobe* (kloma) *to the slaughterer, who should present it to a Brahmana, if he himself would* not *happen to be a Brahmana. The head is to be given to the Subrahmanya, the skin belongs to him (the Subrahmanya), who spoke,* svah sutyam *(tomorrow at the Soma sacrifice); that part* of *the sacrificial animal at a Soma sacrifice which belongs to Ha (sacrificial food) is common to all the priests; only for the Hotar it is optional. All these portions of the sacrificial animal amount to thirty-six single pieces, each of which represents the pada (foot) of a verse by which the sacrifice is carried up. The Brihati metre consists of thirty-six syllables; and the heavenly worlds are of the Brihati nature. In this way (by dividing the animal into thirty-six parts) they gain life (in this world) and the heavens, and having become established in both (this and that*

> *world) they walk there. To those who divide the sacrificial animal in the way mentioned, it becomes the guide to heaven. But those who make the division otherwise are like scoundrels and miscreants who kill an animal merely (for gratifying their lust after flesh). This division of the sacrificial animal was invented by the Rishi* (Devabhaga, *a son* of Sruta*). When he was departing from this life, he did not entrust (the secret to anyone). But a supernatural being communicated it to* Girija, *the son of* Babhru. *Since his time men study it."*

What is said by the Atreya Brahmana places two things beyond dispute. One is that the Brahmins monopolised the whole of the flesh of the sacrificial animal. Except for a paltry bit they did not even 'allow the sacrificer to share in it. The second is that the Brahmins themselves played the pan of butchers in the slaughter of the animal. As a matter of principle the Brahmins should not eat the flesh of the animal killed at a sacrifice. The principle underlying Yajna is that man should offer himself as sacrifice to the gods. He offers an animal only to release himself from this obligation.

From this it followed that the animal, being only a substitute for the man, eating the flesh of animal meant eating human flesh. This theory was very detrimental to the interest *of* the Brahmins who had a complete monopoly of the flesh of the animal offered for sacrifice. The Atreya Brahamana which had *seen* in this theory the danger of the Brahmins being deprived of the flesh of sacrificial animal takes pains to explain away the theory by a simple negation. It says:

> *"The man who is initiated (into the sacrificial mysteries)* offers *himself to all deities. Agni represents all deities and Soma represents all deities. When he (the sacrificer) offers the animal to Agni-Soma he releases himself (by being represented by the animal) from being offered to all deities. They say: "do not eat from the animal offered to Agni-Soma. Who eats from this animal, eats from human flesh; because the sacrificer releases himself (from being sacrificed) by means of the animal". But this (precept) is not to be attended to."*

Given these facts, no further evidence seems to be necessary to support the statement that the Brahmins were not merely beefeaters but they were also butchers. Why then did the Brahmins change front? Let us deal with their change of front in two stages. First, why did they give up beef-eating?

As has already been shown cow-killing was not legally prohibited by Ashoka. Even if it had been prohibited, a law made by the Buddhist Emperor could never have been accepted by the Brahmins as binding upon them.

Did Manu prohibit beef-eating? If he did, then that would be binding on the Brahmins and would afford an adequate explanation of their change of front. Looking into the Manusmriti one does find the following verses:

"V. 46. He who does not seek to cause the sufferings of bonds and death to living creatures, (but) desires the good of all (beings), obtains endless bliss.

"V. 47. He who does not injure any (creature), attains without an effort what he thinks of, what he undertakes, and what he fixes his mind on.

"V. 48. Meat can never be obtained without injury to living creatures, and injury to sentient beings is detrimental to (the attainment of) heavenly bliss; let him therefore shun (the use of) meat.

"V. 49. Having well considered the (disgusting) origin of flesh and the (cruelty of) fettering and slaying corporeal beings, let him entirely abstain from eating flesh."

If these verses can be treated as containing positive injunctions they would be sufficient to explain why the Brahmins gave up meat-eating and became vegetarians. But it is impossible to treat these verses as positive injunctions, carrying the force of law. They are either exhortations or interpolations introduced after the Brahmins had become vegetarians in praise of the change. That the latter is the correct view is proved by the following verses which occur in the same chapter of the Manusmriti.:

"V. 28: The Lord of creatures (Prajapati) created this whole (world to be) the sustenance of the vital spirit; both the immovable and the movable creation is the food of the vital spirit.

"V. 29. What is destitute of motion is the food of those endowed with locomotion; (animals) without fangs (are the food) of those with fangs, those without hands of those who possess hands, and the timid of the bold.

"V. 30. The eater who daily even devours those destined to be his food, commits no sin; for the creator himself created both the eaters and those who are to be eaten (for those special purposes).

"V. 56. There is no sin in eating meat, in (drinking) spirituous liquor, and in carnal intercourse, for that is the natural way of created beings, but abstention brings great rewards.

"V. 27.. One may eat meat when it has been sprinkled with water, while Mantras were recited, when Brahmanas desire (one's doing it) when one is engaged (in the performance of a rite) according to the law, and when one's life is in danger.

"V. 31. The consumption of meat (is befitting) for sacrifices,' that is declared to be a rule made by the gods, but to persist (in using it) on other (occasions) is said to be a proceeding worthy of Rakshasas.

"V. 32. He who eats meat, when he honours the gods and manes commits no sin, whether *he* has bought it, or himself has killed (the animal) or has received it as a present from others.

"V. 42. A twice-born man who, knowing the true meaning of the Veda, slays an animal for these purposes, causes both himself and the animal to *enter* a most blessed state.

"V. 39. Swayambhu (the self-existent) himself created animals for the sake of sacrifices; sacrifices (have been instituted) for the good of this whole (world); hence the slaughtering (of beasts) for sacrifice is not slaughtering (in the ordinary sense of the word).

"V. 40. Herbs, trees, cattle, birds, and other animals that have been destroyed for sacrifices, receive (being reborn) higher existences."

Manu goes further and makes eating of flesh compulsory. Note the following verse:

"V. 35. But a man who, being duly engaged (to officiate or to dine at a sacred rite), refuses to eat meat, becomes after death an animal during twenty-one existences."

That Manu did not prohibit meat-eating is evident enough. That Manusmriti did not prohibit cow-killing can also be proved from the Smriti itself. In the first place, the only references to cow in the Manusmriti are to be found in the catalogue of rules which are made applicable by Manu to the Snataka. They are set out below:

1. A Snataka should not eat food which a cow has smelt.
2. A Snataka should not step over a rope to which a calf is tied.
3. A Snataka should not urinate in a cowpan.
4. A Snataka should not answer call of nature facing a cow.
5. A Snataka should not keep his right arm uncovered when he enters a cowpan.
6. A Snataka should not interrupt a cow which is sucking her calf, nor tell anybody of it.
7. A Snataka should not ride on the back of the cow.
8. A Snataka should not offend the cow.
9. A Snataka who is impure must not touch a cow with his hand.

From these references it will be seen that Manu did not regard the cow as a sacred animal. On the other hand, he regarded it as an impure animal whose touch caused ceremonial pollution. There are verses in Manu which show that he did not prohibit the eating of beef. In this connection, reference may be made to Chapter III. 3. It says: "He (Snataka) who is famous (for the strict performance of) his duties and has received his heritage, the Veda from his father, shall be honoured, sitting on couch and adomed with a garland with the present of a cow (the honey-mixture)."

The question is why should Manu recommend the gift of a cow to a Snataka? Obviously, to enable him to perform Madhuparka. If that is so, it follows that Manu knew that Brahmins did eat beef and he had no objection to it.

Another reference would be to Manu's discussion of the animals whose meat is eatable and those, whose meat is not. In Chapter V.18. he says: "The porcupine, the hedgehog, the iguana, the rhinoceros, the tortoise, and the hare they declare to be eatable, likewise those (domestic animals) that have teeth in one jaw only, excepting camels."

In this verse Manu gives general permission to eat the flesh of all domestic animals that have teeth in one jaw only. To this rule Manu makes one exception, namely, the camel. In this class of domestic animals those that have teeth in one jaw only-falls not only the camel but also the cow. It is noteworthy that Manu does not make an exception in the case of the cow. This means that Manu had no objection to the eating of the cow's flesh.

Manu did not make the killing of the cow an offence. Manu divides sins into two classes (i) mortal sins and (ii) minor sins. Among the mortal sins Manu includes:

"XI. 55. Killing a Brahmana, drinking (the spirituous liquor called Sura) stealing the (gold of Brahmana) a adultery with a Gum's wife, and associating with such offenders." Among minor sins Manu includes:

"XI. 60. Killing the cow, sacrificing for those unworthy to sacrifice, adultery, setting oneself, casting off one's teacher, mother, father or son, giving up the (daily) study of the Veda and neglecting the (sacred domestic) fire."

From this it will be clear that according to Manu cow-killing was only a minor sin. It was reprehensible only if the cow was killed without good and sufficient reason. Even if it was otherwise, it was not heinous or inexplicable. The same was the attitude of Yajnavalkya.

All this proves that for generations the Brahmins had been eating beef. Why did they give up beef-eating? Why did they, as an extreme step, give up meat eating altogether and become vegetarians? It is two revolutions rolled into one. As has been shown it has not been done as a result of the preachings of Manu, their Divine Lawmaker. The revolution has taken place in spite of Manu and contrary to his directions. What made the Brahmins take this step? Was philosophy responsible for it? Or was it dictated bystrategy?

Two explanations are offered. One explanation is that this deification of the cow was a manifestation of the Advaita philosophy that one supreme entity pervaded the whole universe, that on that account all life human as well as animal was sacred. This explanation is obviously unsatisfactory. In the first place, it does not fit in with facts. The Vedanta Sutra which proclaims the doctrine of oneness of life does not prohibit the killing of animals for sacrificial purposes as is evident from 11.1.28. In the second place, if the transformation was due to the desire to realise the ideal of Advaita then there is no reason why it should have stopped with the cow. It should have extended to all other animals.

Another explanation more ingenious than the first, is that this transformation in the life of the Brahmin was due to the rise of the doctrine of the Transmigration of the Soul. Even this explanation does not fit in with facts. The Brahadamyaka Upanishad upholds the doctrine of transmigration (vi.2) and yet recommends that if a man desires to have a learned son born to him he should prepare a mass of the flesh of the bull or ox or of other flesh with rice and ghee.

Again, how is it that this doctrine which is propounded in the Upanishads did not have any effect on the Brahmins upto the time of the Manusmriti, a period of at least 400 years. Obviously, this explanation is no explanation. Thirdly, if Brahmins became vegetarians by reason of the doctrine of transmigration of the soul how is it, it did not make the non-Brahmins take to vegetarianism?

To my mind, it was strategy which made the Brahmins give up beef-eating and start worshipping the cow. The clue to the worship of the cow is to be found in the struggle between Buddhism and Brahmanism and the means adopted by Brahmanism to establish its supremacy over Buddhism. The strife between Buddhism and Brahmanism is a crucial fact in Indian history. Without the realisation of this fact, it is impossible to explain some of the features of Hinduism. Unfortunately students of Indian history have entirely missed the importance of this strife. They knew there was Brahmanism. But they seem to be entirely unaware of the struggle for supremacy in which these creeds were engaged and that their struggle, which extended for 400 years has left some indelible marks on religion, society and politics of India.

This is not the place for describing the full story of the struggle. All one can do is to mention a few salient points. Buddhism was at one time the religion of the majority of the people of India. It continued to be the religion of the masses for hundreds of years. It attacked Brahmanism on all sides as no religion had done before. Brahmanism was on the wane and if not on the wane, it was certainly on the defensive. As a result of the spread of Buddhism, the Brahmins had lost all power and prestige at the Royal Court and among the people. They were smarting under the defeat they had suffered at the hands of Buddhism and were making all possible efforts to regain their power and prestige. Buddhism had made so deep an impression on the minds of the masses and had taken such a hold of them that it was absolutely impossible for the Brahmins to fight the Buddhists except by accepting their ways and means and practising the Buddhist creed in its extreme form. After the death of Buddha his followers started setting up the images of the Buddha and building stupas. The Brahmins followed it. They, in their turn, built temples and installed in them images of Shiva, Vishnu and Ram and Krishna etc.—all with the object of drawing away the crowd that was attracted by the image worship of Buddha.

That is how temples and images which had no place in Brahmanism came into Hinduism. The Buddhists rejected the Brahmanic religion which consisted of Yajna and animal sacrifice, particularly of the cow. The objection to the sacrifice of the cow had taken a strong hold of the minds of the masses especially as they were an agricultural population and the cow was a very useful animal. The Brahmins in all probability had come to be hated as the killer of cows in the same way as the guest had come to be hated as *Gognha,* the killer of the cow by the householder, because whenever he came a cow had to be killed in his honour. That being the case, the Brahmins could do nothing to improve their position against the Buddhists except by giving up the Yajna as a form of worship and the sacrifice of the cow.

That the object of the Brahmins in giving up beef-eating was to snatch away from the Buddhist Bhikshus the supremacy they had acquired is evidenced by the adoption of vegetarianism by Brahmins. Why did the Brahmins become vegetarian? The answer is that without becoming vegetarian the Brahmins could not have recovered the ground they had lost to their rival namely Buddhism. In this connection it must be remembered that there was one aspect in which Brahmanism suffered in public esteem as compared to Buddhism.

That was the practice of animal sacrifice which was the essence of Brahmanism and to which Buddhism was deadly opposed. That in an agricultural population there should be respect for Buddhism and revulsion against Brahmanism which involved slaughter of animals including cows and bullocks is only natural. What could the Brahmins do to recover the lost ground? To go one better than the Buddhist Bhikshus not only to give up meat-eating but to become vegetarians-which they did. That this was the object of the Brahmins in becoming vegetarians can be proved in various ways.

If the Brahmins had acted from conviction that animal sacrifice was bad, all that was necessary for them to do was to give up killing animals for sacrifice. It was unnecessary for them to be vegetarians. That they did go in for vegetarianism makes it obvious that their motive was far-reaching. Secondly, it was unnecessary for them to become vegetarians. For the Buddhist Bhikshus were not vegetarians. This statement might surprise many people owing to the popular belief that the connection between Ahimsa and Buddhism was immediate and essential. It is generally believed that the Buddhist Bhikshus eschewed animal food. This is an error. The fact is that the Buddhist Bhikshus were permitted to eat three kinds of flesh that were deemed pure. Later on they were extended to five classes. Yuan Chwang, the Chinese traveller was aware of this and spoke of the pure kinds of flesh as *San-Ching,* The origin of this practice among the Bhikshus is explained by Mr. Thomas Walters. According to the story told by him:

> *"In the time of Buddha there was in Vaisali a wealthy* general *named Siha who was a convert to Buddhism. He became a liberal supporter of the Brethren and kept them constantly supplied with good flesh-food. When it was noticed abroad that the Bhikshus were in the habit of eating such food specially provided for them, the Tirthikas made the practice a matter of angry reproach. Then the abstemious ascetic Brethren, learning this, reported the circumstances to the Master, who thereupon called the Brethren together. When they assembled, he announced to them the law that they were not to eat the flesh of any animal which they had seen put to death for them, or about which they had been told that it had*

been slain for them. But he permitted to the Brethern as 'pure' (that is, lawful) food the flesh of animals the slaughter of which had not been seen by the Bhikshus, not heard of by them, and not suspected by them to have been on their account. In the Pali and Ssu-fen *Vinaya it was after a breakfast given by Siha to the Buddha and some of the Brethren, for which the carcass of a large ox was procured that the Nirgianthas reviled the Bhikshus and Buddha instituted this new rule declaring fish and flesh 'pure' in the three conditions. The animal food now permitted to the Bhikshus came to be known as the 'three pures' or 'three pure kinds of flesh', and it was tersely described as 'unseen, unheard, unsuspected', or as the Chinese translations sometimes have it 'not seen, not heard nor suspected to be on my account'. Then two more kinds of animal food were declared "lawful for the Brethren viz., the flesh of animals which had died a natural death, and that of animals which had been killed by a bird of prey or other savage creature. So there came to be five classes or descriptions of flesh which the professed Buddhist was at liberty to use as food. Then the 'unseen, unheard, unsuspected' came to be treated as one class, and this together with the 'natural death' and 'bird killed' made a* san-ching"

As the Buddhist Bhikshus did eat meat the Brahmins had no reason to give it up. Why then did the Brahmins give up meat-eating and become vegetarians? It was because they did not want to put themselves merely on the same footing in the eyes of the public as the Buddhist Bhikshus.

The giving up of the Yajna system and abandonment of the sacrifice of the cow could have had only a limited effect. At the most it would have put the Brahmins on the same footing as the Buddhists. The same would have been the case if they had followed the rules observed by the Buddhist Bhikshus in the matter of meat-eating. It could not have given the Brahmins the means of achieving supremacy over the Buddhists which was their ambition. They wanted to oust the Buddhists from the place of honour and respect which they had acquired in the minds of the masses by their opposition to the killing of the cow for sacrificial purposes. To achieve their purpose the

Brahmins had to adopt the usual tactics of a wreckless adventurer. It is to beat extremism by extremism. It is the strategy which all rightists use to overcome the leftists. The only way to beat the Buddhists was to go a step further and be vegetarians.

There is another reason which can be relied upon to support the thesis that the Brahmins started cow-worship gave up beef-eating and became vegetarians in order to vanquish Buddhism. It is the date when cow-killing became a mortal sin. It is well-known that cow-killing was not made an offence by Ashoka. Many people expect him to have come forward to prohibit the killing of the cow. Prof. Vincent Smith regards it as surprising. But there is nothing surprising in it.

Buddhism was against animal sacrifice in general. It had no particular affection for the Cow. Ashoka had therefore no particular reason to make a law to save the cow. What is more astonishing is the fact that cow-killing was made a *Mahapataka,* a mortal sin or a capital offence by the Gupta Kings who were champions of Hinduism which recognised and sanctioned the killing of the cow for sacrificial purposes. As pointed out by Mr. D. R. Bhandarkar:

> *"We have got the incontrovertible evidence of inscriptions to show that early in the 5th century A.D. killing a cow was looked upon as an offence of the deepest turpitude, turpitude as deep as that involved in murdering a Brahman. We have thus a copperplate inscription dated 465 A.D. and referring itself to the reign of Skandagupta of the Imperial Gupta dynasty. It registers a grant and ends with a verse saying: 'Whosoever will transgress this grant that has been assigned (shall become as guilty as) the slayer of a cow, the slayer of a spiritual preceptor (or) the slayer of a Brahman. A still earlier record placing* go-hatya *on the same footing as* brahma hatya *is that of Chandragupta II, grandfather of Skandagupta just mentioned. It bears the Gupta date 93, which is equivalent to 412 A.D. It is engraved on the railing which surrounds the celebrated Buddhist stupa at Sanchi, in Central India. This also speaks of a benefaction made by an officer of Chandragupta and ends as follows:...... "Whosoever shall interfere with this*

arrangement.. he shall become invested with (the guilt of) the slaughter of a cow or of a Brahman, and with (the guilt of) the five anantarya" *Here the object of this statement is to threaten the resumer of the grant, be he a Brahminist or a Buddhist, with the sins regarded as mortal by each community. The* anantaryas *are the five* mahapatakas *according to Buddhist theology. They are: matricide, patricide, killing an Arhat, shedding the blood of a Buddha, and causing a split among the priesthood. The* mahapatakas *with which a Brahminist is here threatened are only two: viz., the killing of a cow and the murdering of a Brahman. The latter is obviously a* mahapataka *as it is mentioned as such in all the Smritis, but the former has been specified only an upapataka by Apastamba, Manu, Yajnavalkya and so forth. But the very fact that it is here associated with* brahma-hatya *and both have been put on a par with the* anantaryas *of the Buddhists shows that in the beginning of the fifth century A.D., it was raised to the category of* mahapatakas. *Thus* go-hatya *must have come to be considered a* mahapataka *at least one century earlier, i.e., about the commencement of the fourth century A.D."*

The question is why should a Hindu king have come forward to make a law against cow-killing, that is to say, against the Laws of Manu? The answer is that the Brahmins had to suspend or abrogate a requirement of their Vedic religion in order to overcome the supremacy of the Buddhist Bhikshus. If the analysis is correct then it is obvious that the worship of the cow is the result of the struggle between Buddhism and Brahminism. It was a means adopted by the Brahmins to regain their lost position.

Why should Beef-eating make Broken Men Untouchables?

The stoppage of beef-eating by the Brahmins and the non-Brahmins and the continued use thereof by the Broken Men had produced a situation which was different from the old. This difference lay in the face that while in the old situation everybody ate beef, in the new-situation one section did not and another did. The difference was a glaring difference. Everybody could see it. It divided society as nothing else did before. All the same, this difference need not have given rise to such extreme division of society as is marked by Untouchability. It could have remained a social difference. There are many cases where different sections of the community differ in their foods. What one likes the other dislikes and yet this difference does not create a bar between the two.

There must therefore be some special reason why in India the difference between the Settled Community and the Broken Men in the matter of beef eating created a bar between the two. What can that be? The answer is that if beef-eating had remained a secular affair-a mere matter of individual taste-such a bar between those who ate beef and those who did not would not have arisen. Unfortunately beef-eating, instead of being treated as a purely secular matter, was made a matter of religion. This happened because the Brahmins made the cow a sacred animal. This made beef-eating a sacrilege. The Broken Men being guilty of sacrilege necessarily became beyond the pale of society.

The answer may not be quite clear to those who have no idea of the scope and function of religion in the life of the society. They may ask: Why should religion make such a difference? It will be clear if the following points regarding the scope and function of religion are borne in mind.

To begin with the definition of religion. There is one universal feature which characterises all religions. This feature lies in religion being a unified system of beliefs and practices which (1) relate to sacred things and (2) which unite into one single community all those who adhere to them. To put it slightly differently, there are two elements in every religion. One is that religion is inseparable from sacred things. The other is that religion is a collective thing inseparable from society.

The first element in religion presupposes a classification of all things, real and ideal, which are the subject-matter of man's thought, into two distinct classes which are generally designated by two distinct terms the *sacred* and the *profane,* popularly spoken of as secular.

This defines the scope of religion. For understanding the function of religion the following points regarding things sacred should be noted: The first thing to note is that things sacred are not merely higher than or superior in dignity and status to those that are profane. They are just different. The sacred and the profane do not belong to the same class. There is a complete dichotomy between the two. As Prof. Durkhiem observes:

> *"The traditional opposition of good and bad is nothing beside this; for the good and the bad are only two opposed species of the same class, namely, morals, just as sickness and health are two different aspects of the same order of facts, life, while the sacred and the profane have always and everywhere been conceived by the human mind as two distinct classes, as two worlds between which there is nothing in common."*

The curious may want to know what has led men to see in this world this dichotomy between the sacred and the profane. We must however refuse to enter into this discussion as it is unnecessary for the immediate purpose we have in mind.

Confining ourselves to the issue the next thing to note is that the circle of sacred objects is not fixed. Its extent varies infinitely from religion to religion. Gods and spirits are not the only sacred things. A rock, a tree, an animal, a spring, a pebble, a piece of wood, a house, in a word anything can be sacred.

Things sacred are always associated with interdictions otherwise called *taboos*. To quote Prof. Durkhiem again: "Sacred things are those which the interdictions protect and isolate; profane things, those to which these interdictions are applied and which must remain at a distance from the first"

Religious interdicts take multiple forms. Most important of these is the interdiction on contact. The interdiction on contact rests upon the principle that the profane should never touch the sacred. Contact may be established in a variety of ways other than touch. A look is a means of contact. That is why the sight of sacred things is forbidden to the profane in certain cases. For instance, women are not allowed to see certain things which are regarded as sacred. The word (*i.e.*, the breath which forms part of man and which spreads outside him) is another means of contact. That is why the profane is forbidden to address the sacred things or to utter them. For instance, the Veda must be uttered only by the Brahmin and not by the Sudra. An exceptionally intimate contact is the one resulting from the absorption of food. Hence comes the interdiction against eating the sacred animals or vegetables.

The interdictions relating to the sacred are not open to discussion. They are beyond discussion and must be accepted without question. The sacred is 'untouchable' in the sense that it is beyond the pale of debate. All that one can do is to respect and obey. Lastly the interdictions relating to the sacred are binding on all. They are not maxims. They are injunctions. They are obligatory but not in the ordinary sense of the word. They partake of the nature of a categorical imperative. Their breach is more than a crime. It is a sacrilege.

The above summary should be enough for an understanding of the scope and function of religion. It is unnecessary to enlarge upon the subject further. The analysis of the working of the laws of the sacred which is the core of religion should enable any one to see that my answer to the question why beef-eating should make the Broken Men untouchables is the correct one. All that is necessary to reach the answer I have proposed is to read the analysis of the working of the laws of the sacred with the cow as the sacred object. It will be found that Untouchability is the result of the breach of the interdiction against the eating of the sacred animal, namely, the cow.

As has been said, the Brahmins made the cow a sacred animal. They did not stop to make a difference between a living cow and a dead cow. The cow was sacred, living or dead. Beef-eating was not merely a crime. If it was only a crime it would have involved nothing more than punishment. Beef-eating was made a sacrilege. Anyone who treated the cow as profane was guilty of sin and unfit for association. The Broken Men who continued to eat beef became guilty of sacrilege.

Once the cow became sacred and the Broken Men continued to eat beef, there was no other fate left for the Broken Men except to be treated unfit for association, *i.e.*, as Untouchables. Before closing the subject it may be desirable to dispose of possible objections to the thesis. Two such objections to the thesis appear obvious. One is what evidence is there that the Broken Men did eat the flesh of the dead cow. The second is why did they not give up beef-eating when the Brahmins and the non-Brahmins abandoned it. These questions have an important bearing upon the theory of the origin of untouchability advanced in this book and must therefore be dealt with.

The first question is relevant as well as crucial. If the Broken Men were eating beef from the very beginning, then obviously the theory cannot stand. For, if they were eating beef from the very beginning and nonetheless were not treated as Untouchables, to say that the Broken Men became Untouchables because of beef-eating would be illogical if not senseless. The second question is relevant, if not crucial. If the Brahmins gave up beef-eating and the non-Brahmins imitated them why did the Broken Men not do the same? If the law made the killing of the cow a capital sin because the cow became a sacred animal to the Brahmins and non-Brahmins, why were the Broken Men not stopped from eating beef? If they had been stopped from eating beef there would have been no Untouchability.

The answer to the first question is that even during the period when beef-eating was common to both, the Settled Tribesmen and the Broken Men, a system had grown up whereby the Settled Community ate fresh beef, while the Broken Men ate the flesh of the dead cow. We have no positive evidence to show that members of the Settled Community never ate the flesh of the dead cow. But we have negative evidence which shows that the dead cow had become an exclusive possession and perquisite of the Broken Men. The evidence consists of facts which relate to the Mahars of the Maharashtra to whom reference has already been made. As has already been pointed out, the Mahars of the Maharashtra claim the right to take the dead animal. This right they claim against every Hindu in the village. This means that no Hindu can eat the flesh of his own animal when it dies. He has to surrender it to the Mahar. This is merely another way of stating that when eating beef was a common practice the Mahars ate dead beef and the Hindus ate fresh beef. The only questions that arise are: Whether what is true of the present is true of the ancient past? Can this fact which is true of the Maharashtra be taken as typical of the arrangement between the Settled Tribes and the Broken Men throughout India.

In this connection reference may be made to the tradition current among the Mahars according to which they claim that they were given 52 rights against the Hindu villagers by the

Muslim King of Bedar. Assuming that they were given by the King of Bedar, the King obviously did not create them for the first time. They must have been in existence from the ancient past. What the King did was merely to confirm them. This means that the practice of the Broken Men eating dead meat and the Settled Tribes eating fresh meat must have grown in the ancient past. That such an arrangement should grow up is certainly most natural. The Settled Community was a wealthy community with agriculture and cattle as means of livelihood.

The Broken Men were a community of paupers with no means of livelihood and entirely dependent upon the Settled Community. The principal item of food for both was beef. It was possible for the Settled Community to kill an animal for food because it was possessed of cattle. The Broken Men could not for they had none. Would it be unnatural in these circumstances for the Settled Community to have agreed to give to the Broken Men its dead animals as part of their wages of watch and ward? Surely not. It can therefore be taken for granted that in the ancient past when both the Settled Community and Broken Men did eat beef the former ate fresh beef and the latter of the dead cow and that this system represented a universal state of affairs throughout India and was not confined to the Maharashtra alone.

This disposes of the first objection. To turn to the second objection. The law made by the Gupta Emperors was intended to prevent those who killed cows. It did not apply to the Broken Men. For they did not kill the cow. They only ate the dead cow. Their conduct did not contravene the law against cow-killing. The practice of eating the flesh of the dead cow therefore was allowed to continue. Nor did their conduct contravene the doctrine of Ahimsa assuming that it has anything to do with the abandonment of beef-eating by the Brahmins and the non-Brahmins. Killing the cow was *Himsa*. But eating the dead cow was not. The Broken Men had therefore no cause for feeling qualms of conscience in continuing to eat the dead cow. Neither the law nor the doctrine of *Himsa* could interdict what they were doing, for what they were doing was neither contrary to law nor to the doctrine.

As to why they did not imitate the Brahmins and the non-Brahmins the answer is two fold. In the first place, imitation was too costly. They could not afford it. The flesh of the dead cow was their principal sustenance. Without it they would starve. In the second place, carrying the dead cow had become an obligation though originally it was a privilege. As they could not escape carrying the dead cow they did not mind using the flesh as food in the manner in which they were doing previously.

The objections therefore do not invalidate the thesis in any way.

Untouchabality and the Date of its Birth

The Impure and the Untouchables

When did Untouchability come into existence? The orthodox Hindus insist that it is very ancient in its origin. In support of their contention reliance is placed on the fact that the observance of Untouchability is enjoined not merely by the Smritis which are of a later date but it is also enjoined by the Dharmasutras which are much earlier and which, according to certain authors, date some centuries before B.C.

In a study devoted to exploring the origin of Untouchability the question one must begin with is: Is Untouchability as old as is suggested to be?

For an answer to this question one has to examine the Dharmasutras in order to ascertain what they mean when they refer to Untouchability and to the Untouchables. Do they mean by Untouchability what we understand by it today? Do the class, to which they refer. Untouchables in the sense in which we use the term Untouchables today?

To begin with the first question. An examination of the Dharmasutras no doubt shows that they speak of a class whom they call Asprashya. There is also no doubt that the term Asprashya does mean Untouchables. The question however remains whether the Asprashya of the Dharmasutras are the same as the Asprashya of modern India. This question becomes important when it is realised that the Dharmasutras also use a variety of other terms such as Antya, Antyaja, Antyevasin and Bahya. These terms are also used by the later Smritis. It might be well to have some idea of the use of these terms by the different Sutras and Smritis. The following table is intended to serve that purpose:-

I. Asprashya

Dharma Sutra	***Smriti***
1. Vishnu V. 104.	1. Katyayana verses 433, 783.

II. Antya

Dharmasutras	***Smriti***
1. Vashishtha. (16-30) 2.	1. Manu IV. 79; VIII.. 68.
2. Apastambha (111.1)	2. Yajnavalkyal 148.197.
	3. Atri 25.
	4. Likhita 92.

III. Bahya

Dharmasutras	***Smriti***
1. Apastambha 1,2,39.18	1. Manu 28.
2. Vishnu 16.14	2. Narada 1.155.

IV. Antyavasin

Dharmasutras	***Smriti***
1. Gautama XXXI; XXIII 32	1. Manu IV. 79; X. 39
2. Vashishtha XVIII.	2. Shanti Parvan of the Mahabharata 141; 29-323.
	3. Madhyamangiras (quoted in Mitakshara on Yaj. 3.280.

V. Antyaja

Dharmasutras	***Smriti***
1. Vishnu 36.7	1. Manu IV. 61; VIII. 2792.
	2. Yajnavalkya 12.733.
	3. Brihadyama Smriti (quoted by Mitakshara on Yajna-valkya III. 260)4.
	4. Atri. 1995.
	5. Veda Vyas 1. 12.. 13.

The next question is whether the classes indicated by the terms Antya, Antyaja, Antyavasin and Bahya are the same as those indicated by the term Asprashya which etymologically means an Untouchable. In other words are they only different names for the same class of people?

It is an unfortunate fact that the Dharmasutras do not enable us to answer this question. The term *Asprashya* occurs in two places (once in one Sutra and twice in one Smriti). But not one gives an enumeration of the classes included in it. The same is the case with the term *Antya.* Although the word *Antya* occurs in six places (in two Sutras and four Smritis) not one enumerates who they are. Similarly, the word *Bahya* occurs in four places (in two Sutras and two Smritis), but none of them mentions what communities are included under this term. The only exception is with regard to the terms Antyavasin and Antyajas. Here again no Dharma Sutra enumerates them. But there is an enumeration of them in the Smritis. The enumeration of the Antyavasin occurs in the Smriti known as Madhyamangiras and that of the Antyajas in the Atri Smriti and Veda Vyas Smriti. Who they are, will be apparent from the following table:

From this table it is quite clear that there is neither precision nor agreement with regard to the use of the terms Antyavasin and Antyaja. For instance Chandala and Shvapaka fall in both the categories Antyavasin and Antyaja according to Madhyamangiras and Veda Vyas. But when one compares Madhyamanagiras with Atri they fall in different categories. The same is true with regard to the term Antyaja. For example while (1) Chandala and (2) Shvapaka are Antyajas according to Veda Vyas, according to Atri they are not. Again according to Atri (1) Buruda and (2) Kayavarta are Antyajas while according to Veda Vyas they are not. Again (1) Virat (2) Dasa (3) Bhatt (4) Kolika and (5) Pushkar are Antyaja according to Veda Vyas but according to Atri they are not.

To sum up the position reached so far: neither the Dharmasutras nor the Smritis help us to ascertain who were included in the category of Asprashya. Equally useless are the Dharmasutras and the Smritis to enable us to ascertain whether the classes spoken of as Antyavasin, Antyaja and Bahya were the same as Asprashya. Is there any other way of ascertaining whether any of these formed into the category of Asprashya or Untouchables? It would be better to collect together whatever information is available about each of these classes.

ANTYAVASIN	ANTYAJA	
Madhyamangiras	*Atri*	*Veda Vyas*
1. Chandala.	1. Nata	1. Chandala*
2. Shvapaka.	2. Meda.	2. Shvapaka.
3. Kshatta.	3. Bhilla.	3. Nata.
4. Suta.	4. Rajaka.	4. Meda.
5. Vaidehika.	5, Charmakar.	5. Bhilla.
6. Magadha.	6. Buruda.	6. Rajaka.
7. Ayogava.	7. Kayavarta.	7. Charmakar.
		8. Virat.
		9. Dasa.
		10. Bhatt.
		11.Kolika.
		12. Pushkar.

What about the Bahyas? Who are they? What are they? Are they Untouchables? They are mentioned by Manu. To understand their position, it is necessary to refer to Manu's scheme of social classification. Manu divides the people into various categories. He first makes a broad division between (1) Vaidikas and (2) Dasyus. He then proceeds to divide the Vaidikas into four sub-divisions: (1) Those inside Chaturvarnya (2) Those outside Chaturvarnya (3) Vratya and (4) Patitas or outcastes.

Whether a person was inside Chaturvarnya or outside, was a question to be determined by the Varna of the parents. If he was born of the parents of the same Varnas, he was inside the Chaturvarnya. If, on the other hand, he was born of parents of different Varnas *i.e.*, he was the progeny of mixed marriages or what Manu calls *Varna Sarnkara,* then he was outside the Chaturvarnya. Those outside Chaturvarnya are further subdivided by Manu into two classes. (1) Anulomas and (2) Pratilomas. Anulamas were those whose fathers were of a higher Varna and mothers of a lower Varna. Pratilomas, on the other hand, were those whose fathers were of a lower Varna and the mothers of a higher Varna. Though both the Anulomas and Pratilomas were alike for the reason that they were outside the Chaturvarnya. Manu proceeds to make a distinction between them. The Anulomas, he calls *Varna Bahya* or shortly *Bahyas,* while Pratilomas he calls *Hinas.* The Hinas are lower than the Bahyas. But neither the Bahyas nor the Hinas does Manu regard as Untouchables.

Antya as a class is mentioned in Manu IV.79. Manu however does not enumerate them. Medhatithi in his comentary suggests that Antya means Miecha, such as Meda etc. Buhler translates Antya as a low-caste man.

There is thus nothing to indicate that the Antyas were Untouchables. In all probability, it is the name given to those people who were living in the outskirts or *end* (Anta) of the village. The reason why they came to be regarded as low is to be found in the story narrated in the Brahadaranyaka Upanishad (1.3) to which reference is made by Mr. Kane The story is that: "Gods and Ashuras had a strike and the gods thought that they might rise superior to the Ashuras by the Udgithana. In this occurs the passage 'this devata (Prana) throwing aside the sin that was death to these devatas (vak etc.) sent it to ends of these devatas there; therefore one should not go to the people outside the Aryan pale nor to *disam anta* (the ends of the quarters) thinking, otherwise I may fall in with *papmani i.e.*, death".

The meaning of Antya turns on the connotation of the phrase 'disam Anta' which occurs in the passage quoted above. If the phrase 'ends of the quarters' can be translated as meaning the end of the periphery of the village, without its being called a far-fetched translation, we have here an explanation of what Antya originally meant. It does not suggest that the Antyas were Untouchables. It only meant that they were living on the outskirts of the village.

As to the Antyajas, what we know about them is enough to refute the view that they were Untouchables. Attention may be drawn to the following facts: In the Shanti Parvan (109.9) of the Mahabharata there is a reference to Antyajas who are spoken of as Soldiers in the Army. According to Sarasvativilasa, Pitamaha speaks of the seven cases of Rajakas included in the term Antyaja as Prakritis. That Prakrids mean trade guilds such as of washermen and others is quite clear from the Sangamner Plate of Bhillama II dated Saka 922 which records the grant of a village to eighteen Prakritis. Viramitrodaya says that Srenis mean the eighteen castes such as the Rajaka etc., which are pollectively called Antyajas. In view of these facts how could the Antyajas be said to have been regarded as the Untouchables?

Coming to the Antyavasin, who were they? Were they Untouchables? The term Antyavasin has been used in two different senses. In one sense it was applied to a Brahmachari living in the house of the Gum during his term of studentship. A Brahmachari was referred to as Antyavasin. It probably meant one who was served last. Whatever the reason for calling a Brahmachari Antyavasin it is beyond dispute that the word in that connection could not connote Untouchability. How could it when only Brahmins, Kshatriyas and Vaishyas could become Brahmacharis. In another sense they refer to a body of people. But even in this sense it is doubtful if it means Untouchables.

According to Vas. Dh. Sutra (18.3) they are the offspring of a Sudra father and Vaishya mother. But according to Manu (V.39) they are the offspring of a Chandala father and a Nishad mother. As to the class to which they belong, the Mitakshara says they are a sub-group of the Antyajas which means that the Antyavasin were not different from the Antyajas. What is therefore true of the Antyajas may also be taken as true of the Antyavasin.

Stopping here to take stock of the situation as it emerges from such information as we have regarding the social condition of the people called Antyavasin, Antya, Antyaja, as is available from ancient literature, obviously it is not open to say that these classes were Untouchables in the modem sense of the term. However, for the satisfaction of those who may still have some doubt, the matter may be further examined from another point of view. Granting that they were described as Asprashya we may proceed to inquire as to what was the connotation of the term in the days of the Dharmasutras.

For this purpose we must ascertain the rules of atonement prescribed by the-Shastras. From the study of these rules we will be able to see whether the term Asprashya had the same connotation in the times of the Dharmasutras as it has now.

Let us take the case of the Chandalas as an illustration of the class called Asprashya. In the first place, it should be remembered that the word Chandala does not denote one single homogenous class of people. It is one word for many classes of people, all different from one another. There are altogether five different classes of Chandalas who are referred to in the Shastras. They are (i) the offspring of a Sudra father and a Brahmin mother (ii) the offspring of an unmarried woman (iii) the offspring of union with a sagotra woman (iv) the offspring of a person who after becoming an ascetic turns back to the householder's life and (v) the offspring of a barber father and a Brahmin mother

It is difficult to say which Chandala calls for purification. We shall assume that purification is necessary in the case of all the Chandalas. What is the rule of purification prescribed by the Shastas? Gautama in his Dharma Sutra (Chapter XIV, Verse 30) also refers to it in the following terms:

> *"On touching an outcaste, a Chandala, a woman impure on account of her confinement a woman in her courses, or a corpse and on touching persons who have touched them, he shall purify himself by bathing dressed in his clothes."*

Below is the text of the rule given by the Vashishtha Dharma Sutra (Chapter IV. Verse 37):

> *"When he has touched a sacrificial post, a pyre, a burial ground, a menstruating or a lately confined woman, impure men or Chandalas and so forth, he shall bathe, submerging both his body and his head."*

Baudhayana agrees with Vashishtha for he too in his Dharma Sutra (Prasna 1, Adhyaya 5, Khanda 6, Verse 5) says:

"On touching a tree standing on a sacred spot, a funeral pyre, a sacrificial post, a Chandala or a person who sells the Veda, a Brahmin shall bathe dressed in his clothes."

The following are the rules contained in Manu:

V. 85: When he (the Brahmin) has touched a Chandala, a menstruating woman, an outcaste, a woman in childbed, a corpse, or one who has touched a (corpse), he becomes pure by bathing.

V. 131: Manu has declared that the flesh of an animal killed by dogs is pure, likewise (that) of a (beast) slain by carnivorous (animals) or by men of low caste (Dasya) such as Chandalas.

V. 143: He who, while carrying anything in any manner, is touched by an impure (person or thing), shall become pure, if he performs an ablution, without pulling down that object.

From these texts drawn from the Dharmasutras as well as Manu, the following points are clear:

(1) That the pollution by the touch of the Chandala was observed by the Brahmin only.

(2) That the pollution was probably observed on ceremonial occassions only.

If these conclusions are right then this is a case of Impurity as distinguished from Untouchability. The distinction between the Impure and the Untouchable is very clear. The Untouchable pollutes all while the Impure pollutes only the Brahmin. The touch of the Impure causes pollution only on a ceremonial occasion. The touch of the Untouchable causes pollution at all times.

There is another argument to which so far no reference has been made which completely disproves the theory that the communities mentioned in the Dharmasutras were Untouchables. That argument emerges out of a comparison of the list of communities given in the Order-in-Council (which is reproduced in Chapter II) with the list given in this chapter prepared from the Smritis. What does the comparison show? As anyone can see, it shows:

Firstly: The maximum number of communities mentioned in the Smritis is only 12, while the number of communities mentioned in the Order-in-Council comes to 429.

Secondly: There are communities which find a place in the Order-in-Council but which do not find a place in the Smritis Out of the total of 429 there are nearly 427 which are unknown to the Smritis.

Thirdly: There are communities mentioned in the Smritis which do not find a place in the Order-in-Council at all.

Fourthly: There is only one community which finds a place in both. It is the Charmakar community

Those who do not admit that the Impure are different from the Untouchables do not seem to be aware of these facts. But they will have to reckon with them. These facts are so significant and so telling that they cannot but force the conclusion that the two are different.

Take the first fact. It raises a very important question.

If the two lists refer to one and the same class of people, why do they differ and differ so widely? How is it that the communities mentioned in the Shastras do not appear in the list given in the Order-in-Council? Contrariwise, how is it that the communities mentioned in the Order-in-Council are not to be found in the list given by the Shastras? This is the first difficulty we have to face.

On the assumption that they refer to the same class of people, the question assumes a serious character. If they refer to the same class of people then obviously Untouchability which was originally confined to 12 communities came to be extended to 429 communities! What has led to this vast extension of the Empire of Untouchability? If these 429 communities belong to the same class as the 12 mentioned by the Shastras why none of the Shastras mention them? It cannot be that none of the 429 communities were not in existence at the time when the Shastras were written. If all of them were not in existence at least some of them must have been. Why even such as did exist find no mention?

On the footing that both the lists belong to the same class of people, it is difficult to give any satisfactory answer to these questions. If, on the other hand, it is assumed that these lists refer to two different classes of people, all these questions disappear. The two lists are different because the list contained in the Shastras is a list of the Impure and the list contained in the Order-in-Council is a list of the Untouchables. This is the reason why the two lists differ. The divergence in the two lists merely emphasizes what has been urged on other grounds, namely, that the classes mentioned in Shastras are only Impure and it is a mistake to confound them with the Untouchables of the present day.

Now turn to the second. If the Impure are the same as the Untouchables, why is it as many as 427 out of 429 should be unknown to the Smritis? As communities, they must have been in existence at the time of the Smritis. If they are Untouchables now, they must have been Untouchables then. Why then did the Smritis fail to mention them?

What about the third? If the Impure and the Untouchables are one and the same, why those communities which find a place in the Smritis do not find a place in the list given in the Order-in-Council? There are only two answers to this question. One is that though Untouchables at one time, they ceased to be Untouchables subsequently. The other is that the two lists contain names of communities who fall in altogether different categories. The first answer is untenable. For, Untouchability is permanent Time cannot erase it or cleanse it. The only possible conclusion is the second.

Take the fourth. Why should Chamar alone find a place in the lists? The answer is not that the two lists include the same class of people. If it was the true answer, then not only the Chamar but all others included in the list given by the Smritis should appear in both the lists. But they do not. The true answer is that the two lists contain two different classes of people. The reason why some of those in the list of the Impure appear in the list of the Untouchables is that the Impure at one time became Untouchables. That the Chamar appears in both is far from being evidence to support the view that there is no difference between the Impure and the Untouchables. It proves that the Chamar who was at one time an Impure, subsequently became an Untouchable and had therefore to be included in both the lists.

Of the twelve communities mentioned in the Smritis as Impure communities, only the Chamar should have been degraded to the status of an Untouchable is not difficult to explain. What has made the difference between the Chamar and the other impure communities is the fact of beef-eating. It is only those among the Impure who were eating beef that became Untouchables, when the cow became sacred and beef-eating became a sin. The Chamar is the only beef-eating community. That is why it alone appears in both the lists. The answer to the question relating to the Chamars is decisive on two points. It is conclusive on the point that the Impure are different from the Untouchables. It is also decisive on the point that it is beef-eating which is the root of Untouchability and which divides the Impure and the Untouchables.

The conclusion that Untouchability is not the same as Impurity has an important bearing on the determination of the date of birth of Untouchability. Without it any attempt at fixing the date would be missing the mark.

When did Broken Men become Untouchables?

The foregoing researches and discussions have proved that there was a time when the village in India consisted of a Settled Community and Broken Men and that though both lived apart, the former inside the village and the latter outside it, there was no bar to social intercourse between the members of the Settled Community and the Broken Men. When the cow became sacred and beef-eating became taboo, society became divided into two-the Settled Community became a touchable community and Broken Men became an untouchable community. When did the Broken Men come to be regarded as Untouchables?

That is the last question that remains to be considered. There are obvious difficulties in the way of fixing a precise date for the birth of Untouchability. Untouchability is an aspect of social psychology. It is a sort of social nausea of one group against another group. Being an outgrowth of social psychology which must have taken some time to acquire form and shape, nobody can venture to fix a precise date to a phenomenon which probably began as a cloud no bigger than man's hand and grew till it took its final all-pervading shape as we know it today. When could the seed of Untouchability be said to have been sown? If it is not possible to fix an exact date, is it possible to fix an approximate date?

An exact date is not possible. But it is possible to give an approximate date. For this the first thing to do is to begin by fixing the upper time-limit at which Untouchability did not exist and the lower time-limit at which it had come into operation.

To begin with the question of fixing the upper limit the first thing to note is that those who are called Antyajas are mentioned in the Vedas. But they were not only not regarded as Untouchables but they were not even regarded as Impure. The following extract from Kane may be quoted in support of this conclusion. Says Kane:

"In the early Vedic literature several of the names of castes that are spoken of in the Smritis as Antyajas occur. We have Carmanna (a tanner of hides) in the Rig Veda (VIII.8,38) the

Chandala and Paulkasa occur in Vaj. S., the Vepa or Vapta (barber) even in the Rig., the Vidalakara or Bidalakar (corresponding to the Buruda of the Smritis) occurs in the Vaj. S. and the Tai, Br-Vasahpalpuli (washer woman) corresponding to the Rajakas of the Smritis in Vaj. S. But there is no indication in these-passages whether they, even if they formed castes, were at all Untouchables."

Thus in Vedic times there was no Untouchability. As to the period of the Dharmasutras, we have seen that there was Impurity but there was no Untouchability.

Was there Untouchability in the time of Manu? This question cannot be answered offhand. There is a passage in which he says that there are only four vamas and that there is no fifth vama. The passage's enigmatical. It is difficult to make out what it means. Quite obviously the statement by Manu is an attempt by him to settle a controversy that must have been going on at the time he wrote. Quite obviously the controversy was about the status of a certain class in relation to the system of Chaturvarnya. Equally obvious is the point which was the centre of the controversy. To put briefly, the point was whether this class was to be deemed to be included within the Chaturvarnya or whether it was to be a fifth vama quite distinct from the original four vamas. All this is quite clear. What is, however, not clear is the class to which it refers. This is because Manu makes no specific mention of the class involved in the controversy.

The verse is also enigmatical because of the ambiguity in the decision given by Manu. Manu's decision is that there is no fifth Vama. As a general proposition it has a meaning which everybody can understand. But what does this decision mean in the concrete application to the class whose status was the subject-matter of controversy. Obviously it is capable of two interpretations. Itihay mean that as according to the scheme of Chaturvama there is no fifth vama the class in question must be deemed to belong to one of the four recognized vamas. But it may also mean that as in the original Vama System there is no provision for a fifth vama the class in question must be deemed to be outside the Varna System altogether.

The traditional interpretation adopted by the orthodox Hindu is that the statement in Manu refers to the Untouchables, that it was the Untouchables whose Status was in controversy and that it was their status which is the subject-matter of Manu's decision. This interpretation is so firmly established that it has given rise to a division of Hindus into two classes called by different names, *Savarnas* or Hindus (those included in the Chaturvama) *aad Avarnas* or Untouchables (those excluded from the Chaturvama). The question is, is this view correct? To whom does the text refer? Does it refer to the Untouchables? A discussion of this question may appear to be out of place and remote from the question under consideration. But it is not so. For if the text does refer to the Untouchables then it follows that Untouchability did exist in the time of Manu-a conclusion which touches the very heart of the quesdon under consideration. The matter must, therefore, be thrashed out.

I am sure this interpretation is wrong. I hold that the passage does not refer to the Untouchables at all. Manu does not say which was the fifth class whose status was in controversy and about whose status he has given a decision in this passage. Was it the class of Untouchables or was it some other class? In support of my conclusion that the passage does not refer to Untouchables at all I rely on two circumstances. In the first place, there was no Untouchability in the time of Manu. There was only Impurity. Even the Chandala for whom Manu has nothing but contempt is only an impure person. That being so, this passage cannot possibly have any reference to Untouchables. In the second place, there is evidence to support the view that this passage has reference to slaves and not to Untouchables.

This view is based on the language of the passage quoted from the Narada Smrid in the chapter on the Occupational Theory of Untouchability. It will be noticed that the Narada Smriti speaks of the slaves as the fifth class. If the expression fifth class in the Narada Smriti refers to slaves, I see no reason why the expression fifth class in Manusmriti should not be taken to have reference to slaves. If this reasoning, is correct, it cuts at the very root of the contention that Untouchability existed in the time of Manu and that Manu was not prepared to include them as part of the Varna System. For the reasons stated, the passage does not refer to Untouchability and there is, therefore, no reason to conclude that there was Untouchability in the time of Manu.

Thus we can be sure of fixing the upper limit for the date of the birth of Untouchability. We can definitely say that Manusmriti did not enjoin Untouchability. There, however, remains one important question. What is the date of Manusmriti? Without an answer to this question it would not be possible for the average to relate the existence or nonexistence of Untouchability to any particular point in time. There is no unanimity among savants regarding the date of Manusmriti. Some regard it as very ancient and some regard it as very recent. After taking all facts into consideration Prof. Buhler has fixed a date which appears to strike the truth.

According to Buhler, Maou Smriti in the shape in which it exists now, came into existence in the Second Century A.D. In assigning so recent a date to the Manusmriti Prof. Buhler is not quite alone. Mr. Daphtary has also come to the same conclusion. According to him Manusmriti came into being after the year 185 B.C. and not before. The reason given by Mr. Daphtary is that Manusmriti has a close connection with the murder of the Buddhist Emperor Brihadratha of the Maurya dynasty by his Brahmin Commander-in-Chief Pushyamitra Sunga and as even that took place in 185 B.C., he concludes that Manusmriti must have been written after 185 B.C. To give support to so important a conclusion it is necessary to establish a nexus between the murder of Brihadratha Maurya by Pushyamitra and the writing of Manusmriti by strong and convincing evidence. Mr. Daphatry has unfortunately omitted to do so. Consequently his conclusion appears to hang in the air. The establishment of such a nexus is absolutely essential. Fortunately there is no want of evidence for the purpose.

The muider of Brihadratha Maurya by Pushyamitra has unfortunately passed unnoticed. At any rate it has not received the attention it deserves. It is treated by historians as an ordinary incident between two individuals as though its origin lay in some personal quarrel between the two. Having regard to its consequences it was an epoch-making event. Its significance cannot be measured by treating it as a change of dynasty-the Sungas succeeding the Mauryas. It was a political revolution as great as the French Revolution, if not greater. It was a revolution-a bloody revolution-engineered by the Brahmins to overthrow the rule of the Buddhist Kings. That is what the murder of Brihadratha by Pushyamitra means.

This triumphant Brahmanism was in need of many things. It of course needed to make Chaturvama the law of the land the validity of which was denied by the Buddhists. It needed to make animal sacrifice, which was abolished by the Buddhists, legal. But it needed more than this. Brahmanism in bringing about this revolution against the rule of the Buddhist Kings had transgressed two rules of the customary law of the land which were accepted by all as sacrosanct and inviolable. The first rule-made it a sin for a Brahmin even to touch a weapon. The second made the King's person sacred and regicide a sin. Triumphant Brahmanism wanted a sacred text, infallible in its authority, to justify their transgressions. A striking feature of the Manusmriti is that it not only makes Chaturvama the law of the land, it not only makes animal sacrifice legal but it goes to state when a Brahmin could justifiably resort to arms and when he could justifiably kill the King.

In this the Manusmriti has done what no prior Smriti has done. It is a complete departure. It is a new thesis. Why should the Manusmriti do this? The only answer is, it had to strengthen the revolutionary deeds committed by Pushyamitra by propounding philosophic justification. This interconnection between Pushyamitra and the new thesis propounded by Manu shows that the Manusmriti came into being some time after 185 B.C., a date not far removed from the date assigned by Prof. Buhler. Having got the date of the Manusmriti we can say that in the Second Century A.D., there was no Untouchability.

Now to turn to the possibility of determining the lower limit to the birth of Untouchability. For this we must go to the Chinese travellers who are known to have visited India and placed on record what they saw of the modes and manners of the Indian people. Of these Chinese travellers Fah-Hian has something very interesting to say. He came to India in 400 A.D. In the course of his observations occurs the following passage-I:

"Southward from this (Mathura) is the so-called middle-country (Madhyadesa). The climate of this cototry is warm and equable, without frost or snow. The people are very well off, without poll-tax or official restrictions. Only those who till the royal lands return a portion of profit of the land. If they desire to go, they go; if they like to stop they stop. The kings govern without corporal punishment; criminals are fined, according to circumstances, lightly or heavily. Even in cases of repeated rebellion they only cut off the right hand. The King's personal attendants, who guard him on the right and left, have fixed salaries. Throughout the country the people kill no living thing nor drink wine, nor do they eat garlic or onion, with the exception of Chandalas only. The Chandalas are named 'evil men' and dwell apart from others; if they enter a town or market, they sound a piece of wood in order to separate themselves; then, men knowing they are, avoid coming in contact with them. In this country they do not keep swine nor fowls, and do not deal in cattle; they have no shambles or wine shops in their marketplaces. In selling they use cowrie shells. The Chandalas only hunt and sell flesh."

Can this passage be taken as evidence of the prevalence of Untouchability at the time of Fah-Hian? Certain parts of his description of the treatment given to the Chandalas do seem to lend support to the conclusion, that is, a case of Untouchability.

There is, however, one difficulty in the way of accepting this conclusion. The difficulty arises because the facts relate to the Chandalas. The Chandala is not a good case to determine the existence or nonexistence of Untouchability. The Brahmins have regarded the Chandalas as their hereditary enemies and are prone to attribute to them abominable conduct; hurl at them low epithets and manufacture towards them a mode of behaviour which is utterly artificial to suit their venom against them. Whatever, therefore, is said against the Chandalas must be taken with considerable reservations.

This argument is not based on mere speculation. Those who doubt its cogency may consider the evidence of Bana's Kadambari for a different description of the treatment accorded to the Chandalas.

The story of Kadambari is a very complex one and we are really not concerned with it. It is enough for our purpose to note that the story is told to King Sudraka by a parrot named

Vaishampayana who was the pet of a Chandala girl. The following passages from the Kadambari are important for our purpose. It is better to begin with Bana's description of a Chandala settlement. It is in the following terms:

> *"I beheld the barbarian settlement, a very marketplace of evil deeds. It was surrounded on all sides by boys engaged in the chase, unleashing their hounds, teaching their falcons, mending snares, carrying weapons, and fishing, horrible in their attire, like demoniacs. Here and there the entrance to their dwellings, hidden by thick bamboo forests, was to be inferred, from the rising of smoke of orpiment. On all sides the enclosures were made with skulls; (627) the dust-heaps on the roads were filled with bones; the yards of the huts were miry with blood, fat, and meat chopped up. The life there consisted of hunting; the food, of flesh; the ointment, of fat; the garments, of coarse silk; the couches, of dried skins; the household attendants, of dogs; the animals for riding, of cows; the men's employment, of wine and women; the oblation to the gods, of blood; the sacrifice, of cattle. The place was the image of all hells."*

It is from such a settlement that the Chandala girl starts with her parrot to the palace of King Sudraka. King Sudraka is sitting in the Hall of Audience with his Chieftains. A portress enters the Hall and makes the following announcement:

> *"Sire,* there *stands at the gate a Chandala maiden from the South, a royal* glory *of the race of that Tricamku who climbed the sky, but fell from it at the order of wrathful Indra, She bears a parrot in a cage, and bids me thus hail your majesty: "Sire, thou, like the ocean, art alone worthy to receive the treasures of whole earth. In the thought that this bird is a marvel and the treasure of the whole earth, I bring it to lay at thy feet, and desire to behold thee. Thou, O king, hast heard her message, and must decide!" So saying, she ended her speech. The king, whose curiosity was aroused, looked at the chiefs around him, and with the words Why not? Bid her enter' gave his permission. Then the portress, immediately on the king's order ushered in the Candala maiden. And she entered."*

The King and the Chieftains did not at first take notice of her. To attract attention she struck a bamboo on the mosaic floor to arouse the King. Bana then proceeds to describe her personal appearance: "Then the king, with the' words, look yonder to his suite, gazed steadily upon the Candala maiden, as she was pointed out by the portress. Before her went a man, whose hair was hoary with age, whose eyes were the colour of the red lotus, whose joints, despite the loss of youth, were firm from incessant labour, whose form, though that of Matanga, was not to be despised, and who wore the white raiment meet fora court. Behind *her* went a Candala boy, with locks falling on either shoulder, bearing a cage, the bars of which, though of gold, shone like emerald from the reflection of the parrot's plumage.

She herself seemed by the darkness of her hue to imitate Krishna when he guilefully assumed a woman's attire to take away the arnritit seized by the demons. She was, as it were, a doll of sapphire walking alone; and over the bine garment, which reached to her ankle, there fell a veil of red silk, like evening sunshine falling on blue lotuses. The circle of her cheek was whitened by the earring that hung from one ear, like the *(ace* of night inlaid with the rays of the rising moon: she had a tawny tilaka of gorocana, as if it woe a third eye, like Parvati in mountaineer's attire, after the fashion of the garb of Civa.

She was like Cri. darkened by the sapphire glory of Narayana reflected on the robe on her breast; or like Rati, stained by smoke which rose as Madana was burnt by the fire of wrathful Civa: *or* like Yamuna, fleeing in fear of being drawn along by the ploughshare of wild Balarama; or, from the rich lac that turned her lotus feet into budding shoots, like Durga, with *her* feet crimsoned by the blood of the Ashura Mahisha she had just trampled upon.

Her nails were rosy from the pink glow of *her* fingers; the mosaic pavement seemed too hard for her touch, and she came for placing her feet like tender twigs upon the ground. The rays of *her* anklets, rising in flame-colour, seemed to encircle her as with the arms of Agni, as though, by his love for her beauty, he would purify the strain of her birth, and so set the Creator at naught. Her girdle was like the stars wreathed on the brow of the elephant of Love; and her necklace was a rope of large bright pearls, like the stream of Ganga just tinged by Yamuna. Like autumn, she opened her lotus eyes; like the rainy season, she had cloudy tresses; like the circle of the Malaya Hills, she was wreathed with sandal; like the zodiac, she was decked with starry gems; like Cri, she had the fairness of a lotus in her hand; like a swoon, she entranced the heart; like a forest, she was endowed with living beauty; like the child of a goddess, she was claimed by no tribe; like sleep, she charmed the eyes; as a lotus-pool in a wood is troubled by elephants, so was she dimmed by her Matanga birth; like spirit, she might *not* be touched; like a letter, she gladdened the eyes alone; like the blossoms of spring she lacked the jati flower, her slender waist, like the line of Love's bow, could be spanned by the hands; with *her* curly hair, she was like the Lakshmi of the Yaksha king in Alaka. She had but reached the flower of *her* youth, and was beautiful exceedingly.

And the king was amazed; and the thought arose in his mind. Ill-placed was the labour of the Creator inproducing this beauty! For if she has been created as though in mockery of her Chandala form, such that all the world's wealth of loveliness is laughed to scorn by her own, why was she born in a race with which none can mate? Surely by thought alone did Prajapati create her, fearing the penalties of contact with the Matanga race, else whence this unsullied radiance, a grace that belongs not to limbs sullied by touch? Moreover, though fair in form, by the baseness of her birth, whereby she, like a Lakshmi of the lower world, is a perpetual reproach to the gods, she, lovely as she is, causes fear in Brahma, the maker of so strange a union.' While the king was thus thinking the maiden, garlanded with flowers, that fell over her ears, bowed herself before him with a confidence beyond her years.

And, when she had made her reverence and stepped on to the mosaic floor, her attendant, taking the parrot, which had just entered the cage, advanced a few steps, and, showing it to the King, said: 'Sire, this parrot, by name Vaicampayana, knows the meaning of all the castras, is expert in the practice of royal policy, skilled in tales, history, and Puranas, and acquainted with songs and with musical intervals. He recites, and himself composes graceful and incomparable modern romances, love-stories, plays, and poems, and the like; he is versed in witticisms and is an unrivalled disciple of the vina, flute, and drum. He is skilled in displaying the different movements of dancing, dextrous in painting, very bold in play, ready in resources to calm a maiden angered in a lover's quarrel, and familiar with the characteristics of elephants, horses, men, and women. He is the gem of the whole earth; and in the thought that treasures belong to thee, as pearis to the ocean, the daughter of my lord has brought him hither to thy feet, O king! Let him be accepted as thine.'

On reading this description of a Chandala girl many questions arise. Firstly, how different it is from the description given by Fa-Hian? Secondly Bana is a Vatsyayana Brahmin. This Vatsyayana Brahmin, after giving a description of the Chandala Settlement, finds no compunction in using such eloquent and gorgeous language to describe the Chandala girl. Is this description compatible with the sentiments of utter scorn and contempt associated with Untouchability? If the Chandalas were Untouchables how could an Untouchable girl enter the King's palace? How could an Untouchable be described in the superb terms used by Bana? Far from being degraded, the Chandalas of Bana's period had Ruling Families among them.

For Bana speaks of the Chandala girl as a Chandala princess Bana wrote some time about 600 A.D., and by 600 A.D. the Chandalas had not come to be regarded as Untouchables. It is, therefore, quite possible that the conditions described by Fa-Hian, though bordering on Untouchability, may not be taken as amounting to Untouchability. It may only be extreme form of impurity practised by the Brahmins who are always in the habit of indulging in overdoing their part in sacerdotalism. This becomes more than plausible if we remember that when Fa-Hian came to India it was the reign of the Gupta Kings. The Gupta Kings were patrons of Brahmanism. It was a period of the triumph and revival of Brahmanism. It is quite possible that what Fa-Hian describes is not Untouchability but an extremity to which the Brahmins were prepared to carry the ceremonial impurity which had become attached to some community, particularly to the Chandalas.

The next Chinese traveller who came into India was Yuan Chwang. He came to India in 629 A.D. He stayed in India for

16 years and has left most accurate records of joumeys up and down the country and of the manners and customs of the people. In the course of his description of general characters of the cities and buildings of India, he says:

> *"As to their inhabited towns and cities the quadrangular walls of the cities (or according to* one *text, of the various regions) are broad and high, while the thoroughfares are narrow tortuous passages. The shops are on the highways and booths, or (inns) line the roads. Butchers, fishermen, public performers, executioners, and scavengers have their habitations marked by a distinguishing sign. They are forced to live outside the city and they sneak along on the left when going about in the hamlets."*

The above passage is too short and too brief for founding a definite conclusion thereon. There is, however, one point about it which is worthy of note. Fa-Hian's description refers to the Chandalas only while the description given by Yuan Chwang applies to communities other than the Chandalas. This is a point of great importance. No such argument can be levelled against the acceptance of a description since it applies to communities other than the Chandalas. It is, therefore, just possible that when Yuan Chwang came to India, Untouchability had emerged.

On the basis of what has been said above we can conclude that while Untouchability did not exist in 200 A.D., it had emerged by 600 A.D.

These are the two limits, upper and lower, for determining the birth of Untouchability. Can we fix an approximate date for the birth of Untouchability? I think we can, if we take beef-eating, which is the root of Untouchability, as the point to start from. Taking the ban on beef-eating as a point to reconnoitre from, it follows that the date of the birth of Untouchability must be intimately connected with the ban on cow-killing and on eating beef. If we can answer when cow-killing became an offence and beef-eating became a sin, we can fix an approximate date for the birth of Untouchability. When did cow-killing become an offence? We know that Manu did not prohibit the eating of beef nor did he make cow-killing an offence. When did it become an offence? As has been shown by Dr. D. R.

Bhandarkar, cow killing was made a capital offence by the Gupta kings some time in the 4th Century A.D.

We can, therefore, say with some confidence that Untouchability was born some time about 400 A.D. It is born out of the struggle for supremacy between Buddhism and Brahmanism which has so completely moulded the history of India and the study of which is so woefully neglected by students of Indian history.

3

Ambedkar on the Riddle of the Sudras

Everybody knows that the Sudras formed the fourth Varna of the Indo-Aryan society. But very few have cared to inquire who were these Sudras and how they came to be the fourth Varna. That such an enquiry is of first-rate importance is beyond question. For, it is worth knowing how the Sudras came to occupy the fourth place, whether it was the result of evolution or it was brought about by revolution.

Any attempt to discover who the Sudras were and how they came to be the fourth Varna must begin with the origin of the *Chaturvarnya* in the Indo-Aryan society. A study of the *Chaturvarnya* must in its turn start with a study of the ninetieth Hymn of the Tenth Mandala of the Rig Veda—a Hymn, which is known by the famous name of *Purusha Sukta.*

What does the Hymn say? It says:

1. Purusha has a thousand heads, a thousand eyes, a thousand feet. On every side enveloping the earth he overpassed (it) by a space of ten fingers.
2. Purusha himself is this whole (universe), Whatever has been and whatever shall be. He is the Lord of immortality, since (or when) by food he expands.
3. Such is his greatness, and Purusha is superior to this. All existences are a quarter to him; and three-fourths of him are that which is immortal in the sky.
4. With three-quarters, Purusha mounted upwards. A quarter of him was again produced here. He was then

diffused everywhere over things which eat and things which do not eat.

5. From him was born Viraj, and from Viraj, Purusha. When born, he extended beyond the earth, both behind and before.
6. When the gods performed a sacrifice with Purusha as the oblation, the spring was its butter, the summer its fuel, and the autumn its (accompanying) offering.
7. This victim, Purusha, born in the beginning, they immolated on the sacrificial grass. With him the gods, the *Sadhyas,* and the *Rishis* sacrificed.
8. From that universal sacrifice were provided curds and butter. It formed those aerial (creatures) and animals both wild and tame.
9. From that universal sacrifice sprang the *Rik* and *Saman* verses, the metres and the *Yajus.*
10. From it sprang horses, and all animals with two rows of teeth; kine sprang from it; from it goats and sheep.
11. When (the gods) divided Purusha, into how many parts did they cut him up? What was his mouth? What arms (had he)? What (two objects) are said (to have been) his thighs and feet?
12. The Brahmana was his mouth, the Rajanya was made his arms; the being called the Vaishya, he was his thighs; the Sudra sprang from his feet.
13. The moon sprang from his soul (manas), the sun from the eye, Indra and Agni from his mouth and Vayu from his breath.
14. From his navel arose the air, from his head the sky, from his feet the earth, from his ear the (four) quarters; in this manner (the gods) formed the worlds.
15. When the gods, performing sacrifices, bound Purusha as a victim, there were seven sticks (stuck up) for it (around the fire), and thrice seven pieces of fuel were made.
16. With sacrifices the gods performed the sacrifice. These were the earliest rites. These great powers have sought the sky, where are the former *Sadhyas,* gods."

The *Purusha Sukta* is a theory of the origin of the Universe. In other words, it is a cosmogony. No nation which has reached an advanced degree of thought has failed to develop some sort of cosmogony. The Egyptians had a cosmogony somewhat analogous with that set out in the *Purusha Sukta.* According to it, it was god *Khnumu,* ' the shaper,' who shaped living things on the potter's wheel, "created all that is, he formed all that exists, he is the father of fathers, the mother of mothers... he fashioned men, he made the gods, he was the father from the beginning... he is the creator of the heaven, the earth, the underworld, the water, the mountains... he formed a male and a female of all birds, fishes, wild beasts, cattle and of all worms." A very similar cosmogony is found in Chapter I of the Genesis in the Old Testament.

Cosmogonies have never been more than matters of academic interest and have served no other purpose than to satisfy the curiosity of the student and to help to amuse children. This may be true of some parts of the *Purusha Sukta.* But it certainly cannot be true of the whole of it. That is because all verse of the *Purusha Sukta* are not of the same importance and do not have the same significance. Verses 11 and 12 fall in one category and the rest of the verses fall in another category. Verses other than 11 and 12 may be regarded as of academic interest. Nobody relies upon them. No Hindu even remembers them. But it is quite different with regard to verses 11 and 12. *Prima facie* these verses do no more than explain how the four classes, namely. (1) Brahmins or priests, (2) Kshatriyas or soldiers, (3) Vaishyas or traders, and (4) Sudras or menials, arose from the body of the Creator. But the fact is that these verses are not understood as being merely explanatory of a cosmic phenomenon. It would be a grave mistake to suppose that they were regarded by the Indo-Aryans as an innocent piece of a poet's idle imagination. They are treated as containing a mandatory injunction from the Creator to the effect that Society must be constituted on the basis of four classes mentioned in the *Sukta. Such* a construction of the verses in question may not be warranted by their language. But there is no doubt that according to tradition this is how the verses are construed, and it would indeed be difficult to say that this traditional construction is not in consonance with the intendon of the author of the *Sukta.* Verses 11 and 12 of the *Purusha Sukta* are, therefore, not a mere cosmogony. They contain a divine injunction prescribing a particular form of the constitution of society.

The constitution of society prescribed by the *Purusha Sukta* is known as *Chaturvarnya.* As a divine injunction, it naturally became the ideal of the Indo-Aryan society. This ideal of *Chaturvarnya* was the mould in which the life of the Indo-Aryan community in its early or liquid state was cast. It is this mould, which gave the Indo-Aryan community its peculiar shape and structure.

This reverence, which the Indo-Aryan society had for this ideal mould of *Chaturvarnya,* is not only beyond question, but it is also beyond description. Its influence on the Indo-Aryan society has been profound and indelible. The social order prescribed by the *Purusha Sukta* has never been questioned by anyone except Buddha. Even Buddha was not able to shake it, for the simple reason that both after the fall of Buddhism and even during the period of Buddhism there were enough law-givers, who made it their business not only to defend the ideal of the *Purusha Sukta* but to propagate it and to elaborate it.

To take a few illustrations of this propaganda in support of the *Purusha Sukta,* reference may be made to the *Apastamba Dharma Sutra* and the *Vashishtha Dharma Sutra.* The *Apastamba Dharma Sutra* states: There are four castes— Brahmins, Kshatriyas, Vaishyas and Sudras. Among these, each preceding (caste) is superior by birth to the one following. For all these excepting Sudras and those who have committed bad actions are ordained (1) the initiation *(Upanayan* or the wearing of the sacred thread), (2) the study of the Veda and (3) the kindling of the sacred fire (*i.e.*, the right to perform sacrifice)

This is repeated by *Vashishtha Dharmasutra* which says: There are four castes (Vamas), Brahmins, Kshatriyas, Vaishyas and Sudras. Three castes. Brahmins, Kshatriyas and Vaishyas (are called) twice-born. Their first birth is from their mother; the second from the investiture with the sacred girdle. In that (second birth) the Savitri is the mother, but the teacher is said to be, the father.

They call the teacher father, because he gives instruction in the Veda. The four castes are distinguished by their origin and by particular sacraments.

There is also the following passage of the Veda: "The Brahmana was his mouth, the Kshatriya formed his arms, the Vaishya his thighs; the Shudia was born from his feet."

It has been declared in the following passage that a Sudra shall not receive the sacraments. Many other law-givers have in parrotlike manner repeated the theme of the *Purusha Sukta* and have reiterated its sanctity. It is unnecessary to repeat their version of it. All those, who had raised any opposition to the sanctity of the ideal set out in the *Purusha Sukta,* were finally laid low by Manu, the architect of the Hindu society. For Manu did two things. In the first place, he enunciated afresh the ideal of the *Purusha Sukta* as a part of divine injunction. He said: For the prosperity of the worlds, he (the creator) from his mouth, arms, thighs and feet created the Brahmin, Kshatriya and Vaishya and the Sudra.

The Brahmin, Kshatriya (and) Vaishya (constitute) the three twice-born castes; but the fourth the sudra has only one birth.

In this he was no doubt merely following his predecessors. But he went a step further and enunciated another proposition in which he said: "Veda is the only and ultimate sanction for Dharma."

Bearing in mind that the Purusha Sukta is a part of the Veda, it cannot be difficult to realise that Manu invested the social ideal of *Chaturvarnya* contained in the *Purusha Sukta,* with a degree of divinity and infallibility which it did not have before.

A critical examination of the *Purusha Sukta* therefore becomes very essential.

It is claimed by the Hindus that the *Purusha Sukta* is unique. This is no doubt a tall claim for an idea which came to birth when the mind of man was primitive and was without the rich endowment of varied thought available in modem times. But there need not be much difficulty in admitting this claim provided it is understood in what respect the *Purusha Sukta* is unique.

The principal ground for regarding the *Purusha Sukta* as unique is that the ideal of social organization, namely, the ideal of *Chaturvarnya* which it upholds, is unique. Is this a sufficient ground for holding the *Purusha Sukta* as unique? The *Purusha Sukta* would really have been unique if it had preached a classless society as an ideal form of society. But what does the *Purusha Sukta* do? It preaches a class-composed society as its ideal. Can this be regarded as unique? Only a nationalist and a patriot can give an affirmative answer to this question. The existence of classes has been the *defacto* condition of every society, which is not altogether primitive. It is a normal state of society all over the world where society is in a comparatively advanced state. Looking at it from this point of view, what uniqueness can there be in the *Purusha Sukta,* when it does no more than recognise the sort of class composition that existed in the Indo-Aryan society?

Notwithstanding this, the *Purusha Sukta* must be admitted to be unique, though for quite different reasons. The unfortunate part of the matter is that many people do not know the true reasons why the *Purusha Sukta* should be regarded as unique. But once the true reasons are known, people will not only have no hesitation in accepting that the *Purusha Sukta* is a unique production of the human intellect but will perhaps be shocked to know what an extraordinary production of human ingenuity it is.

What are the features of the social ideal of the *Purusha Sukta,* which give it the hall mark of being unique? Though the existence of classes is the *de facto* condition of every society, nevertheless no society has converted this *de facto* state of affairs into a *de jure* connotation of an ideal society. The scheme of the *Purusha Sukta* is the only instance in which the real is elevated to the dignity of an ideal.

This is the first unique feature of the scheme set forth in the *Purusha Sukta.* Secondly, no community has given the *de facto* state of class composition a legal effect by accepting it as a *de jure* connotation of an ideal society. The case of the Greeks is a case in point. Class composition was put forth as an ideal social structure by no less an advocate than Plato. But the Greeks never thought of making it real by giving it the sanction of law. The *Purusha Sukta* is the only instance in which an attempt was made to give reality to the ideal by invoking the sanction of law. Thirdly, no society has accepted that the class composition is an ideal.

At the most they have accepted it as being natural. The *Purusha Sukta* goes further. It not only regards class composition as natural and ideal, but also regards it as sacred and divine. Fourthly, the number of the classes has never been a matter of dogma in any society known to history. The Romans had two classes. The Egyptians thought three were enough. The Indo-Iranians also had no more than three classes: (1) The *Athravans* (priests) (2) *Rathaeshtar* (warriors) and (3) the *Vastrya-fshuyat* (peasantry). The scheme of the *Purusha Sukta* makes the division of society into four classes a matter of dogma. According to it, there can be neither more nor less. Fifthly, every society leaves a class to find its place *vis-a-vis* other classes according to its importance in society as may be determined by the forces operating from time to time. No society has an official gradation laid down, fixed and permanent, with an ascending scale of reverence and a descending scale of contempt.

The scheme of the *Purusha Sukta* is unique, inasmuch as it fixes a permanent warrant of precedence among the different classes, which neither time nor circumstances can alter. The warrant of precedence is based on the principle of graded inequality among the four classes, whereby it recognises the Brahmin to be above all, the Kshatriya below the Brahmin but above the Vaishya and the Sudra, the Vaishya below the Kshatriya but above the Sudra and the Sudra below all.

These are the real reasons why the *Purusha Sukta* is unique. But the *Purusha Sukta* is not merely unique, it is also extraordinary. It is extraordinary because it is so full of riddles. Few seem to be aware of these riddles. But anyone who cares to inquire will learn how real in their nature and how strange in their complexion these riddles are. The cosmogony set out in the *Purusha Sukta* is not the only cosmogony one comes across in the Rig Veda. There is another cosmogony which is expounded in the 72nd Hymn of the Tenth Mandala of the Rig Veda. It reads as follows:

1. Let us proclaim with a clear voice of the generation of the gods (the divine company), who, when their praises

are recited, look (favourably on the worshipper) in this latter age.

2. Brahmanaspati filled these (generations of the gods) with breath as a blacksmith (his bellows); in the first age of the gods the existent was born of the nonexistent.
3. In the first age of the gods the existent was born of the nonexistent; after that the quarters (of the horizon) were born, and after them the upward-growing (trees).
4. The earth was born from the upward growing (tree), the quarters were born from the earth; Daksha was born from Adili and afterwards Aditi from Daksha.
5. Aditi, who was thy daughter, Daksha, was born; after her, the gods were born, adorable, freed from the bonds of death.
6. When, gods, you abode in this pool well-arranged, then a pungent dust went forth from you as if you were dancing.
7. When, gods, you Filled the worlds (with your radiance) as clouds (fill the earth with rain) then you brought fourth the sun hidden in the ocean.
8. Eight sons (there were) of Aditi who were born from her body; she approached the gods with seven, she sent forth Martanda on high.
9. With seven sons Aditi went to a former generation, but she bore Martanda for the birth and death (of human beings).

The two cosmologies are fundamentally different in principle as well as in detail. The former explains creation *ex nihilo* 'being was born of non-being'. The latter ascribes creation to a being which it calls *Purusha*. Why in one and the same book two such opposite cosmologies should have come to be propounded? Why did the author of the *Purusha Sukta* think it necessary to posit a *Purusha* and make all creation emanate from' him?

Any one who reads the *Purusha Sukta* will find that it starts with the creation of donkeys, horses, goats, etc., but does not say anything about the creation of man. At a point when it would have been natural to speak of the creation of man, it breaks off the chain and proceeds to explain the origin of the classes in the Aryan society. Indeed, the *Purusha Sukta* appears to make the explaining of the four classes of the Aryan society to be its primary concern. In doing this, the *Purusha Sukta* stands in complete contrast not only with other theologies but with the other parts of the Rig Veda also.

No theology has made it its purpose to explain the origin of classes in society. Chapter I of the Genesis in the Old Testament, which can be said to be analogous in intention and purpose to the *Purusha Sukta,* does nothing more than explain how man was created. It is not that social classes did not exist in the old Jewish society. Social classes existed in all societies. The Indo-Aryans were no exception. Nevertheless, no theology has ever thought it necessary to explain how classes arise. Why then did the *Purusha Sukta* make the explanation of the origin of the social classes its primary concern?

The *Purusha Sukta* is not the only place in the Rig Veda where a discussion of the origin of creation occurs. There are other places in the Rig Veda where the same subject is referred to. In this connection, one may refer to the following passage in the Rig Veda which reads as follows:

Rig Veda, i.96.2:"By the first *nivid,* by the wisdom of Ayu, he (Agni) created these children of men; by his gleaming light the earth and the waters, the gods sustained Agni the giver of the riches."

In this, there is no reference at all to the separate creation of classes, though there is no doubt that even at the time of the *Rig Veda,* the Indo-Aryan Society had become differentiated into classes; yet the above passage in the *Rig Veda* ignores the classes and refers to the creation of men only. Why did the *Purusha Sukta* think it necessary to go further and speak of the origin of the classes?

The *Purusha Sukta* contradicts the *Rig Veda* in another respect. The *Rig Veda* propounds a secular theory regarding the origin of the Indo-Aryans as will be seen from the following texts:

Rig Veda, i.80:16: "Prayers and hymns were formerly congregated in that Indra, in the ceremony which Atharvan, father Manu, and Dadhyanch celebrated.'

Rig Veda, i.I 14.2:"Whatever prosperity or succour father

Manu obtained by sacrifice, may we gain all that under thy guidance, Rudra.

Rig Veda, ii.33.13: "Those pure remedies of yours, O Maruts, those which are most auspicious, ye vigorous gods, those which are beneficent, those which our father Manu chose, those and the blessing and succour of Rudra, I desire.

Rig Veda, viii.52.1:"The ancient friend hath been equipped with the powers of the mighty (gods). Father Manu has prepared hymns to him, as portals of access to the gods.'

Rig Veda, iii.3.6: "Agni, together with the gods, and the children *(jantubhih)* of Manush, celebrating a multiform sacrifice with hymns.

Rig Veda, iv. 37.1: "Ye gods, Vajas, and Ribhukshana, come to our sacrifice by the path travelled by the gods, that ye, pleasing deities, may institute a sacrifice among these people of Manush *(Manusho vikshu)* on auspicious days."

Rig Veda, vi.14.2: "The people of Manush praise in the sacrifice Agni the invoker.

From these texts it is beyond question that the rishis who were the authors of the hymns of the Rig Veda regarded Manu as the progenitor of the Indo-Aryans. This theory about Manu being the progenitor of the Indo-Aryans had such deep foundation that it was carried forward by the *Brahmanas* as well as the *Puranas*. It is propounded in the *Aitareya Brahmana* in the *Vishnu Parana* and the *Matsya Parana*. It is true that they have made Brahma the progenitor of *Manu;* but the *Rig Veda* theory of *Manu* being the progenitor has been accepted and maintained by them. Why does the *Purusha Sukta* make no mention of *Manu*? This is strange because the author of the *Purush Sukta* seems to be aware of the fact that Manu Svayambhuva is called *Viraj* and *Viraj* is called *Adi Purusha,* since he too speaks of *Virajo adhi Purushah* in verse five of the *Sukta*.

There is a third point in which the *Purush Sukta* has gone beyond the *Rig Veda*. The Vedic Aryans were sufficiently advanced in their civilization to give rise to division of labour. Different persons among the Vedic Aryans followed different occupations. That they were conscious of it is evidenced by the following verse:

Rig Veda, i.113.6: "That some may go in pursuit of power, some in pursuit of fame, some in pursuit of wealth, some in pursuit of work, Ushas has awakened people so that each may go in pursuit of his special and different way of earning his livelihood." This is as far as the *Rig Veda* had gone. The *Purusha Sukta* goes beyond. It follows up the notion of division of labour and converts the scheme of division of work into a scheme of division of workers into fixed and permanent occupational categories. Why does the *Purush Sukta* commit itself to such a perversity?

There is another point in which the *Purusha Sukta* departs from the *Rig Veda.* It is not that the *Rig Veda* speaks only of man. It speaks also of the Indo-Aryan nation. This nation was made up of the five tribes, which had become assimilated into one common Indo-Aryan people. The following hymns refer to these five tribes as moulded into a nation:

Rig Veda, vi.ll.4: "Agni, whom, abounding in oblations, the five tribes, bringing offerings, honour with prostrations, as if he were a man.

Rig Veda, vii.l5.2: "The wise and youthful master of the house (Agni)' who has taken up his abode among the five tribes in every house.'

There is some difference of opinion as to who these five tribes are. *Yaska* in his *Nirukta* says that it denotes *Gandharvas, Pitris, Devas, Ashuras and Rakshasas. Aupamanyava* says that it denotes the four *Varnas* and the *Nishadas.* Both these explanations seem to be absurd. Firstly, because the five tribes are praised collectively as in the following hymns:

Rig Veda, ii.2.10: "May our glory shine aloft among the five tribes, like the heaven unsurpassable.

Rig Veda, vi.46.7: "Indra, whatever force or vigour exists in the tribe of Nashusa or whatever glory belongs to the five races bring (for us).

Such laudatory statements could not have been made if the five tribes included the *Sudras.* Besides, the word used is not *Varnas.* The word used is *Janah.* That it refer to the five tribes and not to the four *Varnas* and *Nishadas* is quite clear from the following verse of the *Rig Veda:*

Rig Veda, i. 108.8: "If, O Indra and Agni, ye are abiding among the *Yodus, Turvasas, Druhyus, Anus, Purus,* come hither, vigorous heroes from all quarters, and drink the Soma which has been poured out.

That these five tribes had been moulded into one Aryan people is clear from the Atharva Veda (iii.24.2) which says: "these five regions, the five tribes springings from Manu."

A sense of unity and a consciousness of kind can alone explain why the *Rishis* of the *Rig Vedic* hymns came to refer to the five tribes in such manner. The questions are: why did the *Purusha Sukta* not recognise this unity of the five tribes and give a mythic explanation of their origin? Why instead did it recognise the communal divisions within the tribes? Why did the *Purusha Sukta* regard communalism more important than nationalism?

These are some of the riddles of the *Purush Sukta,* which come to light when one compares it with the *Rig Veda.* There are others, which emerge when one proceeds to examine the *Purusha Sukta* from a sociological point of view.

Ideals as norms are good and are necessary. Neither a society nor an individual can do without a norm. But a norm must change with changes in time and circumstances. No norm can be permanently fixed. There must always be room for revaluation of the values of our norm. The possibility of revaluing values remains open only when the institution is not invested with sacredness. Sacredness prevents revaluation of its values. Once sacred, always sacred. The *Purusha Sukta* makes the *Chaturvarnya* a sacred institution, a divine ordination. Why did the *Purusha Sukta* make a particular form of social order so sacred as to be beyond criticism and beyond change? Why did it want to make it a permanent ideal beyond change and even beyond criticism? This is the first riddle of the *Purusha Sukta* which strikes a student of sociology.

In propounding the doctrine of *Chaturvarnya,* the *Purush Sukta* plays a double game. It proceeds first to raise the real, namely, the existence of the four classes in the Indo-Aryan Society, to the status of an ideal. This is a deception because the ideal is in no way different from facts as they exist. After raising the real to the status of the ideal, it proceeds to make a show of giving effect to what it regards as an ideal. This again is a deception because the ideal already exists in fact. This attempt of the *Purusha Sukta* to idealise the real and to realise the ideal, is a kind of political jugglery, the like of which, I am sure, is not to be found in any other book of religion. What else is it if not a fraud and a deception? To idealise the real, which more often than not is full of inequities, is a very selfish thing to do.

Only when a person finds a personal advantage in things as they are that he tries to idealise the real. To proceed to make such an ideal real is nothing short of criminal. It means perpetuating inequity on the ground that whatever is once settled is settled for all times. Such a view is opposed to all morality. No society with a social conscience has ever accepted it. On the contrary, whatever progress in improving the terms of associated life between individuals and classes has been made in the course of history, is due entirely to the recognition of the ethical doctrine that what is wrongly settled is never settled and must be resettled. The principle underlying the *Purush Sukta* is, therefore, criminal in intent and anti-social in its results. For, it aims to perpetuate an illegal gain obtained by one class and an unjust wrong inflicted upon another. What can be the motive behind this jugglery of the *Purusha Sukta*? This is the second riddle.

The last and the greatest of all these riddles, which emerge out of a sociological scrutiny of the *Purusha Sukta,* is the one relating to the position of the *Sudra.* The *Purusha Sukta* concerns itself with the origin of the classes, and says they were created by God—a doctrine which no theology has thought it wise to propound. This in itself is a strange thing. But what is astonishing is the plan of equating different classes to different parts of the body of the Creator. The equation of the different classes to different parts of the body is not a matter of accident. It is deliberate. The idea behind this plan seems to be to discover a formula which will solve two problems, one of fixing the functions of the four classes and the other of fixing the gradation of the four classes after a preconceived plan. The formula of equating different classes to the different parts of the body of the Creator has this advantage.

The part fixes the gradation of the class and the gradation in its turn fixes the function of the class. The *Brahmin* is equated to the mouth of the Creator. Mouth being the noblest part of the anatomy, the *Brahmin* becomes the noblest of the four classes. As he is the noblest in the scale, he is given the noblest function, that of custodian of knowledge and learning. The *Kshatriya is* equated to the arms of the Creator. Among the limbs of a person, arms are next below the mouth. Consequently, the *Kshatriya* is given an order of precedence next below the *Brahmin* and is given a function which is second only to knowledge, namely, fighting. The *Vaishya* is equated to the thighs of the Creator. In the gradation of limbs the thighs are next below the arms. Consequently, the *Vaishya* is given an order of precedence next below the *Kshatriya* and is assigned a function of industry and trade which in name and fame ranks or rather did rank in ancient times below that of a warrior. The *Sudra* is equated to the feet of the Creator. The feet form the lowest and the most ignoble part of the human frame. Accordingly, the *Sudra* is placed last in the social order and is given the filthiest function, namely, to serve as a menial.

Why did the *Purusha Sukta* choose such a method of illustrating the creation of the four classes? Why did it equate the *Sudras* to the feet? Why did it not take some other illustration to show how the four classes were created. It is not that *Purusha* is the only stock simile used to explain creation. Compare the explanation of the origin of the Vedas contained in the *Chhandogya Upanishad.* It says

"Prajapati infused warmth into the worlds, and from them so heated he drew forth their essences, *viz.,* Agni (fire) from the earth, Vayu (wind) from the air, and Surya (the sun) from the sky. He infused warmth into these three deities, and from them so heated he drew forth their essences,— from Agni the *ric* verses, from Vayu the *yajus* verses and from Surya the *saman* verses. He then infused heat into this triple science, and from it so heated he drew forth its essences—from *ric* verses the syllable *bhuh,* from *yajus* verses *bhuvah,* and from *Saman* verses *svar.*"

Here is an explanation of the origin of the Vedas from different deities. So far as the Indo-Aryans are concerned, there was no dearth of them. There were thirty crores of them. An explanation of the origin of the four *Varnas* from four gods would have maintained equality of dignity by birth of all the four classes. Why did the *Purusha Sukta* not adopt this line of explanation? Again, would it not have been possible for the author of the *Purusha Sukta* to say that the different classes were born from the different mouths of the *Purusha*. Such a conception could not have been difficult because the *Purusha* of the *Purush Sukta* has one thousand heads, enough to assign one species of creation to one of his heads. Such a method of explaining creation could not have been unknown to the author of the *Purusha Sukta*. For we find it used by the *Vishnu Purana* to explain the origin of the different *Vedas* as may be seen from the following extract:

> *"From his eastern mouth Brahma formed the Gayatd, the* ric *verses, the trivrit, the sama-rathantara and of sacrifices, the agnistoma. From his southern mouth he created the* yajus *verses, the trishtubh metre, the panchadasa stoma, the brihatsaman, and the ukthya. From his western mouth he formed the* saman *verses, the jagati metre, the saptadasa stoma, the Vairupa, and the atiratra. From his northern mouth he formed the ekavimsa, the* atharvan, *the aptoryaman with the anushtubh and viraj metres."*

The *Harivansa* has another way of explaining the origin of the Vedas. According to it: "The god fashioned the *Rig Veda* with the Yajus from his eyes, the *Sama Veda* from the tip of his tongue, and the *Atharvan* from his head."

Assuming that for some reason the author of the *Purusha Sukta* could not avoid using the body of the Creator and its different parts for explaining the origin and the relation of the four classes, the question still remains as to why he chose to equate the different parts of *the Purusha* to the different classes in the manner in which he does.

The importance of this question is considerably heightened when one realises that the *Purusha Sukta* is not the only instance in which the different parts of the body of the Creator are used as illustrations to explain the origin of the different classes in society. The same explanation is given by the sage *Vaishampayana* to explain the origin of the various classes of priests employed in the performance of sacrifices. But what a difference is there between the two! The explanation of *Vaishampayana* which is reported in the *Harivarnsa* reads as follows: "Thus the glorious Lord Hari Narayana, covering the entire waters, slept on the world which had become one sea, in the midst of the vast expanse of fluid *(rajas),* resembling a mighty ocean, himself free from passion *(virajaskah),* with mighty arms; Brahmans know him as the undecaying. Invested through austere fervour with the light of his own form and clothed with triple time (past, present and future) the lord then slept. *Purushotiama* (Vishnu) is whatever is declared to be the highest. *Purusha* the sacrifice, and everything else which is known by the name of *Purusha.*

Here how the *Brahmins* devoted to sacrifice, and called *ritvijas,* were formerly produced by him from his own body for offering sacrifices. The Lord created from his mouth the *Brahman,* who is the chief, and the *udgatri,* who chants the *Saman,* from his arms the *hotri* and the *adhvaryu.* He then... created the *prastotri,* the *maitravaruna,* and *the pratishthatri,* from his belly the *pratiharti* and the *potri,* from his thighs the *achhavaka* and the *neshtri,* from his hands the *agnidhra* and the sacrificial *brahmanya,* from his arms the *gravan* and the sacrificial *unnetri.* Thus did the divine Lord of the world create the sixteen excellent *ritvijas,* the utterers of all sacrifices. Therefore this *Purusha* is formed of sacrifice and is called the Veda; and all the Vedas with the Vedangas, Upanishads and ceremonies are formed of his essence."

There were altogether seventeen different classes of priests required for the performance of a sacrifice. It could never be possible for anyone attempting to explain the origin of each by reference to a distinct part of the body of the Creator to avoid using the feet of the *Purusha* as the origin of a class, the limbs of the *Purusha* being so few and the number of priests being so many. Yet what does *Vaishampayana* do? He does not mind using the same part of the Creator's body to explain the origin of more than one class of priests. He most studiously avoids using the feet as the origin of anyone of them.

The situation becomes completely intriguing when one compares the levity with which the *Sudras* are treated in the *Purusha Sukta* with the respect with which the *Brahmins* are treated in the Hari-varnsa in the matter of their respective origins. Is it because of malice that the *Purusha Sukta* did not hesitate to say that the *Sudra* was born from the feet of the *Purusha* and that his duty was to serve? If so what is the cause of this malice? The riddles about the Sudras mentioned above are those which arise out of a sociological scrutiny of the *Purusha Sukta*. There are other riddles regarding the position of the *Sudra* which arise out of later developments of the ideal of *Chaturvarnya*. To appreciate these results it is necessary first to take note of these later developments. The later developments of *Chaturvarnya* are mainly two. First is the creation of the fifth class next below the *Sudras*. The second is the separation of the *Sudras* from the first three *Varnas*. These changes have become so integrated with the original scheme of the *Purusha Sukta* that they have given rise to peculiar terms and expressions so well-known that everybody understands what they stand for. These terms are: *Savarnas, Avarnas, Dvijas, non-Dvijas,* and *Traivarnikas*. They stand to indicate the sub-divisions of the original four classes and the degree of separation between them. It is necessary to take note of the relative position of these classes because they disclose a new riddle. If this riddle has not caught the eye of the people, it is because of two reasons. Firstly, because students have not cared to note that these names are not mere names but that they stand for definite rights and privileges, and secondly, because they have not cared to find out whether the groupings made under these names are logical having regard to the rights and privileges they connote.

Let us therefore see what is the *de jure* connotation of these terms. *Savarna* is generally contrasted with *Avarna*. *Savarna* means one who belongs to one of the four *Varnas*. *Avarna* means one who does not belong to any one of the four *Varnas*. The *Brahmins, Kshatriyas, Vaishyas and Sudras* are *Savarnas*. The Untouchables or *Ati-Sudras* are called *Avarnas,* those who have no *Varna*. Logically, the. *Brahmins, Kshatriyas, Vaishyas* and *Sudras* are within the *Chaturvarnya*. Logically, the Untouchables or the *Ati-Sudras* are outside the *Chaturvarnya*. *Dvija* is generally contrasted with *non-Dvija*. *Dvija* literally means twice-born and *non-Dvija* means one who is born only once. The distinction is based on the right to have *Upanayana*.

The *Upanayana* is treated as a second birth. Those who have the right to wear the sacred thread are called *Dvijas*. Those who have no right to wear it are called *non-Dvijas*. The *Brahmins, Kshatriyas* and *Vaishyas* have the right to wear the sacred thread. Logically, they are *Dvijas*. The *Sudras* and the *Ati-Sudras* have no right to wear the sacred thread. Logically, they are both *non-Dvijas*. The *Traivarnika* is contrasted with the *Sudra*. But there is nothing special in this contrast. It conveys the same distinction which is conveyed by the distinction between the *Dvijas* and the *non-Dvijas* except the fact that the contrast is limited to the *Sudra* and does not extend to the *Ati-Sudra*. This is probably because this terminology came into being before the rise of the *Ati-Sudras* as a separate class.

Bearing in mind that both the *Sudra* and the *Ati-Sudra* are *non-Dvijas,* why then is the *Sudra* regarded as *Savarna* and the *Ati-Sudra* as *Avarna*? Why is the former within and why is the latter outside the *Chaturvarnya*? The *Brahmins, Kshatriyas, Vaishyas* and *Sudras* are all within the four corners of the *Chaturvarnya*. They are all *Savarnas*. Why then is the *Sudra* denied the right of the *Traivarnikas*?

Can there be a greater riddle than the riddle of the *Sudras*? Surely, it calls for investigation and explanation as to who they were and how they came to be the fourth *Varna* in the Aryan Society.

The Origin of the Sudras

Has the Brahmanic literature any explanation to offer which can account for the origin of the Sudras? There is no doubt that the Brahmanic literature is full of legends regarding creation which touch upon the creation of the universe, of man and of the different Vamas. Whether or not they furnish any clue to discover the origin of the Sudras, there can be no doubt that all such theories should find a place in a book which is concerned with the problem of the Sudras if for no other reason than that of assembling all material relating to the Sudras in one place and making their story complete. It would be better to take each piece of the Brahmanic literature separately, and note what contribution it has to make to the subject.

To begin with the *Vedas*. As to the *Rig Veda,* the legend about creation to be found in its *Sukta* known as the *Purusha Sukta* has already been set out in the book. It now remains to take note of the legends contained in the other *Vedas*.

There are two recensions of the *Yajur Veda:* (1) the White *Yajur Veda* and (2) the Black *Yajur Veda*. To take the White

Yajur Veda first. The *Vajasaneyi Samhita* of the White *Yajur Veda* sponsors two theories. One is a mere reproduction of the *Purusha Sukta* of the *Rig Veda* with this difference that it has 22 verses, while the original as it occurs in the *Rig Veda* has only 16 verses. The six additional verses in the White *Yajur Veda* read as follows:

17. Brought forth from the waters and from the essence of the earth, he was produced by Vishvakannan in the beginning. Tvashta gives him form; that is the Universe of Purusha on all sides in the beginning.
18. I know this great Purusha, of the colour of the sun, beyond darkness. Only by knowing him does one go beyond death; there is no other path for going.
19. Prajapati moves in the interior of the womb; though unborn, he is born in many forms. Wise men see his source; wise men desire the place of the Marichis.
20. He who shines for the gods, he who is the priest of the gods, he who was born before the gods,—salutation to that shining offspring of Brahma.
21. The gods, generating the shining offspring of Brahma, said in the beginning; "That Brahmin who knows thus,—the gods will be under his control."
22. Sri and Laxmi are his wives; the day and night his sides; the Stars his ornament; the Ashwins his bright face. Grant me my desires; grant me that; grant me everything.

The second explanation contained in the *Vajasaneyi Samhita* is quite different from the *Purusha Sukta.* It reads as follows:

V.S., xiv,28. "He lauded with one. Living beings were formed. He lauded with three the Brahman was created; *Brahmanaspati* was the ruler. *He* lauded with five existing things were created; bhutanampati was ruler. He lauded with seven: die seven rishis were created: *Dhatri* was the ruler. He lauded with nine: the *Fathers* were created: *Aditi* was the ruler. He lauded with eleven: the seasons were created: the *Artavas* were the rulers. He lauded with thirteen: the months were created: the year was the ruler. He lauded with fifteen: the *Kshatra* (the *Kshatriya)* was created: *Indra* was the ruler. He lauded with seventeen: animals were created: *Vrihaspati* was the ruler. He lauded with nineteen: the *Sudra* and the *Arya (Vaishya)* were created: day and night were the rulers. He lauded with twenty-one: animals with undivided hoofs were created: *Varuna* was the ruler. He lauded with twenty-three: small animals were created: *Pushan* was the ruler. He lauded with twenty-five: wild animals were created: *Vayu* was the ruler (compare R.V., x.90.8). He lauded with twenty-seven: heaven and earth separated: *Vasus, Rudras* and *Adityas* separated after them: they were the rulers. He lauded with thirty-one: living beings were created: the first and second halves of the month were the rulers. He lauded with thirty one: existing things were tranquillized: *Prajapati Parameshthin* was the ruler."

Now to turn to the Black *Yajur Veda*. The *Taittriya Samhita* of the Black *Yajur Veda* gives altogether five explanations. The one at iv. 3, 10 is the same as has been put forth by the *Vajasaneyi Samhita* of the White *Yajur Vedaa-t* (xiv.28) and which has been reproduced earlier. Of the rest those which narrate the origin of the Sudra are set out below:

T.S., ii.4.13.1. **:**"The gods were afraid of the *Rajanya* when he was in the womb. They bound him with bonds when he was in the womb. Consequently, this *Rajanya* is born bound. If he were born unbound he would go on slaying his enemies. In regard to whatever *Rajanya* any one desires that he should be born unbound, and should go on slaying his enemies, let him offer for him this *Aindra-Barhaspatya* oblation. A *Rajanya* has the character of *Indra,* and a Brahman is *Vrihaspati.* It is through the *Brahman* that anyone releases the *Rajanya* from his bond. The golden bond, a gift, manifestly releases from the bond that fetters him."

T.S., vii. 1.1.4.: *Prajapad* desired, may I propagate.' He formed the Trivrit (stoma) from his mouth. After it were produced the deity Agni, the metre Gayain, the Saman (called) Rathantara, of men the Brahmin, of beasts the goats. Hence they are the chief *(mukhyah)* because they were created from the mouth *(mukhatah).* From (his) breast, from his arms, he formed the. Panchadasa *(stoma)* After it were created the god, the indra, the Trishtubh metre, the Saman (called) Brihat, of men the *Rajanya,* of beasts the sheep. Hence they are vigorous, because they were created from vigour. From (his) middle he foamed the Saptadasa (stoma). After it were created the gods (called) the Vishvedevas, the Jagati metre, the Saman called the Vairupa of men the *Vaishya,* of beasts kine. Hence they are to be eaten, because they were created from the receptacle of food. Wherefore they *are* more numerous than others, for the most numerous deities were created after (the Saptadasa), From his foot he formed the Ekavimsa (Stoma.). After it were *created the Anushtubh metre, the saman called vairaja,* of men the *Sudra,* of beasts the horse. Hence these two, both the horse and the *Sudra,* are transporters of (other) creatures. Hence (too) the *Sudra is* incapacitated for sacrifice, because no deities were created after (the Ekavimsa). Hence (too) these two subsist by their feet, for they were created from the foot.

Coming to the *Atharva Veda,* there are altogether four explanations. One of these is the same as the *Purusha Sukta* of the *Rig Veda.* It occurs at xix.6. The others are as stated below:

(1) A.V. iv.6.1.: The *Brahman* was born the first with ten heads and ten faces. He first drank the soma; he made poison powerless.

(2) A.V., xv.S.I.: He (the *Vratya)* became filled with passion thence sprang the *Rajanya.*

(3) A.V., xv.9.1.: Let the king to whose house the *Vratya* who knows this, comes as a guest, cause him to be respected as superior to himself. So doing he does no injury to his royal rank, or to his realm. From him arose the *Brahman (Brahmin)* and the *Kshattra (Kshatriya).* They said Into whom shall we enter,' etc.

To proceed to the Brahmanas. The *Satapatha Brahmana* contains six explanations. There are two which concern themselves with the creation of the *Varnas.* Of the two, the one which speaks of the origin of the *Sudras* is given below:

S.B xiv.4.2.23.: "Brahma (here, according to the commentator, existing in the form of Agni and representing the Brahmana caste) was formerly this (universe), one only. Being one, it did not develop. It energetically created an excellent form, the Kshattra, *viz.,* those among the gods who are powers (Kshattrani), Indra, Varuna, Soma, Rudra, Parjanya, Yama, Mrityu, Isana, Hence nothing is superior to the *Kshatra.* Therefore, the Brahmana sits below the Kshatriya at the

Rajasuya sacrifice; he confers that glory on the Kshattra (the royal power). This, the Brahma, is the source of the Kshattra. Hence although the king attains supremacy, he at the end resorts to the Brahman as his source. Whoever destroys him (the Brahman) destroys his own source. He becomes most miserable, as one who has injured a superior. He did not develop. He created the Vis, *viz.*, those classes of gods who are designated by troops, Vasus, Rudras, Adityas, Visvedevas, Maruts. He did not develop. He created the Sudra class Pushan. This earth is Pushan; for she nourishes all that exists. He did not develop.

He energetically created an excellent form. Justice (Dharma). This is the ruler (Kshattra) of, the ruler (Kshattra), namely. Justice. Hence nothing is superior to Justice. Therefore the weaker seeks (to overcome) the stronger by Justice, as by a king. This justice is truth. In consequence they say of a man who speaks truth, 'he speaks justice.' For this is both of these. This is the Brahma, Kshattra, Vis and Sudra. Through Agni it became Brahma among the gods, the Brahmana among men, through the (divine) Kshatriya a (human) Kshatriya, through the (divine) Vaishya a (human) Vaishya, through the (divine) Sudra a (human) Sudra. Wherefore it is in Agni among the gods and in a Brahman among men that they seek after an abode.

The *Taittriya Brahman* is responsible for the following explanation:

T.B. i.2.6.7.:"The Brahmana caste is sprung from the gods; the Sudras from the Ashuras."

T.B., iii. 2.3.9.:"This Sudra has sprung from nonexistence."

Here is a complete collection of all the Brahmanic speculations on the origin of the four classes and of the Sudras. The ancient Brahmins were evidently conscious of the fact that the origin of the four classes was an unusual and uncommon social phenomenon and that the place of the Sudra in it was very unnatural and that this called for some explanation. Otherwise, it would be impossible to account for these innumerable attempts to explain the origin of the *Chaturvarnya* and of the Sudra.

But what is one to say of these explanations? The variety of them is simply bewildering. Some allege that *Purusha* was the origin of the four *Varnas,* and some attribute their origin to Brahma, some to Prajapati and some to Vratya. The same source gives differing explanations. The White *Yajur Veda* has two explanations, one in terms of *Purusha,* the other in terms of *Prajapati.* The Black *Yajur Veda* has three explanations to offer. Two are in terms of *Prajapati,* the third in terms of Brahman. The *Atharva Veda* has four explanations, one in terms of *Purusha,* second in terms of *Brahman,* third in terms of *Vratya* and fourth quite different from the first three. Even when the theory is the same, the details are not the same.

Some explanations such as those in terms of Prajapti, or Brahma are theological. Others in terms of Manu or Kasyapa are in humanistic terms. It is imagination running riot. There is in them neither history nor sense. Prof. Max Muller commenting on the *Brahmanas* has said: "The Brahmanas represent no doubt a most interesting phase in the history of the Indian mind, but judged by themselves, as literary productions, they are most disappointing. No one would have supposed that at so early a period, and in so primitive a state of society, there could have risen up a literature which for pedantry and downright absurdity can hardly be matched anywhere. There is no lack of striking thoughts, of bold expressions, of sound reasoning, and curious traditions in these collections. But these are only like the fragments of a torso, like precious gems set in brass and lead. The general character of these works is marked by shallow and insipid grandiloquence, by priestly conceit, and antiquarian pedantry. It is most important to the historian that he should know how soon the fresh and healthy growth of a nation can be blighted by priestcraft and superstition. It is most important that we should know that nations are liable to these epidemics in their youth as well as in their dotage. These works deserve to be studied as the physician studies the twaddle of idiots, and the raving of madmen."

On reading these Brahmanic speculations on the origin of the four *Varnas* and particularly of the Sudras one is very much reminded of these words of Prof. Max Muller. All these speculations are really the twaddles of idiots and ravings of madmen and as such they are of no use to the student of history who is in search of a natural explanation of a human problem.

The Status of the Sudras

So much for the Brahmanic view of the origin of the Sudra. Turning to the Brahmanic view of the civil status of the Sudra, what strikes one is the long list of (disabilities, accompanied by a most dire system of pains and-penalties to which the Sudra is subjected by the Brahmaiac law-givers. The disabilities and penalties of the Sudra found in the Samhitas and the Br*ahmanas* were few, as may be seen from the following extracts:

I. According to the *Kathaka Samhita* (xxxi.2) and the *Maitrayani Samhita* (iv.1.3;i.8.3) "A sudra should not be allowed to milk the cow whose milk is used for Agnihotra."

II. The *Satapatha Brahmana* (iii.1.1.10), the *Maitrayani Samita* (vii.l.l.6) and also the *Panchavirnsa Brahmana* (vi.l.ll) say: "The Sudra must not be spoken to when performing a sacrifice and a Sudra must not be present when a sacrifice is being performed."

III. The *Satapatha Brahmana* (xiv.l.31) and the *Kathaka Samhita* (xi.10) further provide that: "The Sudra must not be admitted to Soma drink."

The *Aitareya Brahmana* (vii.29.4) and the *Panchavirnsa Brahmana* (vi.l.ll) reached the culminating point when they say: "Sudra is a servant of another (and cannot be anything else)."

But what in the beginning was a cloud no bigger than a man's hand, seems to have developed into a storm, which has literally overwhelmed the Sudras. For, as will be seen from the extracts given from later penal legislation by the *Sutrakaras* like *Apastamba, Baudhayana,* etc. and the *Smritikaras* like Manu and others, the growth of the disabilities of the Sudras has been at a maddening speed and to an extent which is quite unthinkable.

The disabilities are so deadening that it would be impossible to believe them unless one sees them in cold print. They are, however, so numerous that it is impossible to present them in their fullness. To enable those, who do not know them, to have some idea of these disabilities, I have assembled below in one place illustrative statements by the different Sutrakaras and

Smritikaras relating to the disabilities of the Sudras scattered in their Law Books.

(A) *The Apastamba Dharmasutra* says: "There *are* four castes—Brahmanas, Kshatriyas, Vaishyas and Sudras amongst these, each preceding (caste) is superior by birth to the *one* following:

For all these, excepting Sudras and those who have committed bad actions are ordained. (1) the initiation (Upanayaaa or the wearing of the sacred thread), (2) the study of the Veda and (3) the kindling of the sacred fire (i.e.,, the right to perform sacrifices)."

(B) This is what the *Vashishtha Dharma Sutra* says: "There are four castes (Varna) Brahmanas, Kshatriyas, Vaishyas and Sudras.

Three castes, Brahmanas, Kshatriyas and Vaishyas (are called) twice-born.

Their first-birth is from the mother; the second from the investiture with the sacred girdle. In that (second birth) the Savitri is the mother, but the teacher is said to be the father.

They call the teacher father, because he gives instruction in the Veda.

The four castes are distinguished by their origin and by particular sacraments.

There is also the following passage of the Veda: ' The Brahmana was his mouth, the Kshatriya formed his arms: the Vaishya his thighs; the Sudra was born from his feet.'

It has been declared in the following passage of the Veda that a Sudra shall not receive the sacraments. 'He created the Brahmana with the Gayatri (metre), the Kshatriya with the Trishtubh, the Vaishya with the Jagati, the Sudra without any metre."

(C) The *Manusmriti* propounds the following view on the subject: "For the prosperity of the worlds, he (the creator) from his mouth, arms, thighs and feet created the Brahmana, Kshatriya, Vaishya and Sudra.

The Brahmans, Kshatriya (and) Vaishya constitute the three twice-born castes, but the fourth, the Sudra has only one birth."

(A) The *Apastamba Dharma Sutra* says: "(A Traivarnika) shall never study (the Veda) in a burial ground nor anywhere near it within the throw of a Sarnya.

If a village has been built over a burial ground or its surface has been cultivated as a field, the recitation of the Veda in such a place is not prohibited.

But if that place is known to have been a burial ground, he shall not study (there).

A Sudra and an outcaste are (included by the term) burial-ground, (and the rule given, Sutra 6 applies to them).

Some declare, that (one ought to avoid only to study) in the same house (where they dwell).

But if (a student and) a Sudra woman merely look at each other, the recitation of the Veda must be interrupted.

Food touched by a (Brahmana or other high-caste person) who is impure, becomes impure but not unfit for eating.

But what has been brought (be it touched or not) by an impure Sudra must not be eaten. A Sudra touches him, (then he shall leave off eating)."

(B) The *Vishnu Smriti* says: "He must not cause a member of a twice born caste to be carried out by a Sudra (even though he be a kinsman of the deceased). Nor a Sudra by a member of a twice-born caste.

A father and a mother shall be carried out by their sons; (who are equal in caste to their parents).

But Sudras must never carry out a member of a twice-born caste, even though he be their father."

(C) The *Vashishtha Dharma Sutra* prescribes: "Now therefore, we will declare what may be eaten and what may not be eaten.

Food given by a physician, a hunter, a woman of bad character, a mace-bearer, a thief, an Abhisasta, and eunuch, (or) an outcaste must not be eaten.

Nor that given by a miser, one who has performed the initiatory ceremony of a Srauta-sacrifice, a prisoner, a sick person, a seller of the Soma plant, a carpenter, a washerman, a dealer in spirituous liquor, a spy, an usurer, (or) a cobbler.

Nor that given by a Sudra.

Some call that Sudra race a burial-ground.

Therefore the Veda must not be recited in the presence of a Sudra."

Now they quote also the (following) verses which Yama proclaimed:

The wicked Sudra-race is manifestly a burial-ground. Therefore (the Veda) must never be recited in the presence of a Sudra.

Some become worthy receptacles of gifts through sacred learning, and some through the practice of austerities. But that Brahmana whose stomach does not contain the food of a Sudra, is even the worthiest receptacle of all.

If a Brahmana dies with the food of a Sudra in his stomach, he will become a village pig (in his next life) or be born in the family of that Sudra.

For though a (Brahmana) whose body is nourished by the essence of a Sudra's food may daily recite the Veda, though he may offer (an Agnihotra) or mutter (prayers, nevertheless) he will not find the path that leads upwards.

But if, after eating the food of a Sudra, he has conjugal intercourse, (even) his sons (begotten on a wife of his own caste) will belong to the giver of the food (*i.e.*, to the Sudra) and he shall not ascend to heaven.

(D) The *Manusmriti* says: "He (Brahmin) may not dwell in the kingdom of a Sudra nor in one full of unrighteous people, nor in one invaded by hosts of heretics nor in one possessed by low-born men.

A Brahmin who performs a sacrifice for a Sudra should not be invited to dine with other Brahmins at a Shraddha ceremony. His company will destroy all merit that which may otherwise be obtained from such a dinner.

One should carry out by the southern town-gate a dead Sudra, but the twice-born by the western, northern and eastern (gates) respectively.

(A) The *Apastamba Dharma Sutra* says: "A Brahmana shall salute stretching forward his right arm on a level with his ear, a Kshatriya holding it on a level with the breast, a

Vaishya holding it on a level with the waist, a Sudra holding it low (and) stretching forward the joined hands.

And when returning the salute of (a man belonging) to the first (three) castes, the last syllable of the name of the person addressed is produced to the length of three moras.

If a Sudra comes as a guest (to a Brahmana) he shall give him some work to do. He may feed him, after (that has been performed. To feed him without asking him first to do some work is to do him honour.)

Or the slaves (of the Brahmana householder) shall fetch (rice) from the royal stores, and honour the Sudra as a guest."

(B) The *Vishnu Smriti* prescribes: "The same punishment (payment of hundred Panas) is also ordained for hospitably entertaining a Sudra or religious ascetic at an oblation to the gods or to the manes.'"

(C) The *Manusmriti* enjoins that: One should consider a Brahmana ten years old and a Kshatriya a hundred years old as father and son; but of them the Brahman (is) the father.

Wealth, kindred, age, sects (and) knowledge as the fifth; those are the causes of respect, the most important (is) the last (mentioned).

In whom among the three (higher) castes the most and the best of (those) five may be he is here worthy of respect; a Sudra (is not worthy of respect on the ground of his wealth or knowledge no matter how high they are. It is only on the ground of his age and that too only if) he has attained the tenth (decade of his life that he becomes worthy of respect and not before.)

For not by years, nor by grey hair, not by wealth, nor kindred (is superiority); the seers made the rule—Who knows the Veda completely, he is great among us.

Of Brahmins, superiority (is) by knowledge, but of Kshatriyas by valour, of Vaishyas by reason of property (and) wealth, and of Sudras by age.

One is not, therefore, aged because his head is grey; whoever, although a youth, has perused (the Vedas), him the gods consider an elder.

Now a Kshatriya is not called a guest in a Brahmin's house, nor a Vaishya nor a Sudra; neither is a friend, the kinsman, nor a Guru (of the householder). (That is, a Brahmin has alone the right to have the honour of being treated as a guest in a Brahmin's house).

But if a Kshatriya come as a guest to the house after the said Brahmins have eaten one should give him food (if) he wishes.

If a Vaishya (or) Sudra come to the house as guests, the Brahmin should give them food but with the servants, using kindness."

(A) According to the *Apastamba Dharma Sutra*:

He who has killed a Kshatriya shall give a thousand cows (to Brahmins for the expiation of the act).

He shall give, a hundred cows for the killing of a Vaishya, (only) ten for a Sudra.

(B) According to the *Gautama Dharma Sutra*: "A Kshatriya (shall be fined) one hundred (Karshapanas) if he abuses a Brahmana.

In case of an assault (on a Brahmana) twice as much.

A Vaishya (who abuses a Brahmana, shall pay) one and a half (times as much as a Kshatriya).

But a Brahmana (who abuses) a Kshatriya (shall pay) fifty (Karshapanas).

One half of that amount (if he abuses) a Vaishya. And if he abuses a Sudra nothing."

(C) According to *Vrihaspati's Dharma Shastra*: "For a Brahmin abusing a Kshatriya, the fine shall be half of a hundred (fifty) Panas; for abusing a Vaishya, half of fifty (twenty-five) Panas, for abusing a Sudra twelve and a half.

This punishment has been declared for abusing a virtuous Sudra (*i.e.*, a Sudra who accepts his low status and does willingly the duties attached to that status) who has committed no wrong; no offence is imputable to a Brahmin for abusing a Sudra devoid of virtue.

A Vaishya shall be fined a hundred (Panas) for reviling a Kshatriya; a Kshatriya reviling a Vaishya shall have to pay half of that amount as a fine.

In the case of a Kshatriya reviling a Sudra the fine shall

be twenty Panas; in the case of a Vaishya, the double amount is declared to be the proper fine by persons learned in law.

A Sudra shall be compelled to pay the first fine for abusing a Vaishya; the middling fine for abusing a Kshatriya; and the highest fine for abusing a Brahmin.

(D) According to the *Manu Smrati:* "A Kshatriya who reviles a Brahmin ought to be fined one hundred (Panas); a Vaishya one hundred and fifty or two hundred, but a Sudra ought to receive corporal punishment.

A Brahmin should be fined fifty if he has thrown insult on a Kshatriya, but the fine shall be a half of fifty if on a Vaishya and twelve if on a Sudra."

In the murder of a Kshatriya, one fourth (part) of the penance for slaying a Brahman is declared to be the proper penance; an eighth part in the case of a Vaishya; and in (the case of) a Sudra (who) lives virtuously, one sixteenth part must be admitted (as the proper penance).

But if one of the highest of the twice-born (a Brahmin) slay a Kshatriya involuntarily he may, in order to cleanse himself give a thousand cows and a bull.

Or let him for three years (with senses) subdued and locks braided, follow the observances of one who has slain a Brahmin, living in a place rather far from the town, his dwelling place the foot of a tree.

The highest of a twice-born (the Brahmin) should practise just this expiation for a year on having slain a Vaishya who lives virtuously and give one hundred and one (heads) of cattle.

The slayer of a Sudra should practise exactly all these observances for six months; or he may give to a priest ten white cows and a bull.

(E) According to the *Vishnu Smriti:* "With whatever limb an inferior insults or hurts his superior in caste, of that limb the king shall cause him to be deprived.

If he places himself on the same seat with his superior, he shall be banished with a mark on his buttocks. If he spits on him he shall lose both lips. If he breaks wind against him, he shall lose his hind parts. If he uses abusive language, his tongue.

If a low-born man through pride give instruction (to a member of the highest caste) concerning his duty, let the king order hot oil to be dropped into his mouth.

If a Sudra man mentions the name or caste of a superior revealingly, an iron pin ten inches long shall be thrust into his mouth (red hot)."

(A) According to the *Vrihaspati Smriti:* "A Sudra teaching the precepts of religion or uttering the words of the Veda, or insulting a Brahmin shall be punished by cutting out his tongue."

(B) According to the *Gautama Dharma Sutra:* "Now if he listens intentionally to (a recitation of) the Veda, his ears shall be filled with (molten) tin or lac.

If he recites (Vedic texts), his tongue shall be cut out.

If he remembers them, his body shall be split in twain."

(C) According to the *Manusmriti:* One who teaches for hire, also one who learns by paying hire (a Sudra) teacher and one who learns from him are unfit for being invited at the performance in honour of the Devas and Pitris.

One may not give advice to a Sudra, nor (give him) the remains (of food) or of butter that has been offered.

And one may not teach him the law or enjoin upon him religious observances.

For he who tells him the law and he who enjoins upon him (religious) observances, he indeed together with that (Sudra) sinks into the darkness of the hell called Asamvrita.

One should never recite (the Vedas) indistinctly or in the presence of a Sudra; nor having recited the Veda at the end of the night, (though) fatigued may one sleep again."

This is what the *Manusmriti* says: "A Brahmin may take possession of the goods of a Sudra with perfect peace of mind, for, since nothing at all belongs to this Sudra as his own, he is one whose property may be taken away by his master.

Indeed, an accumulation of wealth should not be made by a Sudra even if he is able to do so, for the sight of mere possession of wealth by a Sudra injures the Brahmin.'"

Here is the advice of the Manusmriti to the king: "He who can claim to be a Brahmin merely on account of his birth, or he who only calls himself a Brahmin, may be, if desired, the declarer of law for the king, but a Sudra never.

If a king looks on while a Sudra gives a judicial decision, his realm sinks into misfortune, like a cow in a quagmire.

A realm which consists chiefly of Sudras and is overrun by unbelievers and destitute of twice-born men is soon totally destroyed, oppressed by famine and disease."

(A) The *Apastamba Dharma Sutra* says: "And those who perform austerities, being intent on fulfilling the sacred laws. And a Sudra who lives by washing the feet (of the Brahmin).

Also blind, dumb, deaf and diseased persons (as long as their infirmities last) are exempt from taxes.

To serve the other three castes is ordained for the Sudra. The higher the caste which he serves the greater is the merit.

(B) The Manusmriti has the following: "Now, for the sake of preserving all this creation, the most glorious (being) ordained separate duties for those who sprang from (his) mouth, arm, thigh and feet.

For Brahmins he ordered teaching, study, sacrifices and sacrificing (as priests) for others, also giving and receiving gifts.

Defence of the people, giving (alms), sacrifice, also study, and absence of attachment to objects of sense, in short for a Kshatriya. Tending of cattle, giving (alms), sacrifice, study, trade, usury, and also agriculture for a Vaishya.

One duty the Lord assigned to a Sudra—service to those (before-mentioned) classes without grudging."

(A) The Apastamba Dharma Sutra says: "A man of one of the first three castes (who commits adultery) with a woman of the Sudra caste shall be banished.

A Sudra (who commits adultery) with a woman of one of the first three castes shall suffer capital, punishment

(B) The *Gautama Dharma Sutra* says: If (the Sudra) has criminal intercourse with an Aryan woman, his organ shall be cut off and all his property be confiscated.

If (the woman had) a protector (*i.e.*, she was under the guardianship of some person) he (the Sudra) shall be executed after having undergone the punishments prescribed above.

(C) The *Manusmriti* says: If a man (of the Sudra caste) makes love to a girl of the highest caste he deserves corporal punishment.

A Sudra cohabiting with a woman of twice-born castes, whether she be guarded or not guarded, is (to be) deprived of his member and of all his property if she be not guarded and of everything if she is guarded.

For twice-born men, at first, a woman of the same caste is approved for marrying; but of those who act from lust, those of lower caste may in order (be wives).

A Sudra woman alone (is) a wife for a Sudra; both she and a woman of his own caste (are) legally (wives) of a Vaishya; they two and also a woman of his own caste (are wives) of a Kshatriya, both they and a woman of his own caste (are wives) of a Brahmin.

A Sudra wife is not indicated in any history for a Brahmin and Kshatriya, even though they be in distress.

Twice-born men marrying a (Sudra) woman out of infatuation will surely bring quickly (their) families and descendants to the condition of Sudras.

A Brahmin having taken a Sudra woman to his bed goes the lower course; having begotten on her a son, he is surely deprived of his Brahminhood. Now of (a man) whose offerings towards gods, manes, and guests depend on her, the manes and gods eat not that offering nor does he go to heaven.

An expiation is not prescribed for him who has drunk the moisture on a Sudra woman's lips, who has been reached by her breath, and who has also begotten a son on her.

(A) The *Vashishtha Dharma Sutra* says: "One may know that bearing grudges, envy, speaking untruths, speaking evil of Brahmins, backbiting and cruelty are the characteristics of a Sudra."

(B) The Vishnu Smriti prescribes that: (The name to be chosen should be) auspicious in the case of a Brahmin. Indicating power in the case of a Kshatriya. Indicating wealth in the case of a Vaishya. And indicating contempt in the case of a Sudra.

(C) The *Gautama Dharma Sutra* says: "The Sudra belongs to the fourth caste, which has one birth (only).

And serves the higher (castes). From them he shall seek to obtain his livelihood. He shall use their cast-off shoes. And eat the remnants of their food.

A Sudra who intentionally reviles twice-born men by Criminal abuse, or criminally assaults them with blows, shall be deprived of the limb with which he offends.

If he assumes a position equal to that of twice-born men in sitting, in lying down, in conversation or on the road, he shall undergo (corporal punishment)"

(D) The Manusmriti follows suit and says: "But if a Brahmin through avarice, and because he possesses the power, compel twice-born men, who have received the initiation (into the caste order), to do the work of a slave when they do not wish it, he shall be fined six hundred panas by the king.

But a Sudra, whether bought or not bought (by the Brahmin) may be compelled to practise servitude, for that Sudra was created by the self-existent merely for the service of the Brahmin.

Even if freed by his master, the Sudra is not released from servitude; for this (servitude) is innate in him; who then can take it from him.

Just in proportion as one pursues without complaining the mode of life (practised) by the good, so free from blame, he gains both this and the other world.

Now the supreme duty of a Sudra and that which ensures his bliss is merely obedience toward celebrated priests who understand the Veda and live as householders.

If he be pure, obedient to the higher (castes), mild in speech, without conceit, and always submissive to the Brahmin, he attains (in the next transmigration) a high birth.

Now a Sudra desiring some means of subsistence may serve a Kshatriya, so (is the rule); or the Sudra (if) anxious to support life, (may do so by) serving a wealthy Vaishya.

But he should serve the Brahmins for the sake of heaven, or for the sake of both (heaven and livelihood); for by him (for whom) the word Brahmin (is always) uttered is thus attained the state of completing all he ought to do.

Merely to serve the Brahmins is declared to be the most excellent occupation of a Sudra; for if he does anything other than this it profits him nothing. His means of life should be arranged by those Brahmins out of their own household (goods) in accordance with what is fitting after examining his ability, cleverness, and (the amount) the dependants embrace.

The leaving of food should be given (to him) and the old clothes, so too the blighted part of the grain, so too the old furniture.

Let a Brahmin's name be auspicious, a Kshatriya's full of power, let a Vaishya's mean wealth, a Sudra's however be contemptible.

Let a Brahmin's (distinctive title) imply prosperity, a Kshatriya's safeguard, a Vaishya's wealth, a Sudra's service.

If (a man) of one birth assault one of the twice-born castes with virulent words, he ought to have his tongue cut, for he is of the lowest origin.

If he makes mention in an insulting manner of their name and caste, a red-hot iron rod, ten fingers long, should be thrust into his mouth.

If this man through insolence gives instruction to the priests in regard to their duty, the king should cause boiling hot oil to be poured into his mouth and ear.

If a man of the lowest birth should with any member injure one of the highest station, even that member of this man shall be cut (off); this is an ordinance of Manu.

If he lift up his hand or his staff (against him), he ought to have his hand cut off; and if he smites him with his feet in anger, he ought to have his feet cut off.

If a low-born man endeavours to sit down by the side of a high-born man, he should be banished after being branded on the hip, or (the king) may cause his backside to be cut off.

If through insolence he spit upon him, the king should cause his two lips to be cut off; and if he makes water upon him, his penis, and if he breaks wind upon him, his anus.

If he seize him by the locks, let the king without hesitation cause both his hands to be cut off, (also if he seize him) by the feet, the beard, the neck or the testicles.

A man who tears (another's) skin and one who causes blood to be seen ought to be fined five hundred (Panas), if he tears the flesh (he should be fined) six niskas, but if he breaks a bone he should be banished.

(D) The *Narada Smriti* says: Men of the Sudra caste, who prefer a false accusation against a member of a twice-born Aryan caste, shall have their tongue split by the officers of the king, and he shall cause them to be put on stakes.

A once-born man (or Sudra) who insults members of a twice-born caste with gross invectives, shall have his tongue cut off; for he is of low origin.

If he refers to their name or caste in terms indicating contempt, an iron-rod, ten angulas long, shall be thrust red-hot into his mouth. If he is insolent enough to give lessons regarding their duty to Brahmins, the king shall order hot oil to be poured into his mouth and ears.

With whatever limb a man of low caste offends against a Brahmin, that very limb of him shall be cut off, such shall be the atonement for his crime.

A low-born man, who tries to place himself on the same seat with his superior in caste, shall be branded on his hip and banished, or (the king) shall cause his backside to be gashed.

If through arrogance he spits on a superior, the king shall cause both his lips to be cut off; if he makes water on him, the penis; if he breaks wind against him, the buttocks."

Such were the laws made against the Sudras by the Brahmanic lawgivers. The gist of them may be summarised under the following heads:

(1) That the Sudra was to take the last place in the social order.

(2) That the Sudra was impure and therefore no sacred act should be done within his sight and within his hearing.

(3) That the Sudra is not to be respected in the same way as the other classes.

(4) That the life of a Sudra is of no value and anybody may kill him without having to pay compensation and if at all of small value as compared with that of the Brahmana, Kshatriya and Vaishya.

(5) That the Sudra must not acquire knowledge and it is a sin and a crime to give him education.

(6) That a Sudra must not acquire property. A Brahmin can take his property at his pleasure.

(7) That a Sudra cannot hold office under the State.

(8) That the duty and salvation of the Sudra lies in his serving the higher classes.

(9) That the higher Classes must not intermarry with the Sudra. They can however keep a Sudra woman as a concubine But if the Sudra touches a woman of the higher classes he will be liable to dire punishment.

(10) That the Sudra is born in servility and must be kept in servility for ever.

Anyone who reads this summary will be struck by two considerations. He will be struck by the consideration that Sudra alone has been selected by the Brahmanic law-givers as a victim for their law-making authority. The wonder must be all the greater when it is recalled that in the ancient Brahmanic literature the oppressed class in the ancient Indo-Aryan society was the Vaishya and not the Sudra. In this connection a reference may be made to the *Aitareya Brahmana*. The *Aitareya Brahmana* in telling the story of King Vishvantara and the Shyapama Brahmanas refers to the sacrificial drink to which the different classes are entitled. In the course of the story, it speaks of the Vaishya in the following terms:

> *"Next, if (the priest brings) curds, that is the Vaishya's draught with it thou shall satisfy the Vaishyas. One like a Vaishya shall be born in thy line, one who is tributary to another, who is to be used-(lit eaten) by another, and who may be oppressed at will.*

The question is: why was the Vaishya let off and why the fury directed towards the Sudras?

He will also be struck by the close connection of the disabilities of the Sudra with the privileges of the Brahmin. The Sudra is below the Traivarnikas and is contrasted with the Traivarnikas. That being so, one would expect all the Traivarnikas to have the same rights against the Sudras. But what are the facts? The facts are that the Kshatriyas and Vaishyas have no rights worth speaking of against the Sudras. The only Traivarnika who has special rights and privileges is the Brahmin. For instance, if the Sudra is guilty of an offence against the Brahmin, the Brahmin has the privilege of demanding a higher punishment than what a Kshatriya or a Vaishya could. A Brahmin could take the property of the Sudra without being guilty of an offence if he needed it for the purpose of performing a sacrifice. A Sudra should not accumulate property because he thereby hurts the Brahmin. A Brahmin should not live in a country where the king is a Sudra. Why is this so? Had the Brahmin any cause to regard the Sudra as his special enemy?.

There is one other consideration more important than these. It is, what does the average Brahmin think of these disabilities of the Sudras? That they are extraordinary in their conception and shameful in their nature will be admitted by all. Will the Brahmin admit it? It would not be unnatural if this catalogue of disabilities may not make any impression upon him. In the first place, by long habit and usage his moral sense has become so dulled that he has ceased to bother about the how and why of these disabilities of the Sudras. In the second place, those of them who are conscious of them feel that similar disabilities have been imposed on particular classes in other countries and there is therefore nothing extraordinary nor shameful in the disabilities of the Sudras. It is the second attitude that needs to be exposed.

This attitude is a very facile one and is cherished because it helps to save reputation and slave conscience. It is, however, no use leaving things as they are. It is absolutely essential to show that these disabilities have no parallel anywhere in the world. It is impossible to compare the Brahmanic. Law with every other legal system on the point of rights and disabilities. A comparison of the Brahmanic Law with the Roman Law ought to suffice.

It will be well to begin this comparison by noting the classes which under the Roman Law had rights and those which suffered from disabilities. The Roman jurists divided men into five categories: (1) Patricians and Plebians; (2) Freemen and Slaves; (3) Citizens and Foreigners; (4) Persons who were *sui juris* and persons who were *alieni juris* and (5) Chirstians and Pagans.

Under the Roman Law; persons who were privileged were: (1) Patricians; (2) Freeman; (3) Citizens; (4) *Sui juris* and

(5) Christians. As compared to these, persons who suffered disabilities under the Roman Law were: (1) the Plebians; (2) Slaves; (3) Foreigners; (4) Persons who were *alieni juris* and (5) Pagans.

A Freeman, who was a citizen under the Roman Law, possessed civil rights as well as political rights. The civil rights of a citizen comprised rights of *connubium* and *commercium.* In virtue of the *connubium,* the citizen could contract a valid marriage according to *the jus civile,* and acquire the rights resulting from it, and particularly the paternal power and the civil relationship called agnation, which was absolutely necessary to enable him in law to succeed to the property of persons who died intestate. In virtue of the *commercium* he could acquire and dispose of property of all kinds, according to the forms and with the peculiar privileges of the Roman Law. The political rights of the Roman citizen included *jus suffragii* and *jus honorum,* the right to vote in public elections and the right to hold office.

The slave differed from the Freeman in as much as he was owned by the master and as such had no capacity to acquire rights. Foreigners, who were called *Peregrine,* were not citizens and had none of the political or civil rights which went with citizenship. A Foreigner could obtain no protection unless he was under the protection of a citizen.

The *alieni juris* differed from *sui juris* in as much as the former were subject to the authority of another person, while the latter were free from it. This authority was variously called (1) *Potestas,* (2) *Manus* and (3) *Mancipium,* though they had the same effect. *Potestas* under the Roman Law fell into two classes. Persons subject to *Potestas* were (1) slaves, (2) children, (3) wife in *Manus,* (4) debtor assigned to the creditor by the Court and (5) a hired gladiator. *Potestas* gave to one in whom it was vested rights to exclusive possession of those to whom it extended and to vindicate any wrong done to them by anyone else. The correlative disabilities which persons *alieni juris* suffered as a result of being subject to *Potestas* were: (1) they were not free, (2) they could not acquire property and (3) they could not directly vindicate any wrong or injury done to them.

The disabilities of the Pagans began with the advent of Christianity. Originally, when all the Romans followed the same Pagan worship, religion could occasion no difference in the enjoyment of civil rights. Under the Christian Emperors, heretics and apostates as well as Pagans and Jews, were subjected to vexatious restrictions, particularly as regards their capacity to succeed to property and to act as witnesses. Only orthodox Christians who recognised the decisions of the four oecumenical councils had the full enjoyment of civil rights.

This survey of rights and disabilities of the Roman Law may well give comfort to Hindus that the Brahmanic Law was not the only law which was guilty of putting certain classes under disabilities, although the disabilities imposed by the Roman Law have nothing of the cruelty which characterises the disabilities imposed by the Brahmanic Law. But when one compares the principles of the Roman Law with those of the Brahmanic Law underlying these disabilities, the baseness of the Brahmanic Law becomes apparent.

Let us first ask: What was the basis of rights and disabilities under the Roman Law. Even a superficial student of Roman Law knows that they were based upon (1) *Caput* and (2) *Existimatio.*

Caput meant the civil status of a person. Civil status among the Romans had reference chiefly to three things; liberty, citizenship and family. The status *libertatis* consisted of being a freeman and not a slave. If a freeman was also a Roman citizen, he enjoyed the *status civitatis.* Upon this quality depended not only the enjoyment of political rights, but the capacity of participating in the *jus civile.* Finally, the *status familice* consisted in a citizen belonging to a particular family, and being capable of enjoying certain rights in which the members of that family, in their quality of a gnates, could alone take part.

If an existing status came to be lost or changed, the person suffered what was called a *capitis diminutio,* which extinguished either entirely or to some extent his former legal capacity. There were three changes of state or condition attended with different consequences, called *maxima, media,* and *minima.* The greatest involves the loss of liberty, citizenship, and family; and this happened when a Roman citizen was taken prisoner in war, or condemned to slavery for his crimes. But a citizen who was captured by the enemy, on returning from captivity, was restored to all his civil rights *jure postliminii.* The next change of status consisted of the loss of citizenship and family rights, without any forfeiture of personal liberty; and this occurred when a citizen became a member of another state. He was then forbidden the use of fire and water, so as to be forced to quit the Roman territory, or was sentenced to deportation under the empire.

Finally, when a person ceased to belong to a particular family, without losing his liberty or citizenship, he was said to suffer the least change of state, as for instance, where one *sui juris* came under the power of another by arrogation, or a son who had been under the *patria potestas* was legally emancipated by his father.

Citizenship was acquired first by birth. In a lawful marriage the child followed the condition of the father, and became a citizen, if the father was so at the time of conception. If the child was not the issue *of justoe nuptioe,* it followed the condition of the mother at the time of its birth. Secondly, by manumission, according to the formalities prescribed by law, the slave of a Roman citizen became a citizen. This rule was modified by the laws. Aelia Sentia and Junia Norbana, according to which, in certain cases, the freedman acquired only the status of a foreigner, *peregrinus dedititius* or of a Latin, *Latinus Junianus,* Justinian restored the ancient principle, according to which every slave, regularly enfranchised, became in full right a Roman citizen. Thirdly, the right of citizenship was often granted as a favour, either to a whole community or to an individual, by the people or the senate during the republic, and by the reigning prince during the empire; and this was equivalent to what the moderns call naturalisation.

Citizenship was lost—Firstly, by the loss of liberty—as, for instance, when a Roman became a prisoner of war, secondly, by renouncing the character of Roman citizen, which took place when anyone was admitted a citizen of another state; thirdly, by a sentence of deportation or exile, as a punishment for crime.

The civil status of a person under the Roman Law may or may not be *civis optino jure. Civis optima jure* included not only capacity for civil rights but also capacity for political rights such as *jus suffragii et honorwn, i.e.*, the right to vote and the capacity to hold a public office. Capacity for political rights depended upon *existimatio. Existimatio* means reputation in the eye of the law. A Roman citizen may have *caput* as well as *existimatio.* On the other hand, a Roman may have *caput* but may not have *existimatio.* Whoever had *caput* as well as *existimatio* had civil rights as well as political rights. Whoever had *caput* but had no *existimatio* could claim civil rights only. He could not claim political rights.

A person's *existimatio* was lost in two ways. It was lost by loss of freedom or by conviction for an offence. If a person lost his freedom his *existimatio* was completely extinguished. Loss of *existimatio* by conviction for offence varied according to the gravity of the offence. If the offence was serious the diminution of his *existimatio* was called *infamia.* If the offence was less grave it was called *turpitudo, Infamia* resulted in the existinguishment of *existimatio.* Under the Roman Law a defendant, in addition to ordinary damages, was subjected to *infamia.* Condemnation for theft, robbery, *injuria* or fraud, entailed infamy. So a partner, a *mandatarius,* a *depositarins, tutor,* a mortgagee (in *contractus fidudoe)* if condemned for wilful breach of duty, was held to be infamous.

The consequence of *infamia* was exclusion from political rights, not merely from office (honours), but even from the right to vote in elections *(suffragium).*

From this brief survey of the basis of rights and disabilities in Roman Law, it will be clear that the basis was the same for all. They did not differ from community to community. Rights and disabilities according to Roman Law were regulated by general considerations, such as *caput* and *existimatio.* Whoever had *caput* and *existimatio* had rights. Whoever lost his *caput* and his *existimatio* suffered disabilities. What is the position under the Brahmanic Law? There again, it is quite clear that rights and disabilities were not based on general uniform considerations. They were based on communal considerations. All rights for the first three *Varnas* and all disabilities for the Sudras was the principle on which the Brahmanic Law was based.

The protagonists of Brahmanic Laws may urge that this comparison is too favourable to Roman Law and that the statement that Roman Law did not distribute rights and liabilities on communal basis is not true. This may be conceded. For so far as the relation between the Patricians and Plebians was concerned the distribution of rights and liabilities was communal. But in this connection the following facts must be noted.

In the first place, it must be noted that Plebians were not slaves. They were freemen in as much as they enjoyed jus *commercii* or the right to acquire, hold and transfer property. Their disabilities consisted in the denial of political and social rights. In the second place, it must be noted that their disabilities were not permanent. There were two social disabilities from which they suffered. One arose from the interdict on intermarriage between them and the Patricians imposed by the Twelve Tables. This disability was removed in B.C. 445 by the passing of the Canulenian Law which legalized intermarriage between Particians and Plebians. The other disability was their ineligibility to hold the office of Pontiffs and Augurs in the Public Temples of Rome. This disability was removed by the Ogulnian Law passed in B.C. 300.

As to the political disabilities of the Plebians they had secured the right to vote in popular assemblies *(jus suffragii)* under the Constitution of Servius Tullius the Sixth King of Rome. The political disabilities which had remained unredressed were those which related to the holding of office. This too was removed in course of time after the Republic was established in B.C. 509. The first step taken in this direction was the appointment of Plebian Tribunes in B.C. 494; the Questorship was opened to them, formally in B.C. 421; actually in B.C. 409; the Consulship in B.C. 367; the curule-aedileship in B.C. 366; the dictatorship in B.C. 356; the Censorship in B.C 351; and the Praetorshipin B.C. 336. The Hortensian Law enacted in B.C. 287 marked a complete triumph for the Plebians. By that laws the resolutions of the Assembly of the tribes were to be directly and without modification, control or delay, binding upon the whole of the Roman people.

This marks a complete political fusion of Patricians and Plebians on terms of equality.

Not only were the Plebians placed on the same footing as to political capacity and social status with the Patricians but the road to nobility was also thrown open to them. In Roman society, birth and fortune were the two great sources of rank and personal distinction. But in addition to this, the office of Curule Magistracy was also a source of ennoblement to the holder thereof. Every citizen, whether Patrician or Plebian, who won his way to a Curule Magistracy, from that Aedile upwards, acquired personal distinction, which was transmitted to his descendants, who formed a class called *Nobiles,* or men known, to distinguish them from the *ignobiles,* or people who were not known. As the office was thrown open to the Plebians, many Plebians had become nobles and had even surpassed the Patricians in point of nobility.

It may be that the Roman Law did recognise communal distinction in distributing rights and disabilities. The point is that the disabilities of the Plebians were not regarded as permanent. Although they existed they were in course of time removed. That being so, the protagonists of Brahmanic Law cannot merely take solace in having found a parallel in the Roman Law but have to answer why the Brahmanic Law did not abolish the distinction between the Traivarnikas and the Sudras as the Roman Law did by equating the Plebians with the Patricians? One can therefore contend that the Roman Law of rights and disabilities was not communal while the Brahmanic Law was.

This is not the only difference between the Roman Law and the Brahmanic Law. There are two others. One is equality before law in criminal matters. The Roman Law may not have recognised equality in matters of civil and political rights. But in matters of criminal law it made no distinction between one citizen and another, not even between Patrician and Plebian. The same offence the same punishment, no matter who the complainant and who the accused was. Once an offence was proved, the punishment was the same. What do the *Dharmasutras* and the *Smritis* do? They follow an entirely different principle. For the same offence the punishment varies according to the community of the accused and the community of the complainant. If the complainant is a Sudra and the accused belonged to any one of the three classes the punishment is less than what it would be if the relations were reversed. On the other hand, if the complainant was Traivarnika and the accused a Sudra, the punishment is far heavier than in the first case. This is another barbarity which distinguishes the Brahmanic Law from the Roman Law.

The next feature of the Roman Law which distinguishes it from the Brahmanic Law is most noteworthy. It relates to the extinction of disabilities. Two points need be borne in mind. First is that the disabilities under the Roman Law were only contingent. So long as certain conditions lasted, they gave rise to certain disabilities. The moment the conditions changed, the disabilities vanished and a step in the direction of equality before law was taken. The second point i is that the Roman Law never attempted to fix the conditions for ever and thereby perpetuate the disabilities. On the other hand, it was always ready to remove the conditions to which these disabilities were attached as is evident in the case of the Plebians, the Slaves, the Foreigners and the Pagans.

If these two points about the disabilities under the Roman Law are borne in mind, one can at once see what mischief the *Dharmasutras* and the *Smritis* have done in imposing the disabilities upon the Sudras. The imposition of disabilities would not have been so atrocious if the disabilities were dependent upon conditions and if the disabled had the freedom to outgrow those conditions. But what the Brahmanic Law does is not merely to impose disabilities but it tries to fix the conditions by making an act which amounts to a breach of those conditions to be a crime involving dire punishment. Thus, the Brahmanic Law not only seeks to impose disabilities but it endeavours to make them permanent. One illustration will suffice. A Sudra is not entitled to perform Vedic sacrifices as he is not able to repeat the Vedic *Mantras*. Nobody would quarrel with such a disability. But the Dharmasutras do not stop here. They go further and say that it will be a crime for a Sudra to study the Vedas or hear it being pronounced and if he does commit such a crime his tongue should be cut or molten lead should be poured into his ear. Can anything be more barbarous than preventing a man to grow out of his disability? What is the explanation of these disabilities? Why did the Brahmanic Law-givers take such a cruel attitude towards the Sudras?

The Brahmanic Law books merely state the disabilities. They say that the Sudras have no right to *Upanayana*. They say that the Sudras shall hold no office. They say that the Sudras shall not have property. But they do not say why. The whole thing is arbitrary. The disabilities of the Sudra have no relation to his personal conduct. It is not the result of infamy. The Sudra is punished just because he was a Sudra. This is a mystery which requires to be solved. As the Brahmanic Law books do not help us to solve it, it is necessary to look for explanation elsewhere.

Sudras versus Aryans

From what has been said before, it is clear that the Brahmanic writers do not give us any clue as to who the Sudras were and how they came to be the fourth *Varna*. It is, therefore, necessary to turn to the Western writers and to see what they have to say about the subject. The Western writers have a definite theory about the origin of the Sudras. Though all of them are not agreed upon every aspect of the theory, there are points on which there seems to be a certain amount of unity among them. They comprise the following:

1. The people who created the Vedic literature belonged to the Aryan race.
2. This Aryan race came from outside India and invaded India.
3. The natives of India were known as Dasas and Dasyus who were racially different from the Aryans.
4. The Aryans were a white race. The Dasas and Dasyus were a dark race.
5. The Aryans conquered the Dasas and Dasyus.
6. The Dasas and Dasyus after they were conquered and enslaved were called Sudras.
7. The Aryans cherished colour prejudice and therefore formed the *Chaturvarnya* whereby they separated the white race from the black race such as the Dasas and the Dasyus.

These are the principal elements in the Western theory about the origin and position of the Sudras in the Indo-Aryan society. Whether it is valid or not is another matter. But this much must certainly be said about it that after reading the Brahmanic theories with their long and tedious explanations attempting to treat a social fact as a divine dispensation, one cannot but feel a certain amount of relief in having before oneself a theory, which proceeds to give a natural explanation of a social fact. One can do nothing with the Brahmanic theories except to call them senseless ebullitions of a silly mind. They leave the problem as it is. With the modem theory, one is at least on the road to recover one's way.

To test the validity of the theory, the best thing to do is to examine it piece by piece and see how far each is supported by evidence.

The foundation on which the whole fabric of the theory rests is the proposition that there lived a people who were Aryan by race. It is in the fitness of things therefore to grapple with this question first. What is this Aryan race? Before we consider the question of Aryan race we must be sure as to what we mean by the word "race". It is necessary to raise this question because it is not impossible to mistake a people for a race. The best illustration of such a mistake is the Jews. Most people believe that the Jews are a race. To the naked eye, they appear to be so. But what is the verdict of the experts? This is what Prof. Ripley has to say about the Jews: "Our final conclusion, then, is this: This is paradoxical yet true, we affirm. The Jews are not a race, but only a people after all. In their faces we read its confirmation; while in respect of their other traits, we are convinced that such individuality as they possess—by no means inconsiderable—is of their own making from one generation to the next, rather than a product of an unprecedented purity of physical descent."

What is a race? A race may be defined as a body of people possessing certain typical, traits which are hereditary. There was a time when it was believed that the traits which constitute a race are: (1) the form of the head, (2) the colour of the hair and eyes, (3) the colour of the skin, and (4) the stature. Today the general view is that pigmentation and stature are traits, which vary according to climate and habitat, and consequently they must be ruled out as tests for determining the race of the people. The only stable trait is the shape of the human head—by which is meant the general proportions of length, breadth and height and that is why anthropologists and ethnologists regard it as the best available test of race.

The use of head-forms for determining the race to which an individual belongs has been developed by anthropologists into an exact science. It is called anthropometry. This science of anthropometry has devised two ways of measuring the headform: (1) cephalic index, and (2) facial index. The index is the mark of the race.

Cephalic index is the breadth of the head above the ears expressed in percentage of its length from forehead to back. Assuming that this length is 100, the width is expressed as a fraction of it. As the head becomes proportionately broader—that is more fully rounded, viewed from the top down—this cephalic index increases. When it rises above 80, the head is called brachycephalic. When it falls below 75, the term dolichocephalic is applied to it. Indexes between 75 and 80 are characterised as mesocephalic. These are technical terms. They constantly crop up in literature dealing with questions of race and if one does not know what they denote it obviously becomes very difficult to follow the discussion intelligently. It would not therefore be without advantage if I were to stop to give their popular equivalents. The popular equivalent of mesocephalic is medium-headed, having a medium cephalic Index, the breadth of the cranium being between three-fourths and four-fifths of the length. Dolichocephalic means long-headed, having a low cephalic index, the breadth of the cranium being below four-fifths of the length.

Facial index is the correlation between the proportions of the head and the form of the face. In the majority of cases, it has been found that a relatively broad head is accompanied by a rounded face, in which the breadth back of the cheek bones is considerable as compared with the height from forehead to chin. Lack of uniformity in the mode of taking measurements has so far prevented extended observations fit for exact comparison. All the same, it has been found safe to adopt the rule, long head, oval face: short-head and round face.

Applying these measures of anthropometry, Prof. Ripley, an authority on the question of race, has come to the conclusion that the European people belong to three different races in terms of cephalic and facial index. His conclusions are summarised in the table on the next page. Is there an Aryan race in the physical sense of the term? There seem to be two views on the subject. One view is in favour of the existence of the Aryan race. According to it:

The Aryan type.. is marked by a relatively long (dolichocephalic) head; a straight finely-cut (leptorrhine) nose; a long symmetrically narrow face; well developed regular features and a high facial angle. The stature is fairly high—and the general build of the figure well-proportioned and slender rather than massive.

European Racial Types

	Head	*Face*	*Hair*	*Eyes*	** Stature*	*Nose*
1. Teutonic	Long	Long	Very	Blue	Tall	Narrow
			light			acquiline
2. Alpine (Celtic)	Round	Broad	Light	Hazel	Medium	Variable:
			Chestnut	Grey	stocky	rather
						broad
						heavy
3. Mediterranean	Long	Long	Dark	Dark	Medium	Rather
			brown		slender	broad
			or black			

The other view is that of Prof. Max Muller. According to him, the word is used in three different senses. This is what he, in his lectures on the *Science of Language,* says:

In *ar* or *ara,* I recognise one of the oldest names of the earth, as the ploughed land, lost in Sanskrit but preserved in Greek as (era) so that Arya would have conveyed originally the meaning of landholder, cultivator of the land, while Vaishya from Vis meant householder, *Ida* the daughter of Manu is another name of the cultivated earth and probably a modification of *Ara.*

The second sense in which it was used was to convey the idea of ploughing or tilling the soil. As to this. Prof. Max Muller makes the following observations.

I can only state that the etymological signification of Arya seems to be: One who ploughs or tills. The Aryans would seem to have chosen this name for themselves as opposed to the nomadic races, the *Turanians,* whose original name *Tura* implies the swiftness of the horsemen. In the third sense, the word was used as a general name for the Vaishyas, *i.e.*, the general body of the people, who formed the whole mass of the people. For this, Prof. Max Muller relies on Panini (iii.1,103) for his authority. Then, there is the fourth sense, which the word got only towards the later period, in which sense it means 'of noble origin'.

What is however of particular importance is the opinion of Prof. Max Muller on the question of the Aryan race. This is what he says on the subject: There is no Aryan race in blood; Aryan, in scientific language is utterly inapplicable to race. It means language and nothing but language; and if we speak of Aryan race at all, we should know that it means no more than... Aryan speech.

I have declared again and again that if I say Aryas, I mean neither blood nor bones, nor hair nor skull; I mean simply those who speak an Aryan language. The same applies to Hindus, Greeks, Romans, Germans, Celts, and Slavs. When I speak of them I commit myself to no anatomical characteristics. The blue-eyed and fair-haired Scandinavians may have been conquerors or conquered, they may have adopted the language of their darker lords or their subjects, or *vice versa*. I assert nothing beyond their language, when I call them Hindus, Greeks, Romans, Germans, Celts and Slavs; and in that sense, and in that sense only, do I say that even the blackest Hindus represent an earlier stage of Aryan speech and thought than the fairest Scandinavians. This may seem strong language, but in matters of such importance we cannot be too decided in our language. To me, an ethnologist who speaks of Aryan race, Aryan blood, Aryan eyes and hair, is as great a sinner as linguist who speaks of a dolichocephalic dictionary or a brachycephalic grammar. It is worse than a Babylonian confusion of tongues— it is downright theft. We have made our own terminology for the classification of language; let ethnologists make their own for the classification of skulls, and hair and blood.

The value of this view of Prof. Max Muller will be appreciated by those who know that he was at one time a believer in the theory of Aryan race and was largely responsible for the propagation of it.

The two views are obviously not in harmony. According to one view, the Aryan race existed in a physiological sense with typical hereditary traits with a fixed cephalic and facial index. According to Prof. Max Muller, the Aryan race existed in a philological sense, as a people speaking a common language.

In this conflict of views one may well ask: what is the testimony of the Vedic literature? As examination of the Vedic literature shows that there occur two words in the Rig Veda—one is Arya with a short 'a' and the other is Arya with a long 'a'. The word Arya with a short 'a' is used in the Rig Veda in 88 places. In what sense is it used? The word is used in four different senses; as (1) enemy, (2) respectable person, (3) name for India, and (4) owner, Vaishya or citizen.

The word Arya with a long 'a' is used in the Rig Veda in 31 places. But in none of these is the word used in the sense of race.

From the foregoing discussion, the one indisputable conclusion which follows is that the terms 'Arya' and 'Arya' which occur in the Vedas have not been used in the racial sense at all.

One may also ask: what is the evidence of anthropometry? The Aryan race is described as long-headed. This description is not enough. For as will be seen from the table given by Prof. Ripley, there are two races which are long-headed. The question which of the two is the Aryan race still remains open.

Let us take the next premise—namely, that the Aryans came from outside India, invaded India, and conquered the native tribes. It would be better to take these questions separately.

From where did the Aryan race come into India? On the question of locating the original home of the Aryan race, there is a bewildering variety of views and options. According to Benfey, the original home of the Aryan race must be determined by reference to the common vocabulary. His views on the subject have been well summarised by Prof. Isaac Taylor in the following words: The investigation of the vocabulary common to the whole of the Aryan languages might yield a clue to the region inhabited by the Aryans before the linguistic separation. He contended that certain animals, such as the bear and the wolf, and certain trees, such as the beech and the birch with which the primitive Aryans must have been acquainted, are all indigenous to the temperate zone, and above all, to Europe, whereas the characteristic animals and trees of Southern Asia, such as the lion, the tiger and the palm were known only to the Indians and the Iranians. He urged that the absence from the primitive Aryan vocabulary of common names for the two great Asiatic beasts of prey, the lion and the tiger, or for the chief Asiatic beast of transport, the camel, is difficult to explain on the theory of the migration of the Aryans from the region eastward of the Caspian. That the Greeks called the lion by its Semitic name, and the Indians by a name which cannot be referred to any Aryan root, argues that the lion was unknown in the common home of Greeks and Indians.

Benfey's declaration speedily bore fruit, and Geiger forthwith ranged himself in the same camp, but placing the cradle of the Aryans, not as Benfey had done in the region to the North of the Black Sea, but more to the northwest, in Central and Western Germany. Geiger's contribution to the argument was not without its value. He bases his conclusions largely on the tree names which belong to the primitive Aryan vocabulary. In addition to the fir, the willow, the ash, the alder, and the hazel, he thinks the names of the birch, the beech and the oak are specially decisive. Since the Greek (phegos) which denotes the oak is the linguistic equivalent of the Teutonic *beech* and of the Latin *fague* he draws, the conclusion that the Greeks migrated from a land of beeches to a land of oaks, transferring the name which denoted the tree with 'edible' fruit from the one tree to the other.

Another school holds that the original home of the Aryan race was in Caucasia, because the Caucasians like the Aryans are blonds, have a straight, a sharp nose and a handsome face. On this point, the view of Prof. Ripley is worth quoting. This is what Prof. Ripley has to say on the subject:

The utter absurdity of the misnomer Caucasian, as applied to the blue-eyed and fair-headed 'Aryan' (?) race of Western Europe, is revealed by two indisputable facts. In the first place, this ideal blond type does not occur within many hundred miles of Caucasia; and, secondly, nowhere along the great Caucasian chain is there a single native tribe making use of a purely inflectional or Aryan language.

Even the Ossetes, whose language alone is possibly inflectional, have not had their claims to the honour of Aryan made positively clear as yet. And even if Ossetian be Aryan, there is every reason to regard the people as immigrants from the direction of Iran, not indigenous Caucasians at all. Their head form, together with their occupation of territory along the only highway—the Pass of Darriel—across the chain from the South, give tenability to the hypothesis. At all events, whether the Ossetes be Aryan or not, they little deserve pre-eminence among the other peoples about them. They are lacking both in the physical beauty for which this region is justly famous, and in courage as well, if we may judge by their reputation in yielding abjectly and without shadow of resistance to the Russians.

It is not true that any of these Caucasians are even 'somewhat typical'. As a matter of fact they could never be typical of anything. The name covers nearly every physical type and family of language of the Eur-Asian continent except, as we have said, that blond, tall, 'Aryan' speaking one to which the name has been specifically applied. It is all false; not only improbable but absurd. The Caucasus is not a cradle—it is rather a grave—of peoples, of languages, of customs and of physical types. Let us be assured of that point at the outset. Nowhere else in the world probably is so heterogeneous a lot of people, languages and religions gathered together in one place as along the chain of the Caucasus mountains."

Mr. Tilak has suggested that the original home of the Aryan race was in the Arctic region. His theory may be summarised in his own words. He begins by taking note of the astronomical and climatic phenomenon in the region round about the North Pole. He finds that there are: "Two sets of characteristics, or *differentice;* one for an observer stationed exactly at the terrestrial North Pole, and the other for an observer located in the Circum-Polar regions, or tracts of land between the North Pole and the Arctic circle."

Mr. Tilak calls these two sets of *differentice;* as Polar and Circum-Polar, and sums them up as follows:

The Polar Characteristics

(1) The sun rises in the south.

(2) The stars do not rise and set; but *revolve* or spin round and round, in horizontal planes, completing one round in 24 hours. The northern celestial hemisphere is alone overhead and visible during the whole year; and the southern or lower celestial world is always invisible.

(3) The year consists only of one long day and one long night of six months each.

(4) There is only one morning and one evening, or the sun rises and sets only once a year. But the *twilight,* whether of the morning or of the evening, lasts continuously for about *two months,* or 60 periods of 24 hours each. The ruddy light of the morn, or the evening twilight, is not again confined to a particular part of the horizon (eastern or western) as with us; but moves, like the stars at the place, round and round along the horizon, like a potter's wheel, completing one round in every 24 hours. These rounds of the morning light continue to take place, until the orb of the sun comes above the horizon; and then the sun follows the same course for six months, that is, moves, without setting, round and round the observer, completing one round every 24 hours.

The Circum-Polar Characteristics

(1) The sun will always be to the south of the zenith of the observer, but as this happens even in the case of an observer stationed in the temperate zone, it cannot be regarded as a special characteristic.

(2) A large number of stars are *circum-polor,* that is, they are above the horizon during the entire period of their revolution and hence always visible. The remaining stars rise and set as in the temperate zone, but revolve in more oblique circles.

(3) The year is made up of three parts: (i) one long continuous night, occurring at the time of the winter solstice, and lasting for a period, greater than 24 hours and less than six months, according to the latitude of the place; (ii) one long continuous day to match, occurring at the time of the summer solstice; and (iii) a succession of ordinary days and nights during the rest of the year, a nycthemeron, or a day and a night together, never exceeding a period of 24 hours. The day, after the long continuous night, is at first shorter than the night, but goes on increasing until it develops into the long continuous day. At the end of the long day, the night is, at first, shorter than the day, but, in its

turn, it begins to gain over the day, until the commencement of the long continuous night, with which the year ends.

(4) The dawn, at the close of the long continuous night, lasts for several days, but its duration and magnificence is proportionally less than at the North Pole, according to the latitude of the place. For places, within a few degrees of the North Pole, the phenomenon of revolving morning light will still be observable during the greater part of the duration of the dawn. The other dawns *viz.*, those between ordinary days and nights, will, like the dawns in the temperate zone, only last for a few hours. The sun, when he is above the horizon during the continuous day, will be seen revolving, without setting, round the observer, as at the Pole, but in oblique and not horizontal circles, and during the long night he will be entirely below the horizon, while during the rest of the year he will rise and set, remaining above the horizon for a part of 24 hours, varying according to the position of the sun in the ecliptic.

Summing up the position as analysed by him, Mr. Tilak concludes by saying: "Here we have two distinct sets of *differentice* or special characteristics of the Polar and *Circum-Polar* regions—characteristics which are not found anywhere else on the surface of the globe. Again as the Poles of the earth are the same today as they were millions of years ago, the above astronomical characteristics will hold good for all times, though the Polar climate may have undergone violent changes in the Pleistocene period."

Having noted the phenomenon in the Arctic region, Mr. Tilak proceeds to argue that: "If a Vedic description or tradition discloses any of the characteristics mentioned above, we may safely infer that the tradition is Polar or Circum-Polar in origin, and the phenomenon, if not actually witnessed by the poet, was at least known to him by tradition faithfully handed down from generation to generation. Fortunately there are many such passages or references in the Vedic literature, and, for convenience, these may be divided into two parts; the first comprising those passages which directly describe or refer to the long night, or the long dawn; and the second consisting of myths and legends which corroborate and indirectly support the First."

Mr. Tilak is satisfied that the description of natural phenomenon and the myths and legends contained in the Vedas tally with the natural phenomenon as it exists near the North Pole and concludes that the Vedic poets *i.e.*, the Vedic Aryans must have had the Arctic region as their home.

This is of course a very original theory. There is only one point which seems to have been overlooked. The horse is a favourite animal of the Vedic Aryans. It was most intimately connected with their life and their religion. That the queens vied with one another to copulate with the horse in the *Ashvamedha Yajna* shows what place the horse had acquired in the life of the Vedic Aryans. Question is: was the horse to be found in the Arctic region? If the answer is in the negative, the Arctic home theory becomes very precarious.

What evidence is there of the invasion of India by the Aryan race and the subjugation by it of the native tribes? So far as the *Rig Veda* is concerned, there is not a particle of evidence suggesting the invasion of India by the Aryans from outside India. As Mr. P. T. Srinivasa iyengar points out: "A careful examination of the *Manatras* where the words Arya, Dasa and Dasyu occur, indicates that they refer not to race but to cult. These words occur mostly in *Rig Veda Samhita* where *Arya* occurs about 33 times in *mantras* which contain 153,972 words on the whole. The rare occurrence is itself a proof that the tribes that called themselves *Aryas* were not invaders that conquered the country and exterminated the people. For an invading tribe would naturally boast of its achievements constantly." So far the testimony of the Vedic literature is concerned, it is against the theory that the original home of the Aryans was outside India. The language in which reference to the seven rivers is made in the *Rig. Veda* (X.75.5) is very significant. As Prof. D. S. Triveda says —the rivers are addressed as 'my Ganges, my Yamuna, my Saraswati' and so on. No foreigner would ever address a river in such familiar and endearing terms unless by long association he had developed an emotion about it.

As to the question of conquest and subjugation, references can undoubtedly be found in the *Rig Veda* where Dasas and

Dasyus are described as enemics of the Aryas and there are many hymns in which the Vedic *rishis* have invited their gods to kill and annihilate them. But before drawing any conclusion from it in favour of conquest and subjugation by the Aryans, the following points must be taken into consideration.

First is the paucity of references in the *Rig Veda* to wars between the Aryans on the one hand and the Dasas or Dasyus on the other. Out of the 33 places in which the word occurs in the *Rig Veda* only in 8 places is it used in opposition to Dasas and only in 7 places is it used in opposition to the word Dasyus. This may show the occurrence of sporadic riots between the two. It is certainly not evidence of a conquest or subjugation.

The second point about the Dasas is that whatever conflict there was between them and the Aryans, the two seem to have arrived at a mutual settlement, based on peace with honour. This is borne out by references in the *Rig Veda* showing how the Dasas and Aryans have stood as one united people against a common enemy. Note the following verses from the *Rig Veda:*

Rig Veda- vi. 33.3; vii. 83.1; viii 51.9; x 102.3.

The third point to note is that whatever the degree of conflict, it was not a conflict of race. It was a conflict which had arisen on account of difference of religions. That this conflict was religious and not racial is evidenced by the *Rig Veda* itself. Speaking of the Dasyus, it says: "They are *avrata,* without (the Arya) rites (R.V., i. 51.8, 9; i.132.4; iv.41. 2; vi. 14, 3); *apavrata* (R.V., v.42,2), *anyavrata* of different rites (R.V., viii.59, II; x.22, 8), *Anagnitra* fireless (R.V., v.189, 3), *ayajyu, ayajvan,* non-sacrifices (R.V., i.131, 44; i.33, 4; viii.59, II), *abrambha,* without prayers (or also not having Brahmana priest (R.V., iv.15,9; x.105,8). *anrichah,* without Riks (R.V., x.105, 8), *Brahmadvisha,* haters of prayer (or Brahmans) R.V., v.42,9), and *anindra,* without Indra, despisers of Indra, (R.V., i.133, 1: v.2, 3; vii 18; 6; x 27, 6; x.48, 7). 'They pour no milky draughts they heat no cauldron' (R.V., iii.53, 4). They give no gifts to the Brahmana (R.V., v.7, 10)."

Attention may also be drawn to the Rig Veda X.22.8 which says: "We live in the midst of the Dasyu tribes, who do not perform sacrifices, nor believe in anything. They have their own rites and are not entitled to be called men. O! thou, destroyer of enemies, annihilate them and injure the Dasas."

In the face of these statements from the *Rig Veda,* there is obviously no room for a theory of a military conquest by the Aryan race of the non-Aryan races of Dasas and Dasyus.

So much about the Aryans, their invasion of India and their subjugation of the Dasas and Dasyus. The consideration so far bestowed upon the question has been from the Aryan side of the issue. It might be useful to discuss it from the side of the Dasas and the Dasyus. In what sense are the names Dasa and Dasyu used? Are they used in a racial sense?

Those who hold that the terms Dasa and Dasyu are used in the racial sense rely upon the following circumstances: (1) The use in the *Rig Veda* of the terms *Mridhravak and Anasa* as epithets of Dasyus. (2) The description in the *Rig Veda* of the Dasas as being of Krishna Varna.

The term *Mridhravak* occurs in the following places in the *Rig Veda:*

(1) *Rig Veda,* i. 174. 2;

(2) *Rig Veda,* v. 32.8;

(3) *Rig Veda,* vii. 6. 3;

(4) *Rig Veda,* vii. 18. 3.

What does the adjective *Mridhravak* mean? *Mridhravak* means one who speaks crude, unpolished language. Can crude unpolished language be regarded as evidence of difference of race? It would be childish to rely upon this as a basis of consciousness of race difference.

The term *Anasa* occurs in *Rig Veda* V.29.10. What does the word mean? There are two interpretations. One is by Prof. Max Muller. The other is by Sayanacharya. According to Prof. Max Muller, it means 'one without nose 'or' one with a flat nose' and has as such been relied upon as a piece of evidence in support of the view that the Aryans were a separate race from the Dasyus. Sayanacharya says that it means 'mouthless,' *i.e.*, devoid of good speech. This difference of meaning is due to difference in the correct reading of the word *Anasa*.. Sayanacharya reads it as *an-asa* while Prof. Max Muller reads it as *a-nasa.* As read by Prof. Max Muller, it means without nose. Question is: which of the two readings is the correct one? There is no reason to hold that Sayana's reading is wrong. On the other hand there is everything to suggest that it is right.

In the first place, it does not make nonsense of the word. Secondly, as there is no other place where the Dasyus are described as noseless, there is no reason why the word should be read in such a manner as to give it an altogether new sense. It is only fair to read it as a synonym of *Mridhravak.* There is therefore no evidence in support of the conclusion that the Dasyus belonged to a different race.

Turning to Dasas, it is true that they are described as *Krishna Yoni,* in Rig Veda vi.47.21. But there are various points to be considered before one can accept the inference which is sought to be drawn from it. First is that this is the only place in the Rig Veda where the phrase *Krishna Yoni* is applied to the Dasas. Secondly, there is no certainty as to whether the phrase is used in the literal sense or in a figurative sense. Thirdly, we do not know whether it is a statement of fact or a word of abuse. Unless these points are clarified, it is not possible to accept the view that because the Dasas are spoken of as *Krishna Yoni,* they therefore, belonged to a dark race.

In this connection, attention may be drawn to the following verses from the Rig Veda:

Rig Veda, vi.22.10.—"Oh, Vajri, thou hast made Aryas of Dasas, good men out of bad by your power. Give us the same power so that with it we may overcome our enemies."

Rig Veda, x.49.3, (says Indra).—"I have deprived the Dasyus of the title of Aryas."

Rig Veda, i. 151.8—"Oh, Indra, find out who is an Arya and who is a Dasyu and separate them."

What do these verses indicate? They indicate that the distinction between the Aryans on the one hand and the Dasas and Dasyus on the other was not a racial distinction of colour or physiognomy. That is why a Dasa or Dasyu could become an Arya. That is why Indra was given the task to separate them from the Arya.

That the theory of the Aryan race set up by Western writers falls to the ground at every point, goes without saying. This is somewhat surprising since Western scholarship is usually associated with thorough research and careful analysis. Why has the theory failed? It is important to know the reasons why it has failed. Anyone who cares to scrutinise the theory will find that it suffers from a double infection. In the first place, the theory is based on nothing but pleasing assumptions and inferences based on such assumptions. In the second place, the theory is a perversion of scientific investigation. It is not allowed to evolve out of facts. On the contrary the theory is preconceived and facts are selected to prove it.

The theory of the Aryan race is just an assumption and no more. It is based on a philological proposition put forth by Dr. Bopp in his epoch-making book called *Comparative Grammar* which appeared in 1835. In this book. Dr. Bopp demonstrated that a greater number of languages of Europe and some languages of Asia must be referred to a common ancestral speech. The European languages and Asiatic languages to which Bopp's proposition applied are called Indo-Germanic. Collectively, they have come to be called the Aryan languages largely because Vedic language refer to the Aryas and is also of the same family as the Indo-Germanic. This assumption is the major premise on which the theory of the Aryan race is based.

From this assumption are drawn two inferences: (1) unity of race, and (2) that race being the Aryan race. The argument is that if the languages are descended from a common ancestral speech then there must have existed a race whose mother tongue it was and since the mother tongue was known as the Aryan tongue the race who spoke it was the Aryan race. The existence of a separate and a distinct Aryan race is thus an inference only. From this inference, is drawn another inference which is that of a common original habitat. It is argued that there could be no community of language unless people had a common habitat permitting close communion. Common original habitat is thus an inference from an inference.

The theory of invasion is an invention. This invention is necessary because of a gratuitous assumption which underlies the Western theory. The assumption is that the Indo-Germanic people are the purest of the modern representatives of the original Aryan race. Its first home is assumed to have been somewhere in Europe. These assumptions raise a question: How could the Aryan speech have come to India: This question can be answered only by the supposition that the Aryans must have come into India from outside. Hence the necessity for inventing the theory of invasion.

The third assumption is that the Aryans were a superior race. This theory has its origin in the belief that the Aryans are a European race and as a European race it is presumed to be superior to the Asiatic races. Having assumed its superiority, the next logical step one is driven to take is to establish the fact of superiority. Knowing that nothing can prove the superiority of the Aryan race better than invasion and conquest of native races, the Western writers have proceeded to invent the story of the invasion of India by the Aryans and the conquest by them of the Dasas and Dasyus.

The fourth assumption is that the European races were white and had a colour prejudice against the dark races. The Aryans being a European race, it is assumed that it must have had colour prejudice. The theory proceeds to find evidence for colour prejudice in the Aryans who came into India. This it finds in the *Chaturvarnya*— an institution by the established Indo-Aryans after they came to India and which according to these scholars is based upon *Varna* which is taken by them to mean colour.

Not one of these assumptions is borne out by facts. Take the premise about the Aryan race. The theory does not take account of the possibility that the Aryan race in the physiological sense is one thing and an Aryan race in the philological sense quite different, and that it is perfectly possible that the Aryan race, if there is one, in the physiological sense may have its habitat in one place and that the Aryan race, in the philological sense, in quite a different place. The theory of the Aryan race is based on the premise of a common language and it is supposed to be common because it has a structural affinity. The assertion that the Aryans came from outside and invaded India is not proved and the premise that the Dasas and Dasyus are aboriginal tribes of India is demonstrably false.

Again to say that the institution of *Chaturvarnya* is a reflection of the innate colour prejudice of the Aryans is really to assert too much. If colour is the origin of class distinction, there must be four different colours to account for the different classes which comprise *Chaturvarnya*. Nobody has said what those four colours are and who were the four coloured races who were welded together in *Chaturvarnya.* As it is, the theory starts with only two opposing people, Aryas and Dasas—one assumed to be white and the other assumed to be dark.

The originators of the Aryan race theory are so eager to establish their case that they have no patience to see what absurdities they land themselves in. They start on a mission to prove what they want to prove and do not hesitate to pick such evidence from the Vedas as they think is good for them. Prof. Michael Foster has somewhere said that 'hypothesis is the salt of science.' Without hypothesis there is no possibility of fruitful investigation. But it is equally true that where the desire to prove a particular hypothesis is dominant, hypothesis becomes the poison of science. The Aryan race theory of Western scholars is as good an illustration of how hypothesis can be the poison of science as one can think of.

The Aryan race theory is so absurd that it ought to have been dead long ago. But far from being dead, the theory has a considerable hold upon the people. There are two explanations which account for this phenomenon. The first explanation is to be found in the support which the theory receives from Brahmin scholars. This is a very strange phenomenon. As Hindus, they should ordinarily show a dislike for the Aryan theory with its express avowal of the superiority of the European races over the Asiatic races. But the Brahmin scholar has not only no such aversion but he most willingly hails it. The reasons are obvious. The Brahmin believes in the two-nation theory. He claims to be the representative of the Aryan race and he regards the rest of the Hindus as descendants of the non-Aryans. The theory helps him to establish his kinship with the European races and share their arrogance and their superiority. He likes particularly that part of the theory which makes the Aryan an invader and a conqueror of the non-Aryan native races. For it helps him to maintain and justify his overlordship over the non-Brahmins.

The second explanation why the Aryan race theory is not dead is because of the general insistence by European scholars that the word *Varna* means *colour* and the acceptance of that view by a majority of the Brahmin scholars. Indeed, this is the mainstay of the Aryan theory. There is no doubt that as long as this interpretation of the *Varna* continues to be accepted, the Aryan theory will continue to live. This part of the Aryan theory is therefore very important and calls for fuller examination. It needs to be examined from three different points of view: (1) Were the European races fair or dark? (2) Were the Indo-Aryans fair? and (3) What is the original meaning of the world *Varna*?

On the question of the colour of the earliest Europeans Prof. Ripley is quite definite that they were of dark complexion. Prof. Ripley goes on to say: "We are strengthened in this assumption that the earliest Europeans were not only long-headed but also dark complexioned, by various points in our Enquiry thus far. We have proved the prehistoric antiquity of the living Cro-Magnon type in Southern France; and we saw that among these peasants, the prevalence of black hair and eyes is very striking. And comparing types in the British Isles we saw that everything tended to show that the Brunet populations of Wales, Ireland and Scotland constituted the most primitive stratum of population in Britain. Furthermore, in that curious spot in Garfagnana, where a survival of the ancient Ligurian population of Northern Italy is indicated, there also are the people characteristically dark. Judged, therefore, either in the light of general principles or of local details, it would seem as if this earliest race in Europe must have been very dark.... It was Mediterranean in its pigmental affinities, and not Scandinavian."

Turning to the Vedas for any indication whether the Aryans had any colour prejudice, reference may be made to the following passages in the Rig Veda:

In Rig Veda, i. 117.8, there is a reference to *Ashvins* having brought about the marriage between *Shyavya* and *Rushati* *Shyavya* is black and *Rushati* is fair.

In Rig Veda, i. 117.5, there is a prayer addressed to *Ashvins* for having saved Vandana who is spoken as of golden colour.

In Rig Veda, ii.3.9, there is a prayer by an Aryan invoking the Devas to bless him with a son with certain virtues but of *(pishanga)* tawny (reddish brown) complexion.

These instances show that the Vedic Aryans had no colour prejudice. How could they have? The Vedic Aryans were not of one colour. Their complexion varied; some were of copper complexion, some white, and some black. Rama the son of Dasharatha has been described as *Shyama i.e.*, dark in complexion, so is Krishna the descendant of the Yadus, another Aryan clan. The Rishi Dirghatamas, who is the author of many *mantras* of the Rig Veda must have been of dark colour if his name was given to him after his complexion. Kanva is an Aryan rishi of great repute. But according to the description given in Rig Veda—X.31.11—he was of dark colour.

To take up the third and the last point, namely, the meaning of the word *Varna*. Let us first see in what sense it is used in the Rig Veda. The word *Varna* is used in the Rig Veda in 22 places. Of these, in about 17 places the word is used in reference to decides such as Ushas, Agni, Soma, etc., and means lustre, features or colour. Being used in connection with deities, it would be unsafe to use them for ascertaining what meaning the word *Varna* had in the Rig Veda when applied to human beings. There are four and at the most five places in the Rig Veda where the word is used in reference to human beings. They are:

(1) i.l04.2;

(2) i. 179.6;

(3) ii.l2.4;

(4) iii.34.5;

(5) ix.71.2.

Do these references prove that the word *Varna* is used in the Rig Veda in the sense of colour and complexion?

Rig Veda, iii.34.5 seems to be of doubtful import. The expression 'caused Shukia Varna to increase' is capable of double interpretation. It may mean Indra made Ushas throw her light and thereby increase the white colour, or it may mean that the hymn-maker being of white complexion, people of his *i.e.*, of white colour increased. The second meaning would be quite far-fetched for the simple reason that the expansion of the white colour is the effect and lightening of Ushas is the cause.

Rig Veda, ix.71.2 the expression 'abandons Ashura Varna' is not clear, reading it in the light of the other stanzas in the *Sukta*. The *Sukta* belongs to Soma Pavamana. Bearing this in mind, the expression 'abandons Ashura Varna' must be regarded as a description of Soma. The word Varna as used here is indicative of *roopa.* The second half of the stanza says: 'he throws away his black or dark covering and takes on lustrous covering.' From this it is clear that the word Varna is used as indicative of darkness.

Rig Veda, i. 179.6 is very helpful. The stanza explains that Rishi Agastya cohabitated with Lopamudra in order to obtain *praja,* children and strength and says that as a result two Varnas prospered. It is not clear from the stanza, which are the two Varnas referred to in the stanzas, although the intention is to refer to Aryas and Dasas.

Be that as it may, there is no doubt that the Varna in the stanza means class and not colour.

In Rig Veda, i. 104.2 and Rig Veda, ii.l2.4 are the two stanzas in which the word Varna is applied to Dasa. The question is: What does the word Varna mean when applied to Dasa? Does it refer to the colour and complexion of the Dasa, or does it indicate that Dasas formed a separate class? There is no way of arriving at a positive conclusion as to which of the two meanings is correct.

The evidence of the Rig Veda is quite inconclusive. In this connection, it will be of great help to know if the word occurs in the literature of the Indo-Iranians and if so, in what sense.

Fortunately, the word Varna does occur in the Zend Avesta. It takes the form of *Varana* or *Varena.* It is used specifically in the sense of "Faith, Religious doctrine. Choice of creed or belief." It is derived from the root *Var* which means to put faith in, to believe in. One comes across the word *Varana* or *Varena* in the Gathas about six times used in the sense of faith, doctrine, creed or belief.

It occurs in Gatha Ahunavaiti—Yasna Ha 30 Stanza 2 which when translated in English reads as follows: "Give heed with your ears and contemplate the highest Truth I proclaim; with your illumined mind introspect. Each man for himself must determine his (Avarenao) faith. Before the Great Event, let each individually be awake to the Truth we teach."

This is one of the most famous strophes of the Gatha where Zarathushtra exhorts each one individually to use reasoning faculty and freedom of choice in the selection of his or her faith.

The words occurring here are *'Avarenao vichithahya,' Avarenao* meaning faith, belief and *vichithahya* meaning 'of discriminating, of selecting of determining'.

It occurs in Gatha Ahunavati—Yasna Ha 31 Stanza II. The word used is *Vareneng* accusative plural of *Varena* meaning 'belief, faith.' In this stanza, Zarathushtra propounds the theory of the creation of man. After speaking about man's creation being completed, in the last half line Zarathushtra says "voluntary beliefs are given (to man)".

It occurs in Gatha Ushtavaiti— Yasna Ha 45 Stanza I in the from of *Varena.* In the last line of this strophe, Zarathushtra says 'owing to sinful belief (or evil faith) the wicked is of evil tongue (or invested tongue)'.

It occurs in Gatha Ushtavaid—Yasna Ha 45 Stanza 2 in the same form as above *Varena* in the clear sense of faith, religion, belief, etc. In this stanza, Zarathushtra is propounding his philosophy of good and evil and speaking of dual aspects of human mind. In this stanza, the two mentalities—the good mentality and the evil mentality—are speaking to each other saying "Neither in thought, word, intelligence, faith (or religion or creed) utterance, deed, conscience nor soul do we agree."

It occurs in Gatha Spenta Mainyu,—Yasna Ha 48 Stanza 4 in the form of *Vareneng* meaning religion, faith (root *Vere* Persian *gervidan* = to have faith in). In this stanza Zarathushtra says that "Whosoever will make his mind pure and holy and thus keep his conscience pure by deed and word, such man's desire is in accordance with his faith (religion, belief)."

It occurs in Gatha Spenta Mainyu,—Yasna Ha 49 Stanza 3 as *Varenai* in dative case meaning 'religion'. In the same stanza occurs the word *Thaeshai* which also means religion, creed, religious law. These two words *Varenai* and *Tkaesha* occuring in the same stanza strengthens our argument, as the word *Tkaesha* clearly means religion as is found in the compound *Ahuratkaesha* meaning 'The Ahurian religion'. This word *Tkaesha* is translated in Pahlavi as *Kish* which means religion.

In Vendidad (a book of Zarathushtrian sanitary law written in Avesta language) we come across a word *Anyo Varena.* Here *Anyo* mean other and *Varena* means religion, thus a man of different religion, faith, belief is spoken of *as Anyo-Varena.*

Similarly, we come across in Vendidad the *word Anyo-Tkaosha* also meaning a man of different religion.

We come across many verbal forms in the Gatha derived from this root, *e.g.*, Ahunavaiti Gatha Yasna Ha, 31, Stanza 3. Zarathushtra declares *Ya jvanto vispeng vauraya;* here the verb *vauraya* means I may cause to induce belief, faith (in God) (in all the living ones). In Yasna Ha, 28: Stanza 5, we come across the verb *vauroimaidi,* 'We may give faith to.' We come across another interesting form of this word in Gatha Vahishtaishtish, Yasna Ha, 53, Stanza 9 *Duz-Varenaish.* It is instrumental plural. The first part *Duz* means wicked, false and *Varenai* means believer. Thus the word means "A man belonging to false or wicked religion or a false or wicket believer."

In the Zarathushtrian Confession of Faith, which forms Yasna Ha, 12, we come across the word *Fravarane* meaning 1 confess my faith, my belief in *Mazdayasno Zarathushtrish* 'Mazda worshipping Zara-thushtrian Religion'. This phrase occurs in almost all the Zara-thushtrian prayers. There is yet another form in the Zarathushtrian Confession Yasna, 12, *Ya-V arena.* Here *Ya* is relative pronoun meaning which and *Varena*—faith, religion. Thus, the word means 'the religion to which'. This form *Ya Varena* is used nine times in Yasna 12, and it is used in the clear sense of faith or religion. Here again the word *Varena* is placed along with the word *Tkaesha* which means religion. A very interesting reference is found in Yasna 16 *Zarathushtrahe varenerncha tkaeshemcha yazamaide.* Here the *Varena* and *Tkaesha* of Zarathushtra is worshipped. It is quite clear from the use of these corresponding and co-relative words that the faith and religion of Zarthushtra is meant. The translation of the above line is "We worship the faith and religion of Zarathushtra.'

This evidence from the Zenda Avesta as to the meaning of the word Varna leaves no doubt that it originally meant a class holding to a particular faith and it had nothing to do with colour or complexion.

The conclusions that follow from the examination of the Western theory may now be summarised. They are:

(1) The Vedas do not know any such race as the Aryan race.

(2) There is no evidence in the Vedas of any invasion of India by the Aryan race and its having conquered the Dasas and Dasyus supposed to be natives of India.

(3) There is no evidence to show that the distinction between Aryans, Dasas and Dasyus was a racial distinction.

(4) The Vedas do not support the contention that the Aryas were different in colour from the Dasas and Dasyus.

Aryas against Aryas

Enough has been said to show how leaky is the Aryan theory expounded by Western scholars and glibly accepted by their Brahmin fellows. Yet, the theory has such a hold on the generality of people that what has been said against it may mean no more than scotching it. Like the snake it must be killed. It is therefore necessary to pursue the examination of the theory further with a view to expose its hollowness completely.

Those who uphold the theory of an Aryan race invading India and conquering the Dasas and Dasyus fail to take note of certain verses in the Rig Veda. These verses are of crucial importance.

To build up a theory of an Aryan race marching into India from outside and conquering the non-Aryan native tribes without reference to these verses is an utter futility. I reproduce below the verses I have in mind:

Rig Veda, vi. 33.3.—"Oh, Indra, Thou has killed both of our opponents, the Dasas and the Aryas."

Rig Veda, vi.60.3— "Indra and Agni—these protectors of the good and righteous suppress the Dasas and Aryas who hurt us."

Rig Veda, vii.81.1.— "Indra and Varuna killed the Dasas and Aryas who were the enemies of Sudas and thus protected Sudas from them."

Rig Veda, viii.24.27.—"Oh you, Indra, who saved us from the hands of the cruel Rakshasas and from the Aryas living on the banks of the Indus, do thou deprive the Dasas of their weapons."

Rig Veda, X.38.3.—"Oh you much revered Indra, those Dasas and Aryas who *axe* irreligious and who are our enemies, make it easy for us with your blessings to subdue them. With your help we shall kill them."

Rig Veda, X.86.19.—Oh, You Mameyu, you give him all powers who plays you. With your help we will destroy our Arya and our Dasyu enemies.

Anyone who reads these verses, notes what they say calmly and cooly and considers them against the postulates of the Western theory will be taken aback by them. If the authors of these verses of the Rig Veda were Aryas then the idea which these verses convey is that there were two different communities of Aryas who were not only different but oppose and inimical to each other. The existence of two Aryas is not a mere matter of conjecture or interpretation. It is a fact in support of which there is abundant evidence.

The first piece of such evidence, to which attention may be invited, is the discrimination which existed for a long time in the matter of the recognition of the sacred character of the different Vedas. All students of the Vedas know that there are really two Vedas: (1) the Rig Veda and (2) the Atharva Veda. The Sama Veda and the Yajur Veda are merely different forms of the Rig Veda. All students of the Vedas know that the Atharva Veda was not recognised by the Brahmins as sacred as the Rig Veda for a long time. Why was such a distinction made? Why was the Rig Veda regarded as sacred? Why was the Atharva Veda treated as vulgar? The answer, I like to suggest, is that the two belonged to two different races of Aryans and it is only when they had become one that the Atharva Veda came to be regarded on a par with the Rig Veda.

Besides this, there is enough evidence, scattered through the whole of the Brahmanic literature, of the existence of two different ideologies, particularly relating to creation, which again points to the existence of two different Aryan races. It remains to draw attention to the second type of ideology.

To begin with the Vedas. The following ideology is to be found in the Taittiriya Samhita:

T.S., vi.5.6.1.—"Aditi, desirous of sons, cooked, a Brahmaudana oblation for the gods, the Sadhyas. They gave her the remnant of it This she ate. She conceived seed. Four Adityas were born to her. She cooked a second (oblation). She reflected, 'from the remains of the oblation these sons have been born to me. If I shall eat (the oblation) first, more brilliant (sons) will be born to me.' She ate it first; she conceived seed; an imperfect egg was produced from her. She cooked a third (oblation) for the Adityas, repeating the formula 'may this religious toil have been undergone for my enjoyment.' The Adityas said, Let us choose a boon; let anyone who is produced from this be ours only; let anyone of his progeny who is prosperous be for us a source of enjoyment' In consequence the Aditya Vivasvat was born. This is his progeny, namely, men. Among them he alone who sacrifices is prosperous, and becomes a cause of enjoyment to the gods."

Turning to the Brahmanas. The stories of creation contained in the Satapatha Brahmanas are set out below:

S.B.,1 i.8.1.1—In the morning they brought to Manu water for washing, as men are in the habit of bringing it to wash with the hands. As he was thus washing, a fish came into his hands (which spoke to him) 'preserve me; I shall save thee.' (Manu enquired) From what will thou save me?' (The fish replied) 'A flood shall sweep away all these creatures; from it will I rescue thee.' (Manu asked) 'How (shall) thy preservation (be effected)?'

The fish said: 'So long as we are small, we are in great peril, for fish devours fish; thou shall preserve me first in a jar. When I grow too large for the jar, then thou shall dig a trench, and preserve me in that. When I grow too large for the trench, then thou shall carry me away to the ocean. I shall then be beyond the reach of danger. Straight, away he became a large fish; for he waxes to the utmost. (He said) Now in such and such a year, then the flood will come; thou shall embark in the ship when the flood rises, and I shall deliver thee from it.' Having thus preserved the fish, Manu carried him away to the sea.

Then in the same year which the fish had enjoined, he constructed a ship and resorted to him. When the flood rose, Manu embarked in the ship. The fish swam towards him. He fastened the cable of the ship to the fish's horn. By this means he passed over this northern mountain. The fish said, 1 have delivered thee; fasten the ship to a tree. But lest the water should cut thee off whilst thou art on the mountain, as much as the water subsides so much shall thou descend after it.' He accordingly descended after it as much (as it subsided).

Wherefore also this, *viz.*, ' Manu's descent ' is (the name) of the northern mountain.

Now the flood had swept away all these creatures, so Manu alone was left here. Desirous of offspring, he lived worshipping and toiling in arduous religious rites. Among these he also sacrificed with the *paka* offering. He cast clarified butter, thickened milk, whey and curds as an oblation into the waters. Thence in a year a woman was produced. She rose up as it were unctuous. Clarified butter adheres to her steps. Mitra and Varuna met her. They said to her ' who art thou?' 'Manu's daughter' (she replied). Say (thou art) ours ' (they rejoined). ' No', she said, I am his who begot me.' They desired a share in her. She promised that, or she did not promise that; but passed onward. She came to Manu. Manu said to her, 'who art thou?' Thy daughter' she replied. 'How, glorious one 'asked Manu,' (art thou) my daughter?' "Thou has generated me, ' she said, ' from those oblations, butter, thick milk, whey and curds, which thou didst cast into the waters. I am a benediction. Apply me in the sacrifice. If thou wilt employ me in the sacrifice, thou shall abound in offspring and cattle.

Whatever benediction thou will ask through me, shall accrue to thee.' He (accordingly) introduced her (as) that (which comes in) the middle of the sacrifice; for that is the middle of the sacrifice which (comes) between the introductory and concluding forms. With her he lived worshipping and toiling in arduous religious rites, desirous of offspring. With her he begot this offspring which is this offspring of Manu. Whatever benediction he asked with her, was all vouchsafed to him. This is essentially that which is Ida. Whosoever, knowing this, lives with Ida, begets this offspring which Maim begot Whatever benediction he asks with her, is all vouchsafed to him."

S.B., vi.l.2.11.— "Wherefore they say, "Prajapati having created those worlds was supported upon the earth. For him these herbs were cooked as food. That (food) he ate. He became pregnant. He created the gods from his upper vital airs, and mortal offspring from his lower vital airs. In whatever way he created, so he created. But Prajapati created all this, whatever exists."

S.B. vii.5.2.6.— Prajapati was formerly this (universe), one only. He desired.' Let me create food, and be propagated.' He formed animals from his breath, a man from his soul, a horse from his eye, a bull from his breath, a sheep from his ear, a goat from his voice. Since he formed animals from his breaths, therefore men say, ' the breaths are animals.' The soul is the first of the breaths. Since he formed a man from his 'soul' therefore they say 'man is the first of the animals, and the strongest.' The soul is all the breaths; for all the breaths depend upon the soul. Since he formed man from his soul, therefore they say,' man is all the animals;' for all these are man's."

S.B., x. 1.3.1.— "Prajapati created living beings. From his upper vital airs he created the gods: from his lower vital airs mortal creatures. Afterwards he created death a devourer of creatures."

S.B., xiv.4.2.1.— "This universe was formerly soul only, in the form of Purusha. Looking closely, he saw nothing but himself (or soul). He first said,' This is 1.' Then he became one having the name of 1. Hence even now a man, when called, first says/this is I, 'and then declares the other name when he has. In as much as he, before *(purvah)* all this, burnt up *(aushat)* all sins, he (is called), *purusha.* The man who knows this burns up the person who wishes to be before him. He was afraid. Hence a man when alone is afraid. This (being) considered that ' there is no other thing but myself; of what am I afraid?' Then his fear departed. For why should he have feared? It is of a second person that people are afraid. He did not enjoy happiness. Hence a person when alone does not enjoy happiness. He desired a second. He was so much as a man and a woman when locked in embrace. He caused this same self to fall as under into two parts. Thence arose a husband and wife. Hence Yajnavalkya has said that 'this one's self is like the half of a split pea.' Hence the void is filled up by woman. He cohabited with her. From them Men were born. She reflected how does he, after having produced me from himself, cohabit with me? Ah! let me disappear'; she became a cow, and the other a bull; and he cohabited with her. From them kine were produced. The one became a mare, the other a stallion, the one a she-ass, the other a male-ass. He cohabited with her. From them the class of animals with undivided hoofs were produced. The one became a she-goat, the other a he-goat, the one a ewe, the other a ram. He cohabited with her. From them goats and sheep were produced. In this manner pairs of all creatures whatsoever down to ants, were produced.

The Taitritriya Brahmana has the following:

T.B.1 ii.2.9..—"At first this (universe) was not anything. There was neither sky, nor earth, nor air. Being nonexistent, it resolved let me be.' It became fervent. From that fervour smoke was produced. It again became fervent. From that fervour fire was produced. It again became fervent. From that fervour light was produced. It again became fervent. From that fervour flame was produced.

It again became fervent From that fervour rays were produced. It again became fervent. From that fervour blazes were produced. It again became fervent It became condensed like a cloud. It clove its bladder. That became the sea. Hence men do not drink of the sea. For they regard it as like the place of generation. Hence water issues forth before an animal when it is being born. After that the Dasahotri (a particular formula) was created. Prajapati is the Dasahotri. That man succeeds, who thus knowing the power of austere abstraction (or fervour) practises it.

This was then water, fluid. Prajapati wept (exclaiming). ' For what purpose have I been born, if (I have been born) from this which forms no support.' That which fell into the waters became the earth. That which he wiped away, became the air. That which he wiped away, upward, became the sky. From the circumstance that he wept *(arodit),* these two regions have the name of *rodasi,* (words). They do not weep in the house of the man who knows this. This was the birth of these worlds. He who thus knows the birth of these worlds, incurs no suffering in these worlds. He obtained this (earth as a) basis. Having obtained (this earth as a) basis, he desired. ' May I be propagated.' He practised austere fervour. He became pregnant He created Ashuras from his abdomen. To them he milked out food in an earthen dish. He cast off that body of his.

It became darkness. He desired ' May I be propagated.' He practised austere fervour. He became pregnant. He created living beings *(prajah)* from his organ of generation. Hence they are the most numerous because he created them from-his generative organ. To them he milked out milk in a wooden dish.

He cast off that body of his. It became moonlight He desired 'May I be propagated.' He practised austere fervour. He became pregnant. He created the seasons from his armpits. To them he milked out butter in a silver dish. He cast off that body of his. It became the period which connects day and night He desired ' May I be propagated.' He practised austere fervour. He became pregnant. He created the gods from his mouth. To them he milked out Soma in a golden dish. He cast off that body of his. It became day.

These are Prajapati's milkings. He who thus knows, milks out offspring. ' Day (diva) has come to us:' this (exclamation expresses) the godhead of the gods. He who thus knows the godhead of the gods, obtains the gods. This is the birth of days and nights. He who thus knows the birth of days and nights, incurs no suffering in the days and nights. Mind (or soul, *manas*) was created from the nonexistent. Mind created Prajapati. Prajapati created offspring. All this, whatever exists, rests absolutely on mind. This is that Brahma called Svovasyasa. For the man who thus knows, (Ushas), dawning, dawns more and more bright; he becomes prolific in offspring, and (rich) in cattle; he obtains the rank of Parameshthin."

T.B. ii.3.8.1.— "Prajapati desired, ' May I propagate.' He practised austerity. He became pregnant. He became yellow brown. Hence a woman when pregnant, being yellow, becomes brown. Being pregnant with a foetus, he became exhausted. Being exhausted he became blackish-brown. Hence an exhausted person becomes blackish-brown. His breath became alive. With that breath *(asu)* he created Ashuras. Therein consists the Ashura-nature of Ashuras. He who thus knows this Ashura-nature of Ashuras becomes a man possessing breath. Breath does not forsake him. Having created the Ashuras he regarded himself as a father. After that he created the Fathers (Pitris). That constitutes the fatherhood of the Fathers. He who thus knows the fatherhood of the Fathers, becomes as a father of his own; the Fathers resort to his oblation. Having created the Fathers, he reflected. After that he created men. That constitutes the manhood of men. He who knows the manhood of men, becomes intelligent. Mind does not forsake him. To him, when he was creating men, day appeared in the heaven. After that he created the gods. This constitutes the godhead of the gods.

To him who thus knows the godhead of the gods, day appears in the heavens. These are the four streams, viz; gods, men, fathers and Ashuras. In all of these water is like the air."

T.B., iii.2.3.9.— "This Sudra has sprung from nonexistence."

The following explanation of the origin of creation is given by the Taitririya Aranyaka:

T.A., i.12.3.1.— "This is water, fluid. Prajapati alone was produced on a lotus leaf. Within, in his mind, desire arose, ' Let me create this.' Hence whatever a man aims at in his mind, he declares by speech, and performs by act. Hence this verse has been uttered, 'Desire formerly arose in it, which was the primal germ of mind, (and which) sages, searching with their intellect, have discovered in the heart as the bond between the existent and the nonexistent' (Rig Veda X.129.4). That of which he is desirous comes to the man who thus knows. He practised austere fervour. Having practised austere fervour, he shook his body. From its flesh the rishis (called) Arunas, Ketus and Vatarasanas arose. His nails became the Vaikhanasas, his hairs the Valakhilyas. The fluid (of his body became) a tortoise moving amid the waters.

He said to him ' Thou hast sprung from my skin and flesh.' ' No,' replied the tortoise, ' I was here before.' In that (in his having been 'before" *purvam*) consists the manhood of a man *(purusha).* Becoming a man *Purusha* with a thousand heads, a thousand eyes, a thousand feet (R.V.X.90.1) he arose. Prajapati said to him, 'thou wert produced before me; do thou first make this.' He took water from this in the cavity of his two hands and placed it on the east, repeating the text, 'so be it, O Sun.' From thence the sun arose. That was the eastern quarter. Then Aruna Ketu placed (the water) to the south, saying 'so be it, O Agni.' Thence Agni arose. That was the southern quarter. Then Aruna Ketu placed (the water) to the west, saying ' so be it, O Vayu.' Thence arose Vayu.

That was the western quarter. Then Aruna Ketu placed (the water) to the north, saying 'so be it, O Indra.' Then arose Indra. That is the northern quarter. Then Aruna Ketu placed (the water) in the centre, saying 'so be it, O Pushan.' Thence arose Pushan. That is this quarter. The Aruna Ketu placed (the water) above saying ' so be it, gods.' Thence arose gods, men, Fathers, Gandharvas and Apsarasa. That is the *upper* quarter.

From the drops which fell apart arose the Ashuras, Rakshasas, and Pisachas. Therefore they perished, because they were produced from drops. Hence this text has been uttered; 'when the great waters became pregnant, containing wisdom, and generating Svayambhu, from them were created these creations. All this was produced from the waters. Therefore all this is Brahma Svayambhu.' Hence all this was as it were loose, as it were unsteady. Prajapatiwas that. Having made himself through himself, he entered into that. Wherefore this verse has been uttered; 'Having formed the world, having formed existing things and all intermediate quarters, Prajapati the first born of the ceremonial entered into himself with himself.'"

The Mahabharata has its own contribution to make to the subject. It propounds the theory of creation by Manu.

The Vanaparvan says:

"There was a great rishi, Manu, son of Vivasvat, majestic, in lustre equal to Prajapati. In energy, fiery vigour, prosperity and austere fervour he surpassed both his father and his grand father. Standing with uplifted arm, on one foot, on the spacious Badari,he practised intense austere fervour. This direful exercise he performed with his head downwards, and with unwinking eyes, for 10,000 years. Once, when, clad in dripping rags, with matted hair, he was so engaged, a fish came to him (MI *the banks of the Chirini, and spake: 'Lord, I am a small fish; I dread the stronger ones, and from them you must save me. For the stronger fish devour the weaker; this has been immemorially ordained as our means of subsistence. Deliver me from this flood of apprehension in which I am sinking, and I will requite the deed.' Hearing this, Manu filled with compassion, took the fish in his hand, and bringing him to the water threw him into a jar bright as a moonbeam. In it the fish, being excellently tended, grew; for Manu treated him like a son. After a long time he became very large and could not be contained in the jar. Then, seeing Manu he said again: 'In order that I may thrive, remove me elsewhere.' Manu then took him out of the jar, brought him to a large pond, and threw him in. There he continued to grow for very many years.*

Although the pond was two *yojanas* long and *oneyojana* broad, the lotus-eyed fish found in it no room to move; and again said to Manu. ' Take me to Ganga, the dear queen of the ocean-monarch; in her I shall dwell; or do as thou thinkest best, for I must contentedly submit to thy authority, as through thee I have exceedingly increased.' Manu accordingly took the fish and threw him into the river Ganga. There he waxed for some time, when he again said to Manu, From my great bulk I cannot move in the Ganga; be gracious and remove me quickly to the ocean.' Manu took him out of the Ganga; and cast him into the sea. Although so huge, the fish was easily borne, and pleasant to touch and smell, as Manu carried him. When he had been thrown into the ocean he said to Manu: ' Great Lord, thou hast in every way preserved me; now hear from me what thou must do when the time arrives. *Soon* shall all these terrestrial objects, both fixed and moving, be dissolved.

The time for the purification of the worlds has now arrived. I therefore inform thee what is for thy greatest good. The period dreadful for the universe, moving and fixed, has come. Make for thyself a strong ship, with a cable attached; embark in it with the seven rishis and stow in it, carefully preserved and assorted, all the seeds which have been described of old by Brahmins. When embarked in the ship, look out for me. I shall come recognizable by my horn. So shall thou do; I greet thee and depart These great waters cannot be crossed over without me. Distrust not my word.' Manu replied,' I shall do as thou hast said. ' After taking mutual leave they departed each on his own way. Manu then, as enjoined, taking with him the seeds ' floated on the billowy ocean in the beautiful ship. He then thought on the fish, which knowing his desire, arrived with all speed, distinguished by a horn.

When Manu saw the homed leviathan, lofty as a mountain, he fastened the ship's cable to the horn. Being thus attached the fish dragged the ship with great rapidity, transporting it across the briny ocean which seemed to dance with its waves and thunder with its waters. Tossed by the tempests, the ship whirled like a reeling and intoxicated woman. Neither the earth nor the quarter of the world appeared; there was nothing but water, air, and sky. In the world thus confounded, the seven rishis, Manu and the fish were beheld. So, for *very* many years, the fish, unwearied, drew the ship over the waters; and brought it at length to the highest peak of Himavat. He then, smiling gently, said to the rishis, ' Bind the ship without delay to this peak.' They did so accordingly. And that highest peak of Himavat is still known by the name of Naubandhana ('the Binding of the Ship'.) The friendly fish (or god, *animisha)* then said to the rishis, 'I am the Prajapati Brahma, than whom nothing higher can be reached. In the form of a fish I have delivered you from this great danger. Manu shall create all living beings, gods, ashuras, men, with all worlds, and all things moving and fixed. By my favour and through severe austere fervour he shall attain perfect insight into his creative work, and shall not become bewildered.' Having thus spoken, the fish in an instant disappeared. Manu, desirous to call creatures into existence and bewildered in his work, performed a great act of austere fervour; and then began visibly to create all living beings."

The Adi Parvan of the Mahabharata gives a some what different version of the story of creation:

> "*Vaisuhmpayari said: I shall, after making obeisance to Svayambhu relate to thee exactly the production and destruction of the gods and other beings. Six great rishis are known as the mind-born sons of Brahma,* viz., *Marichi, Atri, Angiras, Pulastya, Pulaha and Kratu. Kasyapa was the son of Marichi: and from Kasyapa sprang these creatures. There were born to Daksha thirteen daughters of eminent rank, Aditi, Dili, Danu, Kala, Danayu, Sirnuka, Krodha, Pradha, Visva, Vinata, Kapila and Muni. Kadni also was of the number. These daughters had valorous sons and grandsons innumerable.*

Daksha, the glorious rishi, tranquil in spirit, and great in austere fervour, sprang from the right thumb of Brahma. From the left thumb sprang that great Muni's wife on whom he begot fifty daughters. Of these he gave ten to Dharma, twenty-seven to Indu (Soma), and according to the celestial system, thirteen to Kasyapa. Pitamaha's descendant Manu, the god and the lord of creatures, was his (it does not clearly appear whose) son. The eight Vasus, whom I shall detail, were his sons. Dividing the right breast of Brahma, the glorious Dharma (Righteousness), issued in a human form, bringing happiness to all people. He had three eminent sons, Sama, Kama, and Harsha (Tranquillity, Love, and Joy), who are the delight of all creatures, and by their might support the world.... Arushi, the daughter of Manu was the wife of that sage (Chyavana, son of Bhrigu)... There are two other sons of Brahma, whose mark remains in the world, Dhatri, and Vidhatri, who remained with Manu. Their sister was the beautiful goddess Lakshmi, whose home is the lotus. Her mind-born sons are the steeds who move in the sky... When the creatures who were desirous of food, had devoured one another, Adharma (Uprighteousness) was produced, the destroyer of all beings. His wife was Nirriti, and hence the Rakshasas are called Nairritas, or the offspring of Nirriti. She had three dreadful sons, continually addicted to evil deeds, Bhaya, Mahabhaya (Fear and Terror) and Mrityu (Death) the ender of beings. He has neither wife, nor any son, for he is the ender."

"Born all with splendour, like that of great rishis, the ten sons of Prachetas are reputed to have been virtuous and holy; and by them the glorious beings were formerly burnt up by the fire springing from their mouths. From them was born Daksha Prachetasa; and from Daksha, the Parent of the world (were produced) these creatures. Cohabiting with Virini, the Muni Daksha begot a thousand sons like himself, famous for their religious observances, to whom Narada taught the doctrine of final liberation, the unequalled knowledge of the Sankhya. Desirous of creating offspring, the Prajapati Daksha next formed fifty daughters, of whom he gave ten to Dharma, thirteen to Kasyapa, and twenty-seven devoted to the regulation of time to Indu (Soma)... On Dakshayani, the most excellent of his thirteen wives, Kasyapa, the son of Marichi, begot the Adityas, headed by Indra and distinguished by their energy, and also Vivasvat. To Vivasvat was born a son, the mighty Yama Vaivasvata. To Martanda (*i.e.*, Vivasvat, the Sun) was born the wise and mighty Manu, and also the renowned Yama, his (Manu's) younger brother. Righteous was this wise Manu, on whom a race was founded. Hence this (family) of men became known as the race of Manu. Brahmins, Kshatriyas, and other men sprang from this Manu. From him, O king, came the Brahmin conjoined with the Kshatriya. Among them the Brahmins, children of Manu, held the Veda with the Vedangas.

The children of Manu are said to have been Vena, Dhrishnu, Narishyanta, Nabhaga, Ikshvaku, Karusha, Saryati, and the eighth, Prishadra the ninth, who was addicted to the duties of a Kshatriya, and Nabhagarishta, the tenth. Manu had also fifty other sons; but they all, as we have heard, perished in consequence of mutual dissensions. Subsequently, the wise Pururavas was born of Ila, who, we heard, was both his mother and his father."

The Ramayana also deals with the subject of creation. One account of it will be found in the second Kanda. It says:

> *"Perceiving Rama to be incensed, Vashishtha replied.' 'Jabali also knows the destruction and renovation of this world. But he spoke as he did from a desire to induce you to return. Learn from me, lord of the earth, this (account* of*) the origin of the world. The universe was nothing but water. In it the earth was fashioned. Then Brahma Svayambhu came into existence, with the deities. He next, becoming a boar, raised up the earth, and created the entire world, with the saints, his sons, Brahma, the eternal, unchanging, and undecaying, was produced from the ether (akasa). From him sprang Marichi, of whom Kasyapa was the son. From Kasyapa sprang Vivasvat: and from him was descended Manu, who was formerly the lord of creatures (Prajapati). Ikshvaku was the son of Manu, and to him this prosperous earth was formerly given by his father. Know that this Ikshvaku was the former king in Ayodhya."*

There is besides this another story of creation. It occurs in the third Kanda and is in the following terms:

> *"Having heard the words of Rama, the bird (Jatayu) made known to him his own race, and himself, and the origin of all beings. "Listen while I declare to you from the commencement all the Prajapatis (lords of creatures) who came into existence in the earliest time. Kardama was the first, then Vikrita, Sesha, Samsraya, the energetic Bahuputra, Sthanu, Marichi, Atri, the strong Kratu, Pulastya, Angiras, Prachetas, Pulaha, Daksha, then Vivasvat, Arishtanemi, and the glorious Kasyapa, who was the last. The Prajapati Daksha is famed to have had sixty daughters. Of these Kasyapa took in*

marriage eight elegant maidens, Aditi, Diti, Danu, Kalaka, Tamra, Krodhavasa, Manu and Anala. Kasyapa, pleased, then, said to these maids: ' ye shall bring forth sons like me, preservers of the three worlds.' Aditi, Diti, Danu and Kalaka assented; but the others did not agree. Thirty-three gods were borne by Aditi, the Adityas, Vasus, Rudras, and the two Asvins. 'Manu, (wife) of Kasyapa, produced men. Brahmins, Kshatriyas, Vaishyas, and Sudras. 'Brahmins were born from the mouth, Kshatriyas from the breast, Vaishyas from the thighs, and Sudras from the feet' so says the Veda. Anala gave birth to all trees with pure fruits."

As an illustration of what the Puranas have to say, I extract the following passages from the Vishnu Purana:

"Before the mundane egg existed the divine Brahma Hiranyagarbha the eternal originator of all worlds, who was the form and essence of Brahma, who consists of the divine Vishnu, who again is identical with the Rik, Yajus, Saman and Atharva-Vedas. From Brahma's right thumb was born the Prajapati Daksha; Daksha had a daughter Aditi; from her was born Vivasvat; and from him sprang Manu. Manu had sons called Ikshvaku, Nriga, Dhrishta, Saryati, Narishyanta, Pramsu, Nabhaganedishta, Karusha, and Prishadhra. Desirous of a son, Manu sacrificed to Mitra and Varuna. But in consequence of a wrong invocation through an irregularity of the hotri-priesta daughter called Ila was born. Then through the favour of Mitra and Varuna she became to Manu a son called Sudyunma. But being again changed into a female through the wrath of Isvara (Mahadeva) she wandered near the hermitage of Buddha the son of Soma (the Moon); who becoming enamoured of her had by her a son called Pururavas. After his birth, the god who is formed of sacrifice, of the Rik, Yajus, Saman, and Atharva Vedas, of all things, of mind, of nothing, he who is in the form of the sacrificial Male, was worshipped by the rishis of infinite splendour who desired that Sudyumna should recover his manhood. Through the favour of this god Ila became again Sudyumna."

The Vishnu Purana then proceeds to give the following particulars regarding the sons of Manu:

(i) Prishadhra became a Sudra in consequence of his having killed his religious preceptor's cow.

(ii) From Karusha the Karushas Kshatriyas of great power were descended.

(iii) Nabhaga, the son of Nedishta became a Vaishya."

The above is the story of the Solar race. The Vishnu Purana has also a parallel story relating to the Lunar race which according to it sprang from Atri just as the Solar race from Manu:

> *"Atri was the son of Brahma, and the father of Soma (the moon), whom Brahma installed as the sovereign of plants. Brahmins and stars. After celebrating the* rajasuya *sacrifice, Soma became intoxicated with pride, and carried off Tara (Slar), the wife of Vrihaspati, the preceptor of the gods, whom, although admonished and entreated by Brahma, the gods, and rishis, Soma refused to restore. Soma's part was taken by Usanas; and Rudra, who had studied under Angiras, aided Vrihaspati. A fierce conflict ensued between the two sides supported respectively by the gods and the Daityas, etc., Biahma interposed, and compelled Soma to restore Tara to her husband. She had, however, in the meantime become pregnant, and bore a son Buddha (the planet Mercury), of whom when strongly urged, she acknowledged Soma to be the father. Pururavas was the son of this Buddha by Ila, the daughter of Manu. Pururavas had six sons, of whom the eldest was Ayus. Ayus had five sons; Nahusha, Kshattravriddha, Rambha, Raji and Anenas.*

Kshattravriddha had a son Sunahotra who had three sons, Kasa, Lesa and Gritsamada. From the last sprang Saunaka, who originated the system of four castes. Kasa had a son, Kasiraja, of whom again Dirghatamas was the son, as Dhanvantari was of Dirghatamas."

Compare these ideologies of creation with those set out in Chapter 2 and what do we find? I think the result of comparison may be set down in the following propositions: (1) one is sacerdotal in colour and character, the other is secular; (2) one refers to a human being Manu as the progenitor, the other refers to God Brahma or Prajapati as the originator; (3) one is historical in its drift, the other is supernatural; (4) one speaks of the deluge, the other is completely silent about it; (5) one aims at explaining the four *Varnas,* the other aims at explaining the origin of society only.

These differences are many and fundamental. Particularly fundamental seems to be the difference in regard to *Chaturvarnya.* The sacerdotal ideology recognizes it, but the secular ideology does not. It is true that an attempt is made to combine the two by explaining, as is done in the Ramayana and the Puranas, how Manu's progeny developed into four *Varnas.* But obviously this is an attempt to mould the two ideologies into one. This attempt is deliberate and calculated. But the difference between the two ideologies is so fundamental that inspite of this attempt they persist as two separate ideologies. All that has happened is that instead of one we have two explanations of *Chaturvarnya,* supernatural *Chaturvarnya* produced by Purusha, and natural Chaturvarnya as developed among Manu's sons. That the result should be so clumsy shows that the two ideologies are fundamentally different and irreconcilable.. It is a pity that the existence of two such ideologies recorded in the Brahmanic literature has not been noticed by scholars who have dealt with the subject. But the fact of their existence and their significance cannot be ignored. What is the significance of the existence of two such ideologies fundamentally different and irreconcilable? To me, it seems that they are the ideologies of two different Aryan races— one believing in *Chaturvarnya* and the other not believing in *Chaturvarnya*— who at a later stage became merged into one. If this reasoning is well-founded then this difference in ideologies disclosed by the Brahmanic literature furnishes further evidence in support of the new theory.

The third and the most unimpeachable evidence in support of my view comes from the anthropometrical survey of the Indian people. Such a survey was first made by Sir Herbert Risley in 1901. On the basis of cephalic index, he came to the conclusion that the people of India were a mixture of four different races: (1) Aryan, (2) Dravidian, (3) Mongolian, and (4) Scythian. He even went to the length of defining the areas where they were massed. The survey was a very rough one. His conclusions have been tested by Dr. Guha in 1936. His Report on the subject forms a very valuable document in the field of Indian anthropology. The map prepared by Dr. Guha on which he has plotted so to say the distribution of the Indian people according to their head measurements throws a flood of light on the racial composition of the people of India. Dr. Guha's conclusion is that the Indian people are composed of two racial stocks: (1) long headed, and short-headed, and that the long-headed are in the interior of India and the short-headed are on the outskirts.

The evidence of skulls found in different parts of India also goes to confirm this. This is how Dr. Guha sums up the evidence on this point:

> *"The accounts of the human remains from prehistoric sites given above, though extremely meagre, with the exception of those of the Indus Valley, enable us nevertheless to visualise the broad outlines of the racial history of India in these times. From the beginning of the 4th Millennium B.C. Northwestern India seems to have been in the occupation of a long-headed race with a narrow prominent nose. Side by side with them we find the existence of another very powerfully built race also long-headed, but with lower cranial vault, and equally long-faced and narrow nose, though the latter was not so high pitched as that of the former.*
>
> *A third type with broader head and apparently Armenoid affinities also existed, but its advent occurred probably somewhat later judged by the age of the site as Harappa from which most of these latter type of skulls came."*

Speaking in terms of the Alpine and the Mediterranean race, one can say that the Indian people are composed of two stocks: (1) The Mediterranean or the long-headed race, and (2) the Alpine or the short-headed race.

About the Mediterranean race, certain facts are admitted. It is admitted that it is a race which spoke the Aryan language. It is admitted that its home was in Europe round about the Mediterranean basin and from thence it migrated to India. From its localisation, it is clear that it must have come to India before the entry of the Alpine race.

Similar facts about the Alpine race remain to be ascertained. First is about the home of the Alpine race and second is about its native speech. According to Prof. Ripley, the home of the Alpine race was in Asia somewhere in the Himalayas. His reasons may be given in his own words. Says Prof. Ripley: "What right have we for the assertion that this infiltration of population from the East-it was not a conquest, everything points to it as a gradual peaceful immigration, often merely the settlement of unoccupied territory—marks the advent of an overflow from the direction of Asia? The proof of this rests largely upon our knowledge of the people of that continent, especially of the Pamir region, the Western Himalayan highlands. Just here on the ' roof of the world,' where Max Muller and the early philologists placed the primitive home of Aryan civilisation, a human type prevails which tallies almost exactly with our ideal Alpine or Celtic European race.

The researches of De Ujfaivy, Topinard, and others localise its peculiar traits over a vast territory hereabouts. The Galchas, mountain Tadjiks, and their fellows are grey-eyed, dark-haired, stocky in build, with cephalic indexes ranging above 86 for the most part. From this region a long chain of peoples of a similar physical type extends.uninterruptedly westward over Asia Minor and into Europe. The only point which the discovery of a broad area in Western Asia occupied by an ideal Alphine type settles, is that it emphasises the affinities of this peculiar race. It is no proof of direct immigration from Asia at all, as Tappeiner observes. It does, however, lead us to turn our eyes eastward when we seek for the origin of the broad-headed type. Things vaguely point to an original ethnic base of supplies somewhere in this direction.

It could not lie westward, for everywhere along the Atlantic the race slowly disappears, so to speak. That the Alpine type approaches all the other human millions on the Asiatic continent, in the head form especially, but in hair, colour and stature as well, also prejudices us in the matter; just as the increasing long-headedness and extreme brunetness of our Mediterranean race led us previously to derive it from some type parent to that of the African Negro. These points are then fixed; the roots of the Alpine race run eastward; those of the Mediterranean type towards the south."

On the question of its language there is a certain amount of dispute as to who introduced the Aryan language in Europe, whether the Nordics (the purest of the Indo-Germans) or the Alpines. But there is no dispute that the language of the Alpine race was Aryan and therefore it is entitled to be called Aryan race in philological sense.

From the foregoing statement of facts, it will be seen that there is a solid foundation in anthropometry and history, in support of the Rig Veda that there were in India two Aryan races and not one. Having regard to this, one cannot refuse to admit that here there is a direct conflict between the Western theory and the testimony of the Rig Veda. Whereas the Western theory speaks of one Aryan race, the Rig Veda speaks of two Aryan races. The Western theory is thus in conflict with the Rig Veda on a major issue. The Rig Veda being the best evidence on the subject the theory which is in conflict with it must be rejected. There is no escape.

This conflict on the major issue also creates a conflict on the issue of invasion and conquest. We do not know which of the two Aryan races came to India first. But if they belonged to the Alpine race then its home being near the Himalayas, there is no room for the theory of invasion from outside. As to the conquest of the native tribes, assuming it to be a fact, the matter is not quite so simple as Western writers have supposed. On the footing that the Dasas and Dasyus were racially different from the Aryans, the theory of conquest must take account not merely of a possible conquest of Dasas and Dasyus by Aryans but also of a possible conquest of Aryans by Aryans. It must also explain which of the two Aryans conquered the Dasas and Dasyus if they conquered them at all.

The Western theory, it is clear, is only a hurried conclusion drawn from insufficient examination of facts and believed to be correct because it tallied with certain preconceived notions about the mentality of the ancient Aryans which they were supposed to have possessed on no other grounds except that their alleged modern descendants, namely, the Indo Germanic races are known to possess. It is built on certain selected facts which are assumed to be the only facts. It is extraordinary that a theory with such a slender and insecure foundation in fact should have been propounded by Western scholars for serious scholars and should have held the field for such a long time. In the face of the discovery of new facts set out in this Chapter the theory can no longer stand and must be thrown on the scrap heap.

Sudras and Dasas

It has been shown how untenable the Western theory is. The only part of the theory that remains to be considered is: who are the Sudras? Mr. A. C. Das says: "The Dasas and the Dasyus were either savages ornon-Vedic Aryan tribes. Those of them that were captured in war were probably made slaves and formed the Sudra caste."

Mr. Kane another Vedic scholar and upholder of the Western theory, holds the view that: "The word 'Dasa' in later literature means a 'scrf or a slave'. It follows that the Dasa tribes that we see opposed to the Aryas in the Rig Veda were gradually vanquished and were then made to serve the Aryas. In the Manusmriti (VIII, 413) the Sudra is said to have been created by God for service *(dasya)* of the Brahmana. We find in the Tai. Samhita, the Tai. Brahmana and other Brahmana works that the Sudra occupied the same position that he does in the Smritis. Therefore it is reasonable to infer that the *Dasas* or *Dasyus* conquered by the Aryans were gradually transformed into the Sudras."

According to this view the Sudras are the same as Dasas and Dasyus and further the Sudras were the non-Aryan original inhabitants of India and were in a primitive and a savage state of civilisation. It is these propositions which we must now proceed to examine. To begin with the first proposition. It is not one proposition but is really two propositions rolled in one. One is that the Dasas and Dasyus are one and the same people. The other is that they and the Sudras are one and the same people.

That the *Dasas* and *Dasyus* are one and the same people is a proposition of doubtful validity. Such references to them as are to be found in the Rig Veda are not decisive. In some places the terms *Dasa* and *Dasyu* are used in a way as though there was no difference between the two. Shambara, Shushna, Vritra and Pipru are described both as Dasas and Dasyus. Both Dasas and Dasyus are described as the enemies of Indra and

Devas and specially the Ashvins. The cities of both Dasas as well as of the Dasyus are described to have been levelled down by Indra and Devas. The defeat of both Dasas as well as Dasyus is described as producing the same effect, namely, release of water and the emergence of light. In describing the release of Dabhiti both are referred to, at one place he is said to have been released from the Dasas and at another place he is said to have been released from the Dasyus.

While these references suggest that the Dasas and Dasyus were the same, there are other references which suggest that they were different. This is clear from the fact that the Dasas are referred to separately in 54 places and Dasyus are referred to separately in 78 places. Why should there be so many separate references if they did not form two distinct entities? The probability is that they refer to two different communities.

About the second proposition that the Sudras are the same as the Dasas and Dasyus, one can definitely say that it is without any foundation whatsoever. To make out a case that the Sudras are the same as the Dasas and Dasyus an attempt is made to treat the word Sudra as a derivative word. The word is said to be derived from *Shuc* (sorrow) and *dm* (overcome) and means one overcome by sorrow. In this connection reliance is placed on the story told in the Vedanta Sutra (i.3.34) of *Janasruti* who is said to have been overcome by sorrow on hearing the contemptuous talk of the flamingoes about himself. The same derivation is given by the Vishnu Purana.

How far are these statements well-founded? To say that Sudra is not a proper name but is a derivative word is too silly for words. The Brahmanic writers excel everybody in the art of inventing false etymologies. There is no word for which they will not design some sort of etymology. Speaking of the different etymologies of the word Upanishad given by Brahmanic writers, Prof. Max Muller said: "These explanations seem so wilfully perverse that it is difficult to understand the unanimity of native scholars. We ought to take into account, however, that very general tendency among half-educated people, to acquiesce in any etymology which accounts for the most prevalent meaning of a word. The Aranyakas abound in such etymologies, which probably were never intended as real etymologies, in our sense of the word, but simply as plays on words, helping to account somehow for their meaning." This warning equally well applies to the attempt of the Vedanta Sutra and of the Vayu Purana to make the word Sudra a derivative word suggesting that it meant a 'sorrowful people' and we must therefore reject it as being absund and senseless. We have, however, direct evidence in support of the proposition that Sudra is a proper name of a tribe or a clan and is not a derivative word as is sought to be made out.

Various pieces of evidence can be adduced in favour of this proposition. The historians of Alexander's invasion of India have described a number of republics as free, independent and autonomous whom Alexander encountered. These are, no doubt, formed of different tribes and were known by the name borne by those tribes. Among these is mentioned a people called *Sodari.* They were a fairly important tribe, being one of those which fought Alexander though it suffered a defeat at his hands. Lassen identified them with the ancient *Sudras.* Patanjali at 1.2.3 of his Mahabhasya mentions Sudras and associates them with the Abhiras. The Mahabharata in Chapter XXXII of the Sabha parvan speaks of the republic of the Sudras. The Vishnu Purana as well as the Markandeya Purana and the Brahma Purana refer to the Sudras as a separate tribe among many other tribes and fix their location in the Western part of the country above the Vindhyas.

Let us now turn to the second proposition and examine the various elements of which it is composed. There are two elements in the proposition. First is: Are the words Dasyus and Dasas used in the racial sense indicative of their being non-Aryan tribes? The second element is that assuming they were, is there anything to indicate that they were the native tribes of India? Unless and until these two questions are answered in the affirmative, there is no possibility of identifying the Dasyus and Dasas with the Sudras.

About the Dasyus, there is no evidence to show that the term is used in a racial sense indicative of a non-Aryan people. On the other hand, there is positive evidence in support of the conclusion that it was used to denote persons who did not observe the Aryan form of religion. In this connection, reference may be made to Verse 23 of Adhyaya 65 of the Shantiparvan of the Mahabharata. It reads as follows:

Driüshyante manushe leeke sarvavarneshu dasyavah!
Linganntharey varthamana
ashrameshuchathushrvapi!!

The verse says: "In all the Vamas and in all the Ashrams, one finds the existence of Dasyus."

What is the origin of the word Dasyu it is difficult to say. But a suggestion has been put forth that it was the word of abuse used by the Indo-Aryans to the Indo-Iranians. There is nothing unnatural or far-fetched in this suggestion. That the two had come into conflict is borne out by history. It is therefore quite possible for the Indo-Aryans to have coined such a contemptuous name for their enemies. If this is true, then Dasyus cannot be regarded as the natives of India.

Regarding the Dasas, the question is whether there is any connection between them and the Azhi-Dahaka of the Zend Avesta. The name Azhi-Dahaka is a compound name which consists of two parts. *Azhi* means serpent, dragon and *Dahaka* comes from root *Dah* meaning ' to sting, to do harm'. Thus *Azhi-Dahaka* meaning a stinging dragon. It is a proper name of a person commonly known in Indo-Iranian traditions as *Zohak*. He is mentioned in Yasht literature many a times. He is credited to have lived in Babylon where he had built a palace. He is also credited to have built a great observatory in Babylon. This mighty devil Azhi-Dahaka was created by the Archdemon Angra Mainyu in order to destroy the kingdom of holiness of the corporeal world. This Azhi-Dahaka went to war against Yima the renowned king of the Indo-Iranians and not only vanquished him, but killed him in battle.

Yima is always spoken of in Avesta as *Kshaeta* meaning shining or ruling. Root *Kshi* has two meanings, to shine or to rule. There is another ephithet commonly used for Yima and that is *Hvanthwa* meaning 'possessing good flock'. This Avesta Yima Khshaita became in later Persian language *Jamshid.* According to traditions, king Jamshid son of Vivanghvant was the great hero of the Iranian history, the founder of a great Persian civilization. He was a king of the Peshdiadyan dynasty. In Yasna 9 and 5 (Koema Yashi) it is stated that 'Vivanshas' was the first man who unceremoniously pounded Hasma (Sk. Sasma) in this corporeal world and the boon he received was: to him was born a son nobly who was Yima the shining and of good flock, who was most glorious amongst the living ones, who was like a glowing sun amongst mankind, during whose kingship he made noblemen and cattle (animals) immortal, made waters and trees undrying. He possessed undiminishing (ever fresh) divine glory. During the kingship of famous Yima there was neither extreme cold nor extreme heat, there was no old age, death and envy.

Is Dahaka of the Zenda Aveshta the same as Dasa of the Rig Veda? If similarity in name can be relied upon as evidence, then obviously it points to their being the names of one and the same person. Dasa in Sanskrit can easily be Daha in Aveshta since *sa* in the former is natural conversion to *ha* in the latter. If this were the only evidence the suggestion that Dasa of the Rig Veda and Dahaka of the Zenda Avesta are the same could have been no better than a conjecture. But there is other and more cogent evidence which leaves no doubt about their identity. In Yasna Ha 9 (which is the same as Horn Yashe) Azhi-Dahaka is spoken of as 'three mouthed, three-headed and six-eyed'. What is striking is that this physical description of Dahaka in Aveshta is exactly similar to the description of Dasa in Rig Veda (x.99.6) where he is also described as having three heads and six eyes If the suggestion that the Dasa in the Rig Veda is the same as Dahaka in the Aveshta, is accepted, then obviously the Dasas were not native tribes aboriginal to India.

Were they savages? The Dasas and Dasyus were not a primitive people. They were as civilised as the Aryans and in fact more powerful than the Aryans. Such is the testimony of the Rig Veda. It is well epitomised by Mr. Iyengar when he says that: "The Dasyus lived in cities (R.V., i.53.8; i. 103.3) and under kings the names of many of whom are mentioned. They possessed 'accumulated wealth' (R.V., viii.40.6) in the form of cows, horses and chariots (R.V., ii. 15.4) which though kept in 'hundred-gated cities' (R.V., X.99.3), Indra seized and gave away to his worshippers, the Aryas (R.V., i.176.4). The Dasyus were wealthy (R.V., i.33.4) and owned property 'in the plains and on the hills' (R.V., x.69.6). They were 'adorned with their array of gold and jewels' (R.V., i.33.8). They owned many castles (R.V., i.33.13; viii.17.14). The Dasyu demons and the Arya gods alike lived in gold, silver and iron castles (SS.S., vi.23; A.V., v.28.9; R.V., ii.20.8). Indra overthrew for his worshipper, Divodasa, frequently mentioned in the hymns, a 'hundred stone castles' (R.V., iv.30.20) of the Dasyus. Agni, worshipped by the Arya, gleaming in behalf of him, tore and burnt the cities of the fireless Dasyus. (R.V., vii.5.3). Vrihaspati broke the stone prisons in which they kept the cattle raided from the Aryas (R.V., iv.67.3). The Dasyus owned chariots and used them in war like the Aryas and had the same weapons as the Aryas (R.V., viii.24.27; iii.30.5; ii.15.4)"

That the Dasas and Dasyus were the same as the Sudras is a pure figment of imagination. It is only a wild guess. It is tolerated because persons who make it are respectable scholars. So far as evidence is concerned, there is no particle of it, which can be cited in support of it. As has been said before, the word Dasa occurs in the Rig Veda 54 times and Dasyu 78 times. The Dasas and the Dasyus are sometimes spoken together. The word Sudra occurs only once and that too in a context in which the Dasas and Dasyus have no place.

In the light of these considerations, it is difficult to say how anyone in his senses can say that Sudras are the same as the Dasas and Dasyus. Another fact which is to be noted is that the names Dasas and Dasyus completely disappear from the later Vedic literature.

It means they were completely absorbed by the Vedic Aryans. But it is quite different with the Sudras. The early Vedic literature is very silent about them. But the later Vedic literature is full of them. This shows that the Sudras were different from the Dasas and Dasyus.

Were the Sudras non-Aryans? Mr. Kane says : "A clear line of demarcation was kept between the Arya and the Sudra in the times of the Brahmana works and even in the Dharmasutras. The Tandya Brahmana speaks of a mock fight: 'the Sudra and Arya fight on a hide; out of the two they so arrange that the Arya colour becomes the victor.' The Ap. Dh. S. (I, i.3.40-41) says that a *brahmachari* if he cannot himself eat all the food he has brought by begging, may keep it near an Arya (for his use) or he may give it to a Sudra who is a Dasa (of his teacher). Similarly, Gautama x.69 used the word 'anarya' for Sudra."

On the question of the line of demarcation; between the Sudras and Aryans, the matter needs to be carefully examined.

The strength of the argument that the Sudras were non-Aryans is to be found in the following statements:

A.V., iv.20.4. — "The thousand-eyed god shall put this plant into my right hand; with that do I see everyone, the Sudra as well as the Arya."

Kathaka Samhita, xxxiv.5— "The Sudra and the Arya quarrel about the skin. The gods and the demons quarrelled about the sun; the gods won it (the sun). (By this act of quarrelling with Sudras) the Arya makes the Arya Varna win, makes himself successful. The Arya shall be inside the altar, the Sudra outside the altar. The skin shall be white, circular-the form of the sun."

Vajasaneyi Samhita, xxiii.30-31— "When a deer eats the barley in the field, the (owner of the field) is not pleased with the nourished animal; when a Sudra woman has an Arya as a lover, (the husband) does not long for (the consequent) prosperity."

When a deer eats barley, the (owner of the field) does not approve of the nourished animal. When a Sudra is the lover of an Arya woman, the (husband) does not consent to the prosperity.

These stanzas, which speak of the Sudra and the Arya as separate and opposed form the foundation of the theory that the Sudras are non-Aryans. To say the least, such a conclusion would be a very hasty one.

Two considerations must be borne in mind before any conclusion is drawn from the aforementioned statements. In the first place, it must be borne in mind that according to what has been said before and according to the evidence of the Rig Veda, there are two categories of Aryans, the Vedic and the non-Vedic.

Given this fact, it would be quite easy for an Arya of one class to speak of an Arya of another class, as though the two were separate and opposed. Interpreted in this way, the above statements, in which Sudras are set against the Aryans, do not mean that they were not Aryas. They were Aryas of a different sect or class.

That this is possible can be seen from the following statements in the sacred literature of the Hindus:

A.V., xix.32.8.— "Make me. Oh, Darbha (grass), dear to the Brahmin, and the Rajanya (*i.e.*, Kshalriya), to the Sudra and to the Arya and to him whom we love and to everyone who is able to see."

A.V., xix.62.1.— "Make me beloved among the gods, make me beloved among the princes; make me dear to everyone who sees, to the Sudra and to the Arya."

Vajasaneyi Samhita, xviii.48.— "(Oh, Agni), give to us lustre among Brahmins, give us lustre among kings; lustre among Vaishyas and among Sudras; give to me lustre added to lustre.",

Vajasaneyi Samhita, xx.17.— "Whatever sin we have committed in the village, in the forest, in the assembly, with our senses, against the Sudra or against the Arya, whatever sin one of us (two, the sacrificer and his wife) has committed in the matter of his duty (towards the other),— of that sin, you are the destroyer."

Vajasaneyi Samhita, xviii.48.— "As I speak these auspicious words to the people, to the Brahmin and the Rajanya, to the Sudra and to the Arya and to my own enemy, may I be dear to the gods and to the giver of *dakshinas* here in this world. May this desire of mine be granted. May that (enemy of mine) be subjected to me."

What do these statements show? The first one makes a distinction between the Brahmins and the Aryas. Can it be said that the Brahmins were non-Aryans? The other statements pray for the love and goodwill of the Sudras. If the Sudra was a primitive aboriginal non-Aryan, is such a prayer conceivable? The statements on which reliance is placed do not prove that the Sudras were non-Aryans.

That the Dharmasutras call the Sudra Anarya and the statements in the Vajasaneyi Samhita pouring scorn on the Sudra woman, do not mean anything. There are two arguments against accepting the testimony of the Dharma Sutra. In the first place, as will be shown later, the Dharmasutras and other treatises are books written by the enemies of the Sudra. As such, they have no evidentiary value. It is also doubtful whether such anti-Sudra statements are mere imprecations or statements of facts as they existed. They seem to contradict facts reported in other works.

The Dharmasutras say that a Sudra is not entitled to the Upanayana ceremony and the wearing of the sacred thread. But in Samskara Ganapati there is an express provision declaring the Sudra to be eligible for Upanayana.

The Dharmasutras say that a Sudra has no right to study the Vedas. But the Chhandogya Upanishad (iv:l-2) relates the story of one Janasruti to whom Veda Vidya was taught by the preceptor Raikva. This Janasruti was a Sudra. What is more is that Kavasha Ailusha, was a Sudra. He was a Rishi and the author of several hymns of the Tenth Book of the Rig Veda.

The Dharmasutras say that a Sudra has no right to perform Vedic ceremonies and sacrifices. But Jaimini, the author of the Purva Mimarnsa mentions an ancient teacher by name Badari— whose work is lost— as an exponent of the contrary view that even *Sudras* could perform Vedic sacrifices. The Bharadvaja Srauta Sutra (v.28) admits that there exists another school of thought which holds that a Sudra can consecrate the three sacred fires necessary for the performance of a Vedic sacrifice. Similarly, the commentator of the Katyayana Srauta Sutra (1.4.16) admits that there are certain Vedic texts which lead to the inference that the Sudra was eligible to perform Vedic rites.

The Dharmasutras say that a Sudra is not entitled to the sacred drink of Soma. But in the story of the Ashvins, there is definite evidence that the Sudra had a right to the divine drink of Soma. The Ashvins, as the story goes, once happened to behold Sukanya when she had just bathed and when her person was bare. She was a young girl married to a Rishi by name Chyavana who at the time of marriage was so old as to be dying almost any day. The Ashvins were captivated by the beauty of Sukanya and said "Accept one of us for your husband. It behoveth thee not to spend thy youth fruitlessly." She refused, saying "I am devoted to my husband." They again spoke to her and this time proposed a bargain: "We two are the celestial physicians of note. We will make thy husband young and graceful. Do thou then select one of us as thy husband." She went to her husband and communicated to him the terms of the bargain. Chyavana said to Sukanya "Do thou so"; and the bargain was carried out and Chyavana was made a young man by the Ashvins. Subsequently, a question arose whether the

Ashvins were entitled to Soma, which was the drink of the Gods. Indra objected saying that the Ashvins were Sudras and therefore not entitled to Soma. Chyavana, who had received perpetual youth from the Ashvins, set aside the contention and compelled Indra to give them Soma.

There is another reason why the evidence of the Dharmasutras that the Sudras are non-Aryans should not be accepted. In the first place, it is contrary to the view taken by Manu. In the decision of the issue whether the Sudra was an Aryan or a non-Aryan, the following verses from Manu require to be carefully considered:

> *"If a female of the caste sprung from a Brahmana and a Sudra female, bear (children) to one of the highest castes, the inferior (tribe) attains the highest caste within the seventh generation."*
>
> *"(Thus) a Sudra attains the rank of a Brahmana and (in a similar manner) a Brahmana sinks to the level of a Sudra; but know that it is the same with the offspring of a Kshatriya or of a Vaishya."*
>
> *"If (a doubt) should arise, with whom the pre-eminence (is, whether) with him whom an Aryan by chance begot on a non-Aryan female, or (with the son) of a Brahmana woman by a non-Aryan;"*

The decision is as follows: 'He who was begotten by an Aryan on a non-Aryan female, may become (like to) an Aryan by his virtues; he whom an Aryan (mother) bore to a non Aryan father (is and remains) unlike to an Aryan.'

Verse 64 from Manu is also to be found in Gautama Dharma Sutra (uv.22). There seems to be some controversy as to the correct interpretation of this verse. In summing up the different interpretations, Buhler says:

> *"According to Medh., Gov., Kull., and Ragh., the meaning is that, if the daughter of a Brahmana and of a Sudra female and her descendants all marry Brahmanas, the offspring of the sixth female descendant of the original couple will be a Brahmana. While this explanation agrees with Haradatta's comment on the parallel passage of Gautama, Nar. and Nan. take the verse very differently. They say that if a Parasava, the son of a*

Brahmana and of a Sudra female, marries a most excellent Parasava female, who possesses a good moral character and other virtues, and if his descendants do the same, the child born in the sixth generation will be a Brahmana. Nandana quotes in support of his view, Baudhayana i. 16.13-14 (left out in my translation of the Sacred Books of the East, ii, p. 197)... '(offspring) begotten by a Nishada on a Nishadi, removes within five generations the Sudrahood; one may initiate him (the fifth descendant); one may sacrifice for the sixth.' This passage of Baudhayana the reading of which is supported by a new MS from Madras clearly shows that Baudhayana allowed the male offspring of Brahmanas and Sudra females to be raised to the level of Aryans. It is also not impossible that the meaning of Manu's verse may be the same, and that the translation should be, 'if the offspring of a Brahmana and of a Sudra female begets children with a most excellent (male of the Brahmana caste or female of the Parasava tribe), the inferior (tribe) attains the highest caste in the seventh generation."

Whatever be the interpretation, the fact remains that in the seventh generation a Sudra under certain circumstances could become a Brahmin. Such a conception would have been impossible if the Sudra was not an Aryan.

That the Sudra is a non-Aryan is contrary to the view taken by the school of Arthashastra. As a representative of that school, the opinion of Kautilya on that question is of great value. In laying down the law of slavery, Kautilya says: The selling or mortgaging by kinsmen of the life of a Sudra who is not a born slave, and has not attained majority, but is Arya in birth shall be punished with a fine of 12 panas.

Deceiving a slave of his money or depriving him of the privileges he can exercise as an Arya *(Aryabhava)* shall be punished with half the fine (levied for enslaving the life of an Arya).

Failure to set a slave at liberty on the receipt of a required amount of ransom shall be punished with a fine of 12 panas; putting a slave under confinement for no reason *(samrodhaschakaranat)* shall likewise be punished.

The offspring of a man who has sold himself off as a slave shall be an Arya. A slave shall be entitled not only to what he has earned himself without prejudice to his masters work but also to the inheritance he has received from his father. Here is Kautilya, who calls the Sudra an Aryan in the most emphatic and express terms possible.

Coming to the question of Sudras having been made slaves, it is nonsense, if not mendacious. It is founded on two assumptions.

First is that the Dasas are described as slaves in the Rig Veda. The second is that the Dasas are the same as Sudras. It is true that the word Dasa is used in the Rig Veda in the sense of slave or servant. But the word in this sense occurs in only 5 places and no more. But even if it did occur more than five times, would it prove that the Sudras were made slaves? Unless and until it is proved that the two were the same people, the suggestion is absurd. It is contrary to known facts.

Sudras participated in the coronation of kings. In the post-vedic or the period of the Brahmanas, the coronation of a king was in reality an offer of sovereignty by the people to the king. This was done by the representatives of the people called Ratnis who played a very important part in the investiture of the king.

The Ratnis were so-called because they held the Ratna (jewel), which was a symbol of sovereignty. The king received his sovereignty only when the Ratnis handed over to him the jewel of sovereignty, and on receiving his sovereignty the king went to the house of each of the Ratnis and made an offering to him. It is a significant fact that one of the Ratnis was always a Sudra.

Nilakantha, the author of *Nitimayukha,* describes the coronation ceremony of a later time. According to him, the four chief ministers, Brahmin, Kshatriya, Vaishya and Sudra, consecrated the new king. Then the leaders of each Varna and of the castes lower still, consecrated him with holy water. Then followed acclamation by the twice-born. That the Sudras were invited to be present at the coronation of the king along with Brahmins is evidenced by the description of the coronation of

Yudhishthira, the eldest brother of the Pandavas, which is given in the Mahabharata. Sudras were members of the two political assemblies of ancient times, namely, the Janapada and Paura and as a member of these the Sudra was entitled to special respect even from a Brahmin. This was so even according to the Manusmriti (vi.61) as well as to the Vishnu Smriti (xxi.64). Otherwise there is no meaning in Manu saying that a Brahmin should not live in a country where the king is a Sudra. That means Sudras were kings.

In the Shanti Parvan of the Mahabharata, Bhisma in his lessons on Politics to Yudhishthira says: "I shall, however, tell thee what kinds of ministers should be appointed by thee.

Four Brahmins learned in the Vedas, possessed of a sense of dignity, belonging to the *Snataka* order, and of pure behaviour, and eight Kshatriyas, all of whom should be possessed of physical strength and capable of wielding weapons, and one and twenty Vaishyas, all of whom should be possessed of wealth, and three Sudras, everyone of whom should be humble and of pure conduct and devoted to his daily duties, and one man of the Suta caste, possessed of a knowledge of the Puranas and the eight cardinal virtues should be thy ministers." This proves that the Sudras were ministers and that they were almost equal to the Brahmins in number The Sudras were not poor and lowly. They were rich. This fact is testified by the Maitrayani Samhita (iv.2.7.10) and the Panchavirnsa Brahmana (vi.l.ll).

There are two other aspects to this question. What significance can there be to the enslavement of the Sudras, assuming it was a fact? There would be some significance if the Aryans did not know slavery or were not prepared to turn the Aryans into slaves. But the fact is that the Aryans knew slavery and permitted the Aryans to be made slaves. This is clear from Rig Veda, (vii.86.7;viii. 19.36 and viii.56.3). That being so, why should they particularly want to make slaves of the Sudras? What is more important is why should they make different laws for the Sudra slaves?

In short, the Western theory does not help us to answer our questions, who were the Sudras and how did they become the fourth Varna?

Who were the Sudras?

Sudras were Kshatriyas

Who were the Sudras if they were not a non-Aryan aboriginal race? This question must now be faced. The theory I venture to advance may be stated in the following three propositions:

(1) The Sudras were Aryans.

(2) The Sudras belonged to the Kshatriya class.

(3) The Sudras were so important a class of Kshatriyas that some of the most eminent and powerful kings of the ancient Aryan communities were Sudras.

This thesis regarding the origin of the Sudras is a startling if not a revolutionary thesis. So startling it is that not many people will be ready to accept it, even though there may be enough evidence to support it. My obligation is to produce the evidence, leaving the people to judge its worth.

The primary piece of evidence on which this thesis rests is a passage which occurs in Verses 38-40 of Chapter 60 of the Shanti Parvan of the Mahabharata. It reads as follows: "It *has been heard by us that in the days of old a Sudra of the name of Paijavana gave a Dakshina (in his own sacrifice) consisting of a hundred thousand Purnapatras according to the ordinance called Aindragni."*

The important statements contained in this passage are three: (1) that Paijavana was a Sudra, (2) that this Sudra Paijavana performed sacrifices, and (3) the Brahmins performed sacrifices for him and accepted Dakshina from him.

The passage quoted above is taken from Mr. Roy's edition of the Mahabharata. The first thing is to ascertain whether the text is accurate or whether there are any variant readings. As regards the authenticity of his text, this is what Mr. Roy says: "As far as my edition is concerned it is substantially based on that of Royal Asiatic Society of Bengal, published about forty-five years ago under the superintendence of a few learned Pandits of Bengal aided, as I believe, by an English Orientalist of repute.

Manuscripts had been procured from all parts of India (the South unexcepted) and these were carefully collated. Although edited with such care, I have not, however, slavishly followed the Society's edition. I have compared it carefully with the Maharajah of Burdwan's text in the Bengalee character which was edited with still greater care. About 18 manuscripts procured from different parts of India (the South not excepted) were carefully collated by the Burdwan Pandits before they admitted a single *sloka* as genuine."

Prof. Sukthankar, the erudite editor of the critical edition of the Mahabharata, after examining many editions of the Mahabharata, concluded by saying that: "The *editio princeps* (Calcutta—1856) remains the best edition of the Vulgate, after the lapse of nearly a century."

Although the authenticity of Mr. Roy's edition of the Mahabharata cannot be doubted, it would not be unreasonable if critics were to say that they would like to know what other manuscript support there is behind this text, which is made the basis of this new theory of the origin of the Sudras. In undertaking such an inquiry it is necessary to point to two considerations.

One is that there is no such thing as a Mahabharata manuscript in the sense of complete sets of manuscripts covering all the eighteen Parvans.

Each Parvan is treated as a separate unit with the result that the number of copies of the different Parvans to be found differ by a vast margin. Consequently, the number of manuscripts to be taken as a basis for deciding which is the correct text must vary with each Parvan.

The second consideration to which attention must be drawn is the fact that the text of the Mahabharata has been handed down in two divergent forms; a Northern and a Southern recension, texts, typical of the Aryavrata and the Dakshinapatha.

It is obvious that an examination of manuscript support must be based upon collation from a fair number of manuscripts and a fair distribution of the manuscripts between the Northern and the Southern recensions. Bearing these considerations in mind, the results of the collation of the text of *Shloka* 38 of the 60th chapter of the Shanti Parvan of the Mahabharata with which we are primarily concerned from different manuscripts is presented below:

1.	Sudrah Paijavano nama	(K) S
2.	Sudrah Pailavano nama	(M/l: M/2) S
3.	Sudrah Yailanano nama	(M/3: M/4) S
4.	Shudmh Yaijanano nama	(F)
5.	Shudropi Yajane nama	(L)
6.	Sudrah Paunjalka nama	(TC) S
7.	Shuddho Vaibhavano nama	(G) N
8.	Pura Vaijavano nama	(A, D/2)
9.	Pura Vaijanano nama	(M) N

Here is the result of the collation of nine manuscripts. Are nine manuscripts enough for constituting a text which has a number of variant readings? It is true that the number of manuscripts taken for the critical edition of the different Parvans of the Mahabharata exceeds nine. For the entire Mahabharata the minimum number of manuscripts taken for constituting the text is only ten. It cannot therefore be contended that nine is an insufficient number. The nine manuscripts fall into two geographical divisions. Northern and Southern. M1, M2, M3, M4 and TC belong to the Southern recession. A, M, G, D2 belong to the Northern recession. The selections of the manuscripts therefore satisfy the two tests which experts have laid down.

I am grateful to the Bhandarkar Oriental Research Institute for allowing me to use their collation sheet. Letters in brackets indicate the index number given by the Institute to the manuscript. N or S indicate whether the manuscript comes from the North or South. K is Kumbhakonam.

A scrutiny of the readings shows that:

(1) there is a variation in the description of Paijavana;

(2) there is a variation in the name of Paijavana;

(3) of the nine texts, six agree in describing him as a Sudra. One describes him as Shuddha and two instead of speaking of the class to which he belonged refer to the time when he lived and use the word 'Pura';

(4) with regard to the name, there is no agreement between any two of the nine manuscripts. Each gives a different reading.

Given this result, the question is what is the real text? Taking first the texts relating to the name, it is obvious that this is not a matter in which the question of meaning is involved. It does not raise any questions such as interpretation *versus* emendation or of giving preference to a reading which suggests how other readings might have arisen.

The question is which is the correct name and which readings are scriptural blunders committed by the scribes. There seems to be no doubt that the correct text is Paijavana. It is supported by both the recessions, Southern as well as Northern.

For Vaijavano in No. S is the same as Paijavano. All the rest are variations which are due to the ignorance of the scribes in not being able to read the original copy correctly and then trying to constitute the text in their own way.

Turning to the description of Paijavana, the change from *Sudrah* to *Pura,* it must be granted, is not accidental. It appears to be deliberate. Why this change has occurred it is difficult to say categorically.

Two things appear to be quite clear. In the first place, the change appears to be quite natural. In the second place, the change does not militate against the conclusion that Paijavana was a Sudra. The above conclusion will be obvious if the context, in which verses 38-40 occur, is borne in mind. The context will be clear from the following verses which precede them:

> *"The Sudra should never abandon his master whatever the nature or degree of the distress into which the latter may fall. If the master loses his wealth, he should with excessive zeal be supported by the Sudra servant A Sudra cannot have any wealth that is his own. Whatever he possesses belongs to his master. Sacrifice has been laid down as a duty of the three other orders. It has been ordained for the Sudra also, O! Bharata, A Sudra however is not competent to utter* swaha *and* svadha *or*

any other mantra. *For this reason, the Sudra, without observing the vows laid down in the Vedas, should worship the gods in minor sacrifices called* Pakayajnas. *The gift called Pumapatra is declared to be the Dakshina of such sacrifices."*

Taking the verses 38 to 40 in the context of these verses preceding them, it becomes clear that the whole passage deals with the Sudra. The story of Paijavana is a mere illustration. Against this background, it is unnecessary *to* repeat the word 'Sudra' before Paijavana.

This explains why the word Sudra does not occur before Paijavana in the two manuscripts. As to the reason for the use of the word *pura* in place of Sudra it must be remembered that the case of Paijavana had occurred in very ancient times.

It was therefore quite natural for the scribe to feel that it was desirable to put this fact in express terms. The writer being aware that there was no necessity for describing Paijavana as Sudra since that was made clear from the context, it was not necessary to emphasise it.

On the other hand, knowing that Paijavana had lived in very ancient times and that fact was not made very clear from the context, the writer thought it more appropriate to add the word *Pura* which was necessary and omit the word *Sudrah* which having regard to the context was unnecessary.

If this explanation is well-founded, we may take it as well established that the person referred to in the passage in the Shanti Parvan of the Mahabharata is Paijavana and that this Paijavana was a Sudra. The next question that falls due for consideration is the identification of Paijavana. Who is this Paijavana?

Yaska's Nirukta seems to give us a clue. In Nirukta ii.24 Yaska Says: "The seer Vishvamitra was the purohita of Sudas, the son of Pijavana, Vishvamitra, friend of all. All, moving together. Sudas a bountiful giver. *Paijavana,* son of Pijavana. Again *Pi-javana* one whose speed is enviable or whose gait is inimitable."

From Yaska's Nirukta we get two very important facts: (1) Paijavana means son of Pijavana, and (2) the person who is the son of Paijavana is Sudas. With the help of Yaska, we are able to answer the question: who is Paijavana referred to in the passage in the Shanti Parvan of the Mahabharata? The answer is that Paijavana is simply another name for Sudas.

The next question is who is this Sudas and what do we know about him? A search in the Brahmanic literature discloses three persons with the name Sudas. One Sudas is mentioned in the Rig Veda. His family particulars are given in the following stanzas of the Rig Veda:

Rig Veda, vii.18.21.—" Parashara, the destroyer of hundreds (of Rakshasas), and Vashishtha, they who, devoted to thee, have glorified thee in every dwelling, neglect not the friendship of thee (their) benefactor; therefore prosperous days dawn upon the pious."

Rig Veda, vii. 18.22.— "Praising the liberality of Sudas, the grandson of Devavata, the son of Paijavana, the donor of two hundred cows, and of two chariots with two wives, I, worthy (of the gift), circumambulate thee, Agni, like the ministrant priest in the chamber (of sacrifice)"

Rig Veda, vii.18.23.— "Four (horses), having golden trappings, going steadily on a difficult road, celebrated on the earth, the excellent and acceptable gifts (made) to me by Sudas, the son of Pijavana; bear me as a son (to obtain) food and progeny."

Rig Veda, vii. 18.24.— "The seven worlds praise (Sudas) as if he were Indra; him whose fame (spreads) through the spacious heaven and earth; who, munificent, has distributed (wealth) on every eminent person, and (for whom) the flowing (rivers) have destroyed Yudhyamadhi in war."

Rig Veda, vii.18.25.— "Maruts, leaders (of rites), attend upon this (prince) as you did upon Divodasa, the father of Sudas: favour the prayers of the devout son of Pijavana, and may his strength be unimpaired, undecaying."

The two others are mentioned by the Vishnu Purana. One Sudas is mentioned in Chapter IV as the descendant of Sagara. The genealogical tree connecting this Sudas with Sagara is as follows: "Sumati, the daughter of Kasyapa and Kesini, the daughter of Raja Vidarbha, were the two wives of Sagara. Being without progeny, the king solicited the aid of the sage Aurva with great earnestness, and the Muni pronounced this boon, that one wife should bear one son, the upholder of his race, and the other should give birth to sixty thousand sons; and he left it to them to make their election.

Kesini chose to have the single son; Sumati the multitude; and it came to pass in a short time that the former bore Asamanjas, a prince through whom the dynasty continued; and the daughter of Vinata (Sumati) had sixty thousand sons. The son of Asamanjas was Ansumat.

The son of Ansumat was Dilipa; his son was Bhagiratha, who brought Ganga down to earth, whence she is called Bhagirathi. The son of Bhagiratha was Sruta; his son was Nabhaga; his son was Ambarisha; his son was Sindhudvipa; his son was Ayutashva; his son was Ritupama, the friend of Nala, skilled profoundly in dice. The son of Ritupama was Sarvakama; his son was Sudasa; his son was Saudasa, named also Mitrasaha."

Another Sudas is mentioned in Chapter XIX as a descendant of Puru. The genealogical tree connecting this Sudas with Puru is as follows: "The son of Puru was Janamejaya; his son was Prechinvat; his son was Pravira, his son was Manasyu; his son was Bhayada; his son was Sudhumna; his *son* was Bahugava; his son was Samyati; his son was Bhamyati; his son was Raudrashva, who had ten sons, Riteyu, Kaksheyu, Stnandileyu, Ghriteyu, Jaleyu, Sthaleyu, Dhaneyu, Vaneyu, and Vrateyu.

The son of Riteyu was Rantinara whose sons were Tansu. Aprtiratha, and Dhruva. The son of the second of these was Kanva, and his son was Medhatithi, from whom the Kanvayana Brahmans are descended. Anila was the son of Tansu, and he had four sons, of whom Dushyanta was the elder. The son of Dushyanta was the emperor Bharata.

Bharata had by different wives nine sons, but they were put to death by their own mothers, because Bharata remarked that they bore no resemblance to him, and the women were afraid that he would therefore desert them. The birth of his sons being thus unavailing, Bharata, sacrificed to the Maruts, and they gave him Bharadvaja, the son of Vrihaspati by Mamata the wife of Utathya.

He was also termed Vitatha, in allusion to the unprofitable *(vitatha)* birth of the sons of Bharata. The son of Vitatha was Bhavanmanyu: his sons were many, and amongst them the chief were Brihatkshatra, Mahavirya, Nara and Garga. The *son* of Nara was Sankriti; his sons were Ruchiradhi and Rantideva. The son of Garga was Sini; and their descendants called Gargyas and Sainyas, although Kshatriyas by birth, became Brahmins.

The son of Mahavirya was Urukshaya, who had three sons, Trayyaruna, Pushkarin and Kapi, the last of whom became a Brahmin. The son of Brihatkshatra was Suhotra, whose son was Hastin, who founded the city of Hastinapur.

The sons of Hastin were Ajamidha, Dvimidha and Purumidha. One son of Ajamidha was Kanva, whose son was Medhatithi, his other son was Brihadshu, whose son *was* Brinadvasu; his son was Brihatkarman: his son was Jayadratha, his 'son was Vishvajit, his son was Senajit, whose sons were Ruchirashva, Kasya, Dridhadhanush, and Vasahanu.

The son of Ruchiraswa was Prithusena: his son was Para; his son was Nipa; he had a hundred sons, of whom Samara, the principal, was the ruler of Kampilya.

Samara had three sons, Para, Sampara, Sadashva. The son of Para was Prithu; his son was Sukriti; his son was Vibhratra; his son was Anuha, who married Kritvi, the daughter of Shuka (the son of Vyasa), and had by her Brahmadatta; his son was Vishvaksena; his son was Udaksena; and his son was Bhallata.

The son of Dvimidha was Yavinara; his son was Dhritimat; his son was Satyadhriti; his son was Dridhanemi; his son was Suparshva,' his son was Sumati; his son was Sannatimat; his son was Krita, to whom Hiranyanabha taught the philosophy of the Yoga, and he compiled twenty-four Sanhitas (or compendia) for the use of the eastern Brahmins, who study the Sama-Veda.

The son of Krita was Ugrayudha, by whose prowess the Nipa race of Kshatriyas was destroyed; his son was Kshemya; his son was Suvira; his son was Nripanjaya; his son was Bahuratha. These were all called Pauravas.

Ajamidha had a wife called Nilini, and by her he had a son named Nila: his son was Santi; his son was Susanti; his son was Purujanu; his son was Chakshu; his son was Haryashva, who had five sons.

Mudgala, Srinjaya, Brihadishu. Pravira, and Kampilya. Their father said, "These my five (pancha) sons are able (alam) to protect the countries'; and hence they were termed the Panchalas. From Mudgala descended the Maudgalya Brahmins; he had also a son named Bahvashva, who had two children, twins, a son and daughter, Divodasa and Ahalya.

The son of Divodasa was Mitrayu; his son was Chyavana; his son was Sudasa; his son was Saudasa, also called Sahadeva; his son was Somaka; he had a hundred sons, of whom Jantu was the eldest, and Prishata the youngest. The son of Prishata was Drupada; his son was Dhrishtadyumna; his son was Drishtaketu.

Another son of Ajamidha was named Riksha; his son was Samvarana; his son was Kuru, who gave his name to the holy district Kurukshetra; his sons were Sudhanush, Parikshit, and many others.

The son of Sudhanush was Suhotra; his son was Chyavana; his son was Kritaka; his son was Uparichara the Vasu, who had seven children Brihadratha, Pratyagra, Kushamba, Mavella, Matsya, and others. The son of Brihadratha was Kusagra; his son was Rishabha; his son was Pushpavat; his son was Satyadhrita; his son was Sudhanvan; and his son was Jantu. Brihadratha had another son, who being born in two parts, which were put together *(sandhita)* by a female fiend named Jara, he was denominated Jarasandha; his son was Sahadeva; his son was Somapi; his son was Srutasravas, These were kings of Magadha."

The immediate ancestry of the three Sudasas is put below in parallel columns to facilitate the settlement of the question whether they are one or three different persons:

	Status in Rig	Veda		Sudas in Vishnu Purana
VII, 18:22	*VII, 18:23*	*VII 18:25*	*In the Sagar Family*	*In the Puru Family*
Devavata Pijavana	Pijavana Sudas	Divodasa= Pijavana	Rituparna	Bahvashva
			Sarvakama	Divodasa
Sudas		Sudas		Mitrayu
			Sudas	Chyavana
			Saudasa=	Sudas
			Mitrasaha	Saudasa
				Somaka

From the table two things are as clear as daylight. First is that neither Sudas mentioned in the Vishnu Purana has anything to do with the Sudas mentioned in the Rig Veda. The second point which is clear is that if the Paijavana mentioned in the Mahabharata can be identified with anybody who lived in ancient times it can only be with Sudas mentioned in Rig Veda who was called Paijavana because he was the son of Pijavana which was another name of Divodasa.

Fortunately for me my conclusion is the same as that of Prof. Weber. In commenting upon the passage in the Shanti Parvan of the Mahabharata on which my thesis is based Prof. Weber says: "Here the remarkable tradition is recorded that Paijavana, *i.e.*, Sudas who was so famous for his sacrifices and who is celebrated in the Rig Veda as the patron of Vishvamitra and enemy of Vashishtha, was a Sudra." Prof. Weber unfortunately did not realize the full significance of this passage. This is another matter. It is enough for my purpose to find that he too thinks that the Paijavana of the Mahabharata is no other than Sudas of the Rig Veda. What do we know about Sudas, the Paijavana?

The following particulars are available about him:

1. Sudas was neither Dasa nor Arya. Both the Dasas as well as the Aryas were his enemies. This means that he was a Vedic Aryan.
2. The father of Sudas was Divodasa. He seems to be the adopted son of Vadhryashva. Divodasa was a king. He fought many battles against Turvasas and Yadus, Shambara, Parava, and Karanja and Gungu. There

was a war between Turyavana and Divodasa and his allies Ayu and Kutsa. The victory went to Turyavana.

It seems that at one time Indra was against him particularly in the battle of Turyavana. His purohita was Bharadvaja, to whom Divodasa gave many gifts. Bharadvaja seems to have played the part of a traitor by joining Turyavana against Divodasa.

There is no reference to the mother of Sudas. But there is a reference to the wife of Sudas. His wife's name is given as Sudevi. It is said that the Ashvins procured her for Sudas.

3. Sudas was a king and his coronation ceremony was performed by the Brahma-rishi, Vashishtha. The Aitarreya Brahmana gives the following list of the kings who had the Mahabhisheka ceremony performed and the name of the Purohita who officiated at *it.*

"With this ceremony Sharyata, the son of Manu, was inaugurated by Chyavana, the son of Bhrigu. Thence Sharyata went conquering all over the earth, and sacrificed the sacrificial horse, and was even at the sacrificial session held by the gods, the housefather."

"With this ceremony Samasushama, the son of Vajaratna, inaugurated Shatanika, the son of Satrajit. Thence Shatanika went conquering everywhere over the whole earth up to its ends, and sacrificed the sacrificial horse."

"With this ceremony Parvata and Narada inaugurated Ambashthya. Thence Ambashthya went conquering everywhere over the whole earth up to its ends, and sacrificed the sacrificial horse."

"With this ceremony Parvata and Narada inaugurated Yudhamasraushti, the son of Ugrasena. Thence Yudhamasraushti went conquering everywhere over the whole earth up to its ends, and sacrificed the sacrificial horse."

"With this inauguration ceremony Kashyapa inaugurated Vishva-karma, the son of Bhuvana. Thence

Vishvakarma went conquering everywhere over the whole earth up to its ends, and sacrificed the sacrificial horse." "They say that the earth sang to Vishvakarma the following stanza: "No mortal is allowed to give me away (as donation). O, Vishva-karma, thou hast given me, (therefore) I shall plunge into the midst of the sea. In vain was thy promise made to Kashyapa.'"

"With this ceremony Vashishtha inaugurated Sudas, the son of Pijavana. Thence Sudas went conquering everywhere over the whole earth up to its ends, and sacrificed the sacrificial horse."

"With this inauguration ceremony Samvarta, the son of Angiras, inaugurated Maruta, the son of Avikshit Thence Maruta went conquering everywhere over the whole earth up to *its* ends, and sacrificed the sacrificial horse."

In this list there is a specific mention of Sudas and of his coronation having been performed by Vashishtha. Sudas was the heroin the famous Dasharajna Yuddha or the battle of the ten kings described in the *Rig Veda*. References to this famous battle occur in the various Suktas of the Seventh Mandala of the Rig Veda.

Sukta 83 says:

4. "Indra and Varuna, you protected Sudas, overwhelming the yet unassailed Bheda with your fatal weapons; hear the prayers of these Tertius in time of battle, so that my ministration may have borne them fruit."
5. "Both (Sudas and the Tertius) call upon you two, (Indra and Varuna), in combats for the acquirement of wealth, when you defend Sudas, together with the Tertius, when attacked by the ten Rajas."
6. "The ten confederated irreligious Rajas did not prevail, Indra and Varuna, against Sudas; the praise of the leaders (of rites), the offerers of sacrificial food, was fruitful; the gods were present at their sacrifices."
7. "One of you destroys enemies in battle, the other ever protects religious observances; we invoke you showerers

(of benefits), with praises; bestow upon us, Indra and Varuna, felicity."

Sukta 33 says:

2. "Disgracing (Pashadyumna), they brought from afar the fierce Indra, when drinking the ladle of Soma at his sacrifice, to (receive) the libation (of Sudas); Indra hastened from the effused Soma of Pashadyumna, the son of Vayata, to the Vashishtha."
3. "In the same manner was he, (Sudas), enabled by them easily to cross the Sindhu river; in the same manner, through them he easily slew his foes; so in like manner, Vashishtha, through your prayers, did Indra defend Sudas in the war with the ten kings."

"Suffering from thirst, soliciting (rain), supported (by the Tertius) in the war with the ten Rajas, (the Vashishtha) made Indra radiant as the sun; Indra heard (the praises) of Vashishtha glorifying him, and bestowed a spacious region on the Tertius."

Sukta 19 says:

3. "Undaunted (Indra), thou hast protected with all thy protecti-ons Sudas, the offerer of oblations; thou hast protected, in battles with enemies for the possession of the earth, TRASADASYU, the son of PURUKUTSA and PURU."
6. "Thy favours, Indra, to Sudas, the donor (of offerings), the presenter of oblations, are infinite; showerer (of benefits) I yoke for thee (thy vigorous) steeds; may our prayers, reach thee who art mighty, to whom many rites are addressed."

Sukta 18 of the Seventh Mandala says:

5. "The adorable Indra made the well-known deep waters (of the Parushni) fordable for Sudas, and converted the vehement awakening imprecation of the sacrificer into the calumniation of the rivers."
6. "TURVASHA, who was preceding (at solen rites), diligent in sacrifice, (went to Sudas) for wealth; but like fishes restricted (to the element of water), the Bhrigus and Druhyus quickly assailed them; of these two

everywhere going, the friend (of Sudas, Indra) rescued his friend."

7. "Those who dress the oblation, those who pronounce auspicious words, those who abstain from penance, those who bear horns (in their hands), those who bestow happiness (on the world by sacrifice), glorify that Indra, who recovered the cattle of the Arya from the plunderers, who slew the enemies in battle."
8. "The evil-disposed and stupid (enemies of Sudas), crossing the humble Parushni river, have broken down its banks; but he by his greatness pervades the earth, and KAVI the son of CHAYAMANA, like a falling victim, sleeps (in death)."
9. "The waters followed their regular course to the Parushni, nor (wandered) beyond it; the quick course (of the king) came to the accessible places, and INDRA made the idly-talking enemies, with their numerous progeny, subject among them (to Sudas)."
10. "They who ride on parti-coloured cattle, (the Maruts), despatched by PRISHNI, and recalling the engagement made by them with their friend (Indra), came like cattle from the pasturage, when left without a herdsman; the exulting Niyut steeds brought them quickly (against the foe)."
11. "The hero INDRA created the Maruts (for the assistance of the Raja), who, ambitious of fame, slew one and twenty of the men on the two banks (of the Parushni), as a well looking priest lops the sacred grass in the chamber of sacrifice."
12. "Thou, the bearer of the thunderbolt, didst drown SHRUTA, KAVASHA, VRIDDHA, and afterwards DRUHYU in the waters; for they, Indra, who are devoted to thee, and glorify thee, preferring thy friendship, enjoy it."
13. "Indra, in his might, quickly demolished all their strongholds, and their seven (kinds of) cities; he has given the dwelling of the son of ANU to TRITSU; may we, (by propitiating), (Indra) conquer in battle the ill-speaking man."

14. "The warriors of the ANUS and DRUHYUS intending (to carry off the) cattle, (hostile) to the pious (SUDAS), perished to the number of sixty-six thousand six hundred and sixty; such are all the glorious acts of INDRA."
15. "These hostile Tertius, ignorantly contending with INDRA, fled, routed as rapidly as rivers on a downward course, and being discomfited abandoned all their possessions to SUDAS."
16. "INDRA has scattered over the earth the hostile rival of the hero (SUDAS), the senior of INDRA, the appropriator of the oblation; INDRA has baffled the wrath of the wrathful enemy, and the (foe) advancing on the way (against SUDAS) has taken the path of flight."
17. "INDRA has effected a valuable (donation) by a pauper; he has slain an old lion by a goat; he has cut the angles of the sacrificial post with a needle; he has, given all the spoils (of the enemy) to SUDAS."
18. "Thy numerous enemies, INDRA, have been reduced to subjugation,' effect at some time or other the subjugation of the turbulent BHEDA who holds men praising thee as guilty of wickedness; hurl, INDRA, thy sharp thunderbolt against him."
19. "The dwellers on the Yamuna and Tertius glorified INDRA when he killed BHEDA in battle; the Ajas, the Shigrus, the Yakshas, offered to him as a sacrifice the heads of the horses killed in the combat"
20. "Thy favours, INDRA, and thy bounties, whether old or new, cannot be counted like the (recurring) dawns; thou hast slain DEVAKA, the son of MANYAMANA and of thine own will hast cast down SHAMBARA from the vast (mountain)."

In this battle the kings who fought against Sudas were: (1) Shinyu, (2) Turvasha, (3) Druhyu, (4) Kavasha, (5) Puru, (6) Anu, (7) Bheda, (8) Shambara, (9) Vaikama, (10) another Vaikama, (II) Yadu, (12) Matsya, (13) Paktha, (14) Bhalanas, (15) Aleena, (16) Vishanin, (17) Aja, (18) Shiva, (19) Shigru,

(20) Yakshu, (21) Yudhyamadhi, (22) Yadva, (23) Devaka Manyamana, (24) Chayamana Kavi, (25) Sutuka, (26) Uchatha, (27) Shruta, (28) Vriddha, (29) Manyu, and (30) Prithu.

Obviously, the war was a much bigger war than its name indicates. The war must have been a very great event in the history of the Indo-Aryans. No wonder the victorious Sudas became a great hero of his time. We do not know what exactly led to this war. Some indication is given by Rig Veda, vii.83.7, where the kings arrayed against Sudas are described as irreligious which suggests that it was probably a religious war.

4. Sayanacharya, as well as tradition, declare the following hymns of the Rig Veda to have had the under-mentioned kings for their rishis: "Vitahavya (or Bharadva) x.9, Sindhudvipa, son of Ambarisha (or Trisiras, son of Tvashtri) x.75,Sindhukshit, son of Priyamedha; x.133, Sudas, son of Pijavana; x.134, Mandhatri, son of Yuvanasa; x.179, Sibi, son of Usinara, Pratardana, son of Divodasa and king of Kasi, and Vasumanas, son of Rohidasva; and x.148 is declared to have had Prithi Vainya." It will be noticed that in this list there occurs the name of Sudas as a composer of Vedic hymns.
5. Sudas performed Ashvamedha Yajna. There is reference to this in Rig Veda, iii.53. 9. "The great *Rishi,* the generator of the gods, attracted by the deities, the overlooker of the leaders (at holy rites), Vishvamitra arrested the watery stream when he sacrificed for Sudas; Indra with the *Kushikas,* was pleased." 11. "Approach, *Kushikas,* the steed of Sudas; animate (him), and let him loose to (win) riches (for the raja); for the king (of the gods), has slain Vritra in the East, in the West, in the North, therefore let (Sudas) worship him in the best (regions) of the earth."
6. Sudas was known for charity to the Brahmins who called him Atithigva (the doyen) of Philanthrophists. How the Brahmins have praised him for his philanthrophy appears from the following references in the Rig Veda:

i.47.6. "O, impetuous Ashvins, possessing wealth in your car, bring sustenance to Sudas. Send to us from the (aerial) ocean, or the sky, the riches which are much coveted."

i.63.7. "Thou didst then, O, thundering Indra, war against, and shatter, the seven cities for Purukutsa, when thou, O king, didst without effort hurl away distress from Sudas like a bunch of grass, and bestow wealth on Puru."

i.112.19. "Come, O Ashvins, with those succours whereby ye brought glorious power to Sudas."

vii. 19.3. "Though, O fierce Indra, hast impetuously protected Sudas, who offered oblations, with every kind of succour. Thou hast preserved Trasadasyu the son of Purukutsa, and Puru in his conquest of land and in his slaughter of enemies."

vii.20.2 "Indra growing in force slays Vritra; the hero protects him who praises him; he makes room for Sudas (or the liberal sacrificer-Sayana); he gives riches repeatedly to his worshippers."

vii.25.3. "Let a hundred succours come to Sudas, a thousand desirable (gifts) and prosperity. Destroy the weapon of the murderous. Confer renown and wealth on us."

vii.32.10. "No one can oppose or stop the chariot of Sudas. He whom Indra, whom the Marutas, protect, walks in a pasture filled with cattle."

vii.53.3. "And ye, O, Heaven and Earth, have many gifts of wealth for Sudas."

vii.60.8. "Since Aditi, Mitra, and Varuna, afford secure protection to Sudas (or the liberal man), bestowing on him offspring—may we not, O mighty deities, commit any offence against the gods... May Aryaman rid us of our enemies. (Grant) ye vigorous gods, a wide space to Sudas."

These are the biographical bits regarding Paijavana referred to in the Shanti Parvan of the Mahabharata gleaned from the most authentic source, namely, the Rig Veda. From the Rig

Veda, we know that his real name was Sudas, that he was a Kshatriya.

He was more than a Kshatriya. He was a king and a mighty king. To this, the Mahabharata adds a fresh and a new detail, namely that he was a Sudra.

A Sudra to be an Aryan, a Sudra to be a Kshatriya and a Sudra to be a king!! Can there be a greater revelation? Can there be anything more revolutionary?

This search for biographical details may be closed with a discussion of three important questions: Was Sudas an Aryan? If Sudas is, an Aryan what is the tribe to which he belonged? If Sudas is a Sudra, what does Sudra signify?

It might be well to begin with the second. For the determination of this question it is possible to derive some assistance from certain reference in the Rig Veda. The Rig Veda mentions many tribes, most important of which are Tertius, Bharatas, Turvasas, Durhyus, Yadus, Purus and Anus.

But according to the references in the Rig Veda there are only three with whom Sudas was connected. They are Purus, Tertius and the Bharatas. It is enough to confine ourselves to these three and to find out if possible to which of these tribes he belonged.

The most important stanzas bearing on the relation between Tertius and Sudas are the Rig Veda, i.63.7; i. 130.7; vii.l8.15; vii.33.5;vii.33.6; vii.83:4,6.

In i.63,7, Divodasa is spoken of as the king of the Purus and in i.130.7, Divodasa is spoken of as Paurve, *i.e.*, belonging to the Purus.

Rig Veda, vii.l8.15 and vii.83.6, suggest that Sudas was not a Tritsu. The first suggests that Sudas raided the camp of Tertius who ran away and Sudas took possession of their wealth. The second suggests that Tertius and Sudas were on one side in the war against the ten kings, but they are shown as separate. But in vii.35.5 and in vii.83.4, Sudas becomes fully identified with Tertius; indeed, in the former Sudas becomes a king of the Tertius.

On this question of the relation between the Tertius and the Bharatas and between them and Sudas, we have as our evidence Rig Veda, vii.33.6 and v. 16.4, 6, 19. According to the first, Tertius are the same as the Bharatas. According to the second, Divodasa the father of Sudas is spoken of as belonging to the Bharatas.

From these references one thing is certain that the Purus, Tertius and Bharatas were either different branches of one and the same folk or that they were different tribes, who in the course of time became one people, folk. This is not impossible. The only question is: assuming they were different, to whom did Sudas originally belong? To the Purus, the Tertius or to the Bharatas? Having regard to the connection of the Purus and the Bharatas with Divodasa, his father, it seems natural to suppose that Sudas originally belonged either to the Purus or to the, Bharatas—which, iris difficult to say.

Whether he belonged to the Purus or not, there is no doubt that Sudas belonged to the Bharatas if regard is had to the fact that his father Divodasa is spoken of as belonging to the Bharatas.

The next question is: who were these Bharatas and whether they are the people after whom India got the name Bharata Bhumi or the land of the Bharatas. This question is important because most people are not aware of the true facts. When Hindus talk of the Bharatas they have in mind the Daushyanti Bharatas, Bharatas descended from Dushyanta and Shakuntala and who fought the war which is described in the Mahabharata. Not only are they not aware of any other Bharatas but they believe that the name Bharata Bhumi which was given to India was given after the Daushyanti Bharatas.

There are two Bharatas quite distinct from each other. One tribe of the Bharatas are the Bharatas of the Rig Veda, who were descended from Manu and to whom Sudas belonged. The other tribe of Bharatas are the Daushyanti Bharatas. What is more important is that if India has been named Bharata Bhumi it is after the Bharatas of the Rig Veda and not after the Daushyanti Bharatas. This is made clear by the following stanzas from the Bhagavad Purana:

Priyamvadho nama sutho manoh
swayambhuvasya ha!
Thasyagnigrasthatho nabhitrishbhashcha
suthasthathah!!
Avatheerana puthrashatham
thasyasidrahaychaparagham!
Vikyatham varshamethaghyannaamnaa
bharathamuthapram!!

"Manu, the son of Syavambhu, had a son named Priyamvada; his son was Agnidhra: his son was Nabhi: he had a son Rishabha. He had a hundred sons born to him, all learned in the Veda; of them, Bharata was the eldest, devoted to Narayana, by whose name this excellent land is known as Bharata."

This shows to what illustratious line of kings this Sudra Sudas belonged.

The next thing to find out is whether Sudas was an Aryan. The Bharatas were of course Aryans and therefore Sudas must have been an Aryan. If reference is had to Rig Veda, vii. 18.7, this connection with the Tritus to the Aryans seems to throw some doubt on his Aryan origin. This stanza says that Indra rescued the cows of the Aryas from the Tritus and killed the Trtsus, thereby suggesting that the Tertius were the enemies of the Aryas. Griffiths is very much perturbed by the Tertius being shown as non-Aryans which is the result of a literal translation of the stanza, and to avoid it he understands cows to mean comrade. This of course is unnecessary if one bears in mind that the Rig Veda contains the story of two sorts of Aryas, whether differing in race or religion, it is difficult to say. Interpreted in the light of this fact, all that the stanza means is that at the time when it was written the Tertius had not become Aryans by religion. It does not mean that they were not Aryans by race. It is therefore indisputable that Sudas, whether taken as a Bharata or as a Tritsu was an Aryan.

And now to the last question, though it is by no means the least. What does Sudra signify? In the light of this new discovery that Sudas was a Sudra, the word now stands in a totally different light. To old scholars to whom the word was just the name of a servile and aboriginal class this new discovery must come as a surprise for which their past researches cannot possibly furnish an answer. As for myself, I am in no better position. The reason is that the social organisation of the Vedic Aryans has-yet to be studied. We know from the study of primitive societies that they are organised in groups and they act as groups. The groups are of various sons. There are clans, phratries, moieties and tribes. In some cases, the tribe is the primary unit, in others it is the clan, in others the phratry. In some cases tribes are sub-divided into clans. In other cases there are no clans. It is a single cleanless tribe.

The clan embraces the descendants of a single ancestor held together by a sense of common descent. Clans often become associated through common social and ceremonial interests into major units, called phratries or brotherhoods of clans. The bond within the phratry may be relatively loose, that is, the association may not imply more than an informal feeling of preferential friendship. The phratry may become a moiety in which each clan is recognised as part of one of two major units. But moieties may occur without any sub-division, that is, the entire clan may consist of two clans. All these organisations whether it is a clan, a phratry, a moiety or a tribe, are all based on the tie of kinship.

The Vedic Aryans had no doubt some such forms of social organisation. That is clear from the nomenclature. As pointed out by Prof. Senart: "The Vedic hymns are all too indefinite concerning the details of external and social life. We at least see from them that the Aryan population was divided into a number of tribes or small peoples *(janas),* subdivided into clans united by the ties of kinship *(visas),* which in their turn were split up into families.

The terminology of the Rig Veda, is in this respect somewhat indecisive, but the general fact is clear. *Sajata,* that is to say, kinsman' or 'fellow in *Jati,'* of race, seems in the Atharva-Veda to denote fellow in clan *(vis).* Jana, which assumes a wider significance, recalls the Avestic equivalent of the clan, the *zantu,* and the *jati* or caste. A series of terms, vra, *vrijana, vraja, vrata,* appear to be synonyms or subdivisions either of the clan or of the tribes. The Aryan population then lived, at the epoch to which the hymns refer, under the rule of an organisation dominated by the traditions of the tribe and the lower or similar groupings. The very variety of names indicates that-this organisation was somewhat unsettled."

We have, however, no information to determine which of these corresponds to the clan, which to the phratry and which to the tribe. That being so, it is difficult to say whether Sudra was the name of a clan, a phratry or a tribe. It is, however, interesting to refer to the view of Prof. Weber when he comments on the passage from the Satapatha Brahmana (i.1.4.12) where it says that different modes of address should be adopted inviting the sacrificer to proceed with the sacrifice, addressing him as 'come' if he is a Brahmin, 'hasten hither' if he is a Kshatriya, 'hasten hither' if he is a Vaishya and 'run hither' if he is a Sudra.

Prof. Weber says: "The entire passage is of great importance, as it shows (in opposition to what Roth says in the first Volume of this Journal, p. 83) that the Sudras were then admitted to the holy sacrifices of the Aryans, and understood their speech, even if they did not speak it. The latter point cannot certainly be assumed as a necessary consequence, but it is highly probable and I consequently incline to the view of those who regard the Sudras as an Aryan tribe which immigrated into India before the others."

His conclusion that the Sudras were Aryans hits the nail squarely on the head. The only point of doubt is whether the Sudras were a tribe. That they were Aryans and Kshatriyas is beyond doubt.

Bibliography

Ahir, D.C.: *Dr. Ambedkar, Buddhism and Social Change*, BR Publishing, Delhi, 1993.

Bhagat Ram: *Educating Harijans*, Academic Press, Haryana, 1981.

Busi, Subhamani N.: *Mahatma Gandhi and Babasaheb Ambedkar: Crusaders Against Caste and Untouchability*, Andhra Pradesh: Saroja Publications, Hyderabad, 1997.

Chatterjee, Partha: *Caste and Subaltern Consciousness*, Oxford University Press, Delhi, 1994.

Chetty, V.B.: *Scheduled Castes and Development Programmes in India,* Vohra, Allahabad, 1991.

Dubois, Abbe: *Hindu Manners, Customs and Ceremonies*, AES, New Delhi, 1983.

Fisher, F.B.: *Touching the Untouchables, India's Silent Revolution*, MacMillan, New York, 1920.

Fiske, A.: *The Untouchables in Contemporary India*, University of Arizona Press, Tucson, 1972.

Ganesan, L.: *Relevance of Reservation*, Valentina Publications, Madras, 1991.

Glen, M. and Johnson, S. B.: *Social Mobility Among Untouchables*, Vikas, New Delhi, 1979.

Ishwaran, K.: *Shivpur: A South Indian Village*, Routledge, London, 1968.

Jadhav, N.: *Dr. Ambedkar's Economic Thought and Philosophy*, Popular Prakashan, Bombay, 1993.

Jaffrelot, Christophe: *Dr. Ambedkar and Untouchability: Fighting the Indian Caste System*, New York, Columbia University Press, 2005.

Jaffrelot, Christophe:: *Mr. Gandhi and the Emancipation of the Untouchables*, Thacker & Co., Bombay, 1943.

Jeevaratanam, A. G.: *Political Implications of Untouchability*, Kondaveedu Press, Hyderabad, 1973.

Johnson, Glen and Bose, Sipra: *Social Mobility Among Untouchables,* Cohesion and Conflict in Modern India, New Delhi, 1978.

Johnson, S. B.: *Social Mobility Among Untouchables*, Vikas, New Delhi, 1979.

Joshi, B.R.: *Untouchable! Voices of the Dalit Liberation Movement*, Zed and MRG, London, 1986.

Juergensmeyer, Mark: *Religion as Social Vision: The Movement Against Untouchability in 20th Century Punjab*, University of California Press, Berkeley, 1979.

Kananaikil, Jose: *Constitutional Provisions for the Scheduled Castes*, Indian Social Institute, New Delhi, 1984.

Khairmode, C.B.: *Dr. Bhimrao Ramji Ambedkar*, Pratap, Bombay, 1978.

Khare, R. S.: *The Untouchable as Himself: Ideology, Identity and Pragmatism Among the Lucknow Chamars*, Cambridge University Press, London, 1984.

Krishan, Asha: *Ambedkar and Gandhi: Emancipators of Untouchables in Modern India*, Himalaya Pub. House, Mumbai, 1997.

Kshirsagar, R. K.: *Dalit Movement in India and Its Leaders (1857-1956)*, MD Pub. Pvt. Ltd., New Delhi, 1994.

Kuber, W.N.: *Dr. Ambedkar: A Critical Study*, People's Publishing House, New Delhi, 1973.

Lal, Sheo Kumar and Nahar, Umed Raj: *Extent of Untouchability and Pattern of Discrimination*, Mittal Publications, New Delhi, 1990.

Lynch, Owen M.: *The Politics of Untouchability: Social Mobility and Social Change in a City of India*, Columbia University Press, New York, 1969.

Mahar, Michael J.: *The Untouchables in Contemporary India*, University of Arizona Press, Arizona, 1972.

Majumdar, D. N.: *Caste and Communication in an Indian Village*, Asia Publishing House, Bombay, 1958.

Marriott, Mckim: *Village India: Studies in the Little Community*, The University of Chicago Press, Chicago, 1955.

Meyer, Mark J.: *Religion as Social Vision: The Movement Against Untouchability in 20th Century in Punjab*, University of California Press, Berkeley, 1982.

Michael J.: *The Untouchables in Contemporary India*, University of Arizona Press, Arizona, 1972.

Moffatt, Michael: *An Untouchable Community in South India: Structure and Consensus*, Princeton University Press, NJ, 1979.

Mumtaz Ali: *Human Rights and the Dalits*, Uppal Publishing House, New Delhi, 1995.

Nagaraj, D. R.: *The Flaming Feet: A Study of the Dalit Movement*, South Forum Press, Bangalore, 1993.

Naidu, Ch. M.: *Salt Satyagraha in the Coastal Andhra*, Mittal Publications, Delhi, 1986.

Nath, Trilok: *Politics of the Depressed Classes*, Deputy Publications, Delhi, 1987.

O'Malley, L. S. S.: *Indian Caste Customs*, Vikas Publishing House, Delhi, 1974.

Pantavane, G.: *Patrikar Dr. Babasaheb Ambedkar*, Abhijit, Nagpur, 1987.

Paranjpe, A. C.: *Caste, Prejudice and the Individual*, Lalvani Publishing House, New Delhi, 1970.

Parvathamma, C. *New Horizons and Scheduled Castes*. Ashish Publishing House, New Delhi, 1986.

Prabhu, P. N.: *Report of the Seminar on Casteism and Removal of Untouchability*, Indian Conference of Social Work, Bombay, 1955.

Pradhan, A. C.: *The Emergence of the Depressed Classes*, Bookland International, Bhubaneshwar, 1986.

Prahlad G.: *Dalit Movement in Maharashtra*, Kanak Publications, New Delhi, 1991.

Rajasekharaiah, A.M.: *B.R. Ambedkar: the Politics of Emancipation*, Sindhu Publications, Bombay, 1971.

Raju, G.G.: *The Life of B.R. Ambedkar*, Babasaheb Dr. Ambedkar Memorial Society, Hyderabad, 1979.

Rathnaiah, K.: *Social Change Among the Malas: An Ex-Untouchable Caste in South India*, Discovery Publishing House, New Delhi, 1991.

Rayappa, P. Hanumantha and Grover, Deepak: *Employment Planning for the Rural Poor: The Case of Scheduled Castes and Scheduled Tribes*, Sterling Press, New Delhi, 1980.

Rege, Sharmila: *Sati: A Critical Analysis,* University of Poona, Poona, 1989.

Richard, L.: *The Speaing Tree*, Oxford University Press, London, 1971.

Robb, Peter: *Dalit Movements and the Meanings of Labour in India*, Oxford University Press, New Delhi, 1993.

Sarkar, J.: *Caste, Occupation and Change*, B. R. Publishing Co., Delhi, 1984.

Shah, Ghanshyam: *Caste Association and Political Processes in Gujarat*, Popular Prakashan, Bombay, 1975.

Sharma, G. S.: *Legislation and Cases of Untouchability and Scheduled Castes in India*, Allied Publishers, Bombay, 1975.

Sharma, K. L.: *Caste, Class and Social Movements*, Rawat Publications, Jaipur, 1986.

Shashi B.R.: *Ambedkar and Human Rights*, KK Publishers, New Delhi, 1981.

Shetty, V. T. Rajshekar: *Dalit Movement in Karnataka*, Christian Literature Society, Madras, 1978.

Silverberg, James: *Social Mobility in the Caste System in India*, Mouton Publishers, The Hague, 1968.

Singh, S. N.: *Reservation: Problems and Prospects*, Uppal Publishing House, New Delhi, 1987.

Srinivas, M. N.: *Caste in Modern India and Other Essays*, Asia Publishing House, Bombay, 1962.

Suneila, M: *Social Integration of the Scheduled Castes*. Abhinav, New Delhi, 1979.

Tope, T.K.: *Dr. B.R. Ambedkar, A Symbol of Social Revolt*, Maharashtra Information Centre, New Delhi, 1964.

Tripathy, R. B.: *Dalits: A Sub-Human Society*, Ashish Publishing House, New Delhi, 1994.

Varale, B.H.: *Dr. Babasaheb Ambedkarrancha Sangaki*, Shrividya Prakashan, Pune, 1988.

Wolf, G.: *Re-inventing Tradition,* Indian Institute of Advanced Studies, Shimla, 1992.

Index

E

F

G

H

I

J

□□□